DATE DUE

Demco, Inc. 38-293

The Regime Change of Kwame Nkrumah

The Regime Change of Kwame Nkrumah

Epic Heroism in Africa
And the Diaspora

Ahmad A. Rahman

76852320   4-16-08

THE REGIME CHANGE OF KWAME NKRUMAH: EPIC HEROISM IN AFRICA AND THE
DIASPORA

First published in 2007 by
PALGRAVE MACMILLAN™
175 Fifth Avenue, New York, N.Y. 10010 and
Houndmills, Basingstoke, Hampshire, England RG21 6XS.
Companies and representatives throughout the world.

PALGRAVE MACMILLAN is the global academic imprint of the
Palgrave Macmillan division of St. Martin's Press, LLC and of Palgrave
Macmillan Ltd. Macmillan® is a registered trademark in the United States,
United Kingdom and other countries. Palgrave is a registered trademark in
the European Union and other countries.

ISBN-10: 1-4039-6569-2
ISBN-13: 978-1-4039-6569-1

Library of Congress Cataloging-in-Publication Data is available from the
Library of Congress.

A catalogue record for this book is available from the British Library.

Design by Macmillan India Ltd.

First edition: February 2007

10 9 8 7 6 5 4 3 2 1

Printed in the United States of America.

To my grandmother, Mrs. Anzola Lewis, 1902–1985, for her many sacrifices so that we would reach a healthy adulthood.

To my father, James "Doug" Irwin, 1923–2001. If there was ever a man who was generous, gracious, and good, he was my dad, The Man.

And to my children, Khalil Kevin, Saidah Thandiwe, Sundiata Hamadi, and Askia Ahmad. I might not live to see it but they will one day see a real African Union.

Table of Contents

Foreword

The Call, Quest, and Return of Kwame Nkrumah: Epic Heroism in Africa and the Diaspora

Kwame Francis Nwia Nkrumah was born on September 18, 1909, in the small village of Nkroful in Britain's Gold Coast colony. Early in his life his elders identified him as having special mystical powers. But no one could predict that he would grow up to lead the first sub-Saharan African country to independence from European colonialism. He renamed the country Ghana. By this singular event he proved to Africa and the world that under dynamic leadership the seemingly unstoppable trend of 400 years of European conquest and domination could end for one small country. His actions became exemplary for the many other African nations suffering under the exploitation and misrule of Britain, Spain, Portugal, France, Belgium, and Afrikanerdom.

Nkrumah's teachers noticed his quick and precocious mind and chose him to teach his peers while he was still in his early teens. In 1926 a visitor from the Prince of Wales College at Achimota, Ghana, recognized his talent. He selected Nkrumah for higher education. It was at Achimota that he would come under the tutelage of James Aggrey, who introduced him to the ideas of W. E. B. Du Bois and Marcus Garvey. In 1935 he gained admission to Lincoln University, in Pennsylvania, and secured passage to the United States. Lincoln was one of America's premier historically black educational institutions. During the course of the next ten years he received both a bachelor's degree and a degree in theology from Lincoln. He was ordained as a Methodist minister and earned a master's degree from the University of Pennsylvania before being admitted into a PhD program there.

During his sojourn in the United States, Nkrumah would develop the foundations of much that would come to be known as Nkrumaism. He met C. L. R. James, Ralph Bunche, E. Franklin Frazier, and a host of African American luminaries. He worked as a circuit preacher, a dockworker, a student organizer, and an advocate for Africa's independence. In 1945, as World War II ended, he sailed to England. For the next two years Nkrumah immersed himself in the nascent movement for Africa's independence. He collaborated with his hero, W. E. B. Du Bois, on a Pan-African Congress in Manchester, England. Such giants of Pan-African thought as George Padmore and T. Ras Makonnen tutored him. So brightly did his light shine among his peers that members of Britain's Gold Coast colony's small black mercantile and professional elite eventually offered him the leadership of a fledgling and nearly defunct nationalist organization—the United Gold Coast Convention (UGCC). He accepted their offer and returned to Ghana in 1947. Within one year he had built the UGCC into a force that sparked disruptions of the peaceful running of what the British considered their model colony. Prison was his reward, and from its confinement he was catapulted into national leadership as Britain conceded, for the first time, a degree of independence to an African state.

Differences with the gradualist and elitist founders of the UGCC forced him to leave their organization. He founded the Convention People's Party (CPP), which led Ghana to full independence on March 6, 1957. He spoke at midnight to a crowd of over 100,000 newly independent Ghanaians at Accra's Polo Grounds. Using the term "African Personality," which the African American polymath Edward Wilmot Blyden coined in the nineteenth century, he proclaimed: "We must change our attitudes and our minds. . . . We are going to create our own African personality and identity."[1]

His words indeed rang true. This study is as much about the history of Nkrumah's creation of his own personality and identity as it is about his struggle to define a Ghanaian and then a continental African personality and identity. The creation of both personalities was for him a prerequisite to the ultimate goal that he outlined before concluding his midnight address: "Our independence is meaningless unless it is linked up with the total liberation of the African continent."[2]

An important founding thesis of this study is that Nkrumah's battles were contests of consciousness. His ultimate vision was a socialist African continent as politically unified as the United States of America. His ideological commitment drew constant attacks from the combat ideologies of Western political, economic, and racial supremacy, which Nkrumah defined as "imperialism." Previous depictions of Nkrumah have often drawn from these Western viewpoints. They have given inaccurate, simplistic, superficial, and biased accounts of his life.[3]

A synopsis of the problem is evident in the writings on Nkrumah by the scholar Henry Bretton. Bretton was a close observer of Nkrumah who lived and worked in Ghana during Nkrumah's years in power. His writings serve as a representative example of a genre of anti-Nkrumah texts.[4]

> Undoubtedly, Nkrumah's intellectual makeup and political personality are to some extent the product of cultural influences associated with his tribal origins: to sort out the analytically relevant aspects of these origins, however, and to relate them meaningfully to the political behavior of the mature man may be beyond the range of contemporary social-science methodology.[5]

Bretton precisely states here the challenge met by this study: to expand the range of social-science methodology and sort out the analytically relevant aspects of Nkrumah's cultural origins and to then show their causal connection to his political behavior. This requires an unrestrictive social-science methodology that allows for the analysis of praxis, that is, Nkrumah's political actions that incorporated his cultural identity. This study seeks to explore the conceptual horizons that Bretton proclaimed beyond the range of contemporary social-science methodology.

Bretton did not conceptually grasp how a behavioral analysis of a modern African politician, steeped, according to him, in indigenous "superstitions," could employ methodology outside the bounds of modernity. He could not fashion a tool for the task, so he took the shortcut of filling in the lacunae with pejoratives about the subject. He wrote:

> While it is certainly not my intention to elevate rumors to the level of historical fact, Nkrumah's behavior appears to have been more related to tribal superstitions and beliefs than would be indicated by the image of a modern progressive, worldly leader. At any rate it is difficult to discount the possibility that the political decisions of Kwame Nkrumah were not wholly detached from traditional customs.[6]

Bretton researched his book between 1956 and 1965. During those years many Western anthropologists and historians routinely classified all African indigenous religions and spiritual practices that existed outside the Judeo-Christian-Islamic tradition as superstition. Like other authors, Bretton detailed the rise and fall of Nkrumah as a series of his triumphs and defeats, strengths and weaknesses, without analytically weighing the importance of these "superstitions" on his decisions and states of being during specific times and events.

Bretton's book is an example of an entire genre of writings produced in the West during the Cold War about defiant leaders in the developing world. A comprehensive critique of these books is not the province of this study. However, since the influence of these books continues, a few more words concerning Henry Bretton frame the approach of this study to the topic.

Bretton was a professor of political science at the University of Michigan in the 1950s and 1960s. There he sponsored an Association of African Students that also included African American students from Michigan State and Wayne State Universities. One of the consultants for this study, the artist Paa Kwame, a.k.a Leroy Mitchell, was a member of this association and remembered Bretton. In Paa Kwame's Detroit home, on his office wall, is a 1957 photograph of him with Henry Bretton and other members of this association. Paa Kwame would eventually live and teach in Ghana for twenty years, from 1965 to 1985.

"Bretton usually spoke negatively about Nkrumah," said Paa Kwame. He further stated that in the 1950s, during the peak of the Cold War, Bretton and other Western scholars went to Ghana with minds already set firmly in opposition to Pan-African socialism. These preset opinions meant that Bretton had little incentive to look beneath the surface of outer appearances to find less derogatory connotations to Nkrumah's so-called superstitions. Additionally, the funding for research in Africa during the Cold War came from sources not sympathetic to positive interpretations of left-wing politics. "Favorable comments about socialism or somebody considered a communist like Nkrumah could get your money cut off back in those days. And without money from those foundations, you couldn't do nothing in Africa, unless you were financially independent. And how many of us were that?"[7]

Especially during the Cold War, the attempt by authors like Bretton to view African phenomena through the eyes of Africans was constrained by their politics. Viewing Nkrumah favorably, even from a cultural standpoint, could be personally and professionally damaging. They needed understandings rooted in Africa and black America to explain Nkrumah's mysticism as part of his political life. Without these tools for the task, Bretton and other analysts took shortcuts. Where they did not understand Nkrumah's motivations, they substituted pejoratives. They described him with words like "megalomaniac," "personality cult," "dictator," "corrupt," and "superstitious." They wrote impressions that were little different from the colonial genre that attached to a practitioner of African traditional religions the term "witch doctor."[8]

The reactions of most Ghanaians to Nkrumah's leadership fell into three general categories: enthusiastic support, passive apathy, or active opposition. The last category included men who conspired with foreign powers to assassinate or overthrow him. On February 24, 1966, these opponents successfully forced Nkrumah into exile in Conakry, Guinea. These categories were not, however, rigid and inflexible, for some persons slipped into one category for a while only to morph into another one later. Nevertheless, Nkrumah's battles were fought in the realm of consciousness, and his victories and defeats took place first in the minds of his people and in the minds of his foreign enemies.

The largest of these three groups supported Nkrumah. One of the principal leaders of the anti-Nkrumah coup d'état ironically verified Nkrumah's popularity less than a year after overthrowing him. General Akwasi A. Afrifa wrote, "The irony of the present situation in Ghana is that it is quite probable that President Nkrumah and the CPP would command the support of a majority of the electorate, even in genuinely free elections. It is a pity that it is not possible to test this hypothesis."[9] But this hypothesis could have been easily tested by allowing Nkrumah to return from Guinea and holding an election. For all of their rhetoric denouncing Nkrumah's so-called dictatorship and lauding the superiority of Western democracy, neither Afrifa, nor his successors, nor their Western benefactors would ever allow Nkrumah to participate again in this democratic process.

Acknowledgments

SANKOFA: Many people helped me to complete this project, with and without knowing. First I must acknowledge Dr. Aneb Kgositsile (Gloria House) for her unwavering support over the years. And I acknowledge my debt to my brother, Doug "Eddie" Irwin; my Aunt Lynn; my nephew, Abdul Hakim Irwin; and my oldest son, Khalil Kevin, whose Father's Day gift was the laptop on which I finished typing this book. Many others helped along the way. Principal among them were Dr. Melvin Troy Peters, Dr. Nubia Kai Al Nura Salaam Conte, Nsombe Famadou Lo, Nomalanga Ismail, Josephine Gentry Huyghe, Tammy Latrice Armstrong, and Joe and Marsha Lunn. I am also indebted to University of Michigan Vice Provost, Dr. Lester Monts, and Associate Vice Provost, Dr. John Matlock, for their generous support of my endeavors in general and my research in Africa particularly. Sheila Williams in the University of Michigan Department of History was often a big help. Joellen El Bashir, Curator of Manuscripts at the Howard University Moorland-Spingarn Archives provided indispensable assistance. Thanks also to Dr. Sizwe Poe at Lincoln University for helping me to access the Nkrumah Papers and for fostering critical thinking about Nkrumah with his excellent book.

I am especially grateful for the gracious hospitality in Guinea of the late Kwame Ture (Stokely Carmichael) and the support in the diaspora of other members of the All African Peoples Revolutionary Party, particularly Nehanda Omowale and the late Mawina Kouyate. I also appreciate the generosity of time and space of the family of Boubaucar Barry in Dakar, Senegal, and in Conakry and Maumou, Guinea. Thanks for helping me know that I am *Pular Americ*. I am also indebted to my support base in Accra, Ghana. These included Dhoruba Bin Wahad and his Ashanti queen, Abeena, and Makeda Sherman. I must also acknowledge the assistance from the many women and men on the streets and in the market places of Senegal, Guinea, Ghana, and Mali. Casual conversations with these common people were uncommon in providing me with a new perspective on African cultural and historical realities.

Thanks to Emory University Provost, Dr. Earl Lewis, who understood what I meant when I said that I wanted to have a foot on both continents and write a diasporic history. I further acknowledge the assistance of those ancestors whose spirits still participate in the movement to advance Pan-Africanism toward Black Globalism: Toussaint Louverture, Denmark Vesey, Gabriel Prosser, Nat Turner, David Walker, Harriet Tubman, Samori Toure, Henry McNeal Turner, Lat Dior Diop, William Monroe Trotter, Marcus Garvey, W. E. B. Du Bois, Oliver Shows, Fred Hampton, Mark Clark, John Percy Boyd, Spurgeon Jake Winters, Albert Noh Washington, Sam Napier, Amadou Diallo, Zayd Malik Shakur, Amilcar Cabral, Samora Machel, Steve Biko, Ella Baker, Fanny Lou Hamer, Chris Hani, Edwardo Mondlane, Frantz Fanon, Maurice Bishop, C. L. R. James, Thomas Sankara, Modibo Kieta, Ahmed Sekou Toure, Malcolm X, Ossie Davis, Patrice Lumumba, Reverend Dr. Martin Luther King, Jr., Amy Jacques Garvey, and, of course, Reverend Osagyefo Kwame Nwia Nkrumah. Finally I acknowledge the continuing inspiration of my courageous civil rights activist aunt, the late Mrs. Dilla Irwin. She first introduced me to the importance of countering the combat ideologies of oppression in Vicksburg, Mississippi, during Freedom Summer. That's when she entrusted me with the responsibility to distribute fifty copies of the *Vicksburg Citizen's Appeal*. This was the civil rights movement newspaper that she founded, with the assistance of brave student Freedom Riders, on her back porch and produced, despite Ku Klux Klan threats, on her back porch.

Introduction

Kwame Francis Nwia Nkrumah 's modern-day detractors disparage his leadership and his writings for propaganda, myth-making, and symbol manipulation. Hugh Seton-Watson thought that Nkrumah possessed "more the hysteria of Hitler and the vanity of Mussolini, than the genius of Lenin."[1] Ali Mazrui, on the other hand, believed that Nkrumah did resemble Lenin, but as a "Leninist Czar."[2] In so doing, they devalue these qualities as if they presaged Nkrumah's failure or were evidence of his corruption. However, analyzing Nkrumah's social psychology is essential to creating a methodology that goes beyond the perceived limits of social science. The process of colonization was itself a far-reaching psychological operation, called "Psy-Ops" in the parlance of modern warfare. Propaganda, myth-making, and symbol manipulation were the colonialists' essential catechism for centuries. Hence, the anticolonial movement that Nkrumah led had to counter the images colonialism had created in African minds with appropriate decolonizing propaganda, myth-making, and symbol manipulation.

Military power supported the colonialists' psy-ops. Colonialism was, by definition, a projection of force by a metropole that proclaimed itself the "mother country." Following invasion, conquest, and settlement, the omnipresent threat of force was permanently necessary to secure the settlers' confiscation of land and properties without deference to their original owners.

The colonialists' catechism was omnipresent. One aphorism that Africans repeat throughout the continent, in a myriad of different languages, is as symbolically true as it is relevant to this catechism: "When the white man came to Africa, we had the land and he had the Bible. He told us to close our eyes and pray. When we opened our eyes, he had the land and we had the Bible." This simple message captures the process of the colonizing of the African mind with propaganda, myths, and symbols of obedience and reverence. This method of creating a "colonial subject" certainly involved more than the Bible. The Holy Book alone could not colonize the African mind to accept the metropole's new secular laws, taxes, and onerously exploitive labor relations.

The psychiatrist Frantz Fanon and the philosopher Albert Memmi were eloquent resisters of colonialism. Both noted, from first-hand experience, that colonialism created two new beings—the colonizer and the colonized. Within the colony, these two human forces wrestled in a dialectical embrace, neither existing without the other. Like opposite poles on a magnet, European superiority could only exist if it was the antipode of African inferiority. The colonizer taught standards by which civilizations were measured that colonized African minds with their inferiority as "fact." Were not British cities resplendent with tall buildings while Africans lived in villages populated by thatched or mud dwellings? Had not Europeans mastered the oceans with immense ships and then mastered even the skies with flying vessels? Africans still traveled by royal palanquin, ass, horse, dugout canoe, and on foot. Indeed, were not the Europeans also literate and in possession of an obviously superior culture and bearing, for had not God created man in His own image? The yellow-haired, white-skinned, blue-eyed Christian iconography confirmed this everywhere in heavily evangelized countries such as the Gold Coast colony. The physical appearance of Africans, which so little resembled the God they worshipped, confirmed that they were obviously from a lesser stratum of humanity. In 1878, the Afro-Caribbean repatriate Edward Wilmot Blyden, after extensive travels and observations in the United States and in West Africa, penned these observations of successful psy-ops:

> Whenever the Negro is found in Christian lands, his leading trait is not docility, as has been often alleged, but servility. He is slow and unprogressive. Individuals here and there may be found of extraordinary intelligence, enterprise and energy, but there is no Christian community of Negroes anywhere which is self-reliant and independent.[3]

Africans internalized the premise that to be civilized they had to replace their black gods with white deities.. Their passive submission to European domination was further evidence of civilization. Only "uncivilized," "savage," and "barbarous" Africans fought or otherwise resisted their "superiors."

The European colonial myth was an image of the past and a vision of the future. The past image included European grandeur and might. Both the Duke of Wellington and Napoleon became symbols of the inexhaustible tenacity, nay, invincibility, of a European people militarized and dedicated to their duty to subjugate the "white man's burden."

The future vision required a more sophisticated manipulation of myths and symbols. In the image of the future that colonialists projected, Europeans would lift Africans to the heights of what France called "honorary Frenchmen." The British were prepared to regard their Ghanaian subjects as honorary English, akin to the former apartheid regime in South Africa that designated certain privileged persons of color "honorary white." This officially permitted them to avoid the onerous restrictions of apartheid. In this formula, "honorary" functions as a hyphen that attaches the African to the status of human being. In colonial societies, where the economic status of a person and his family rose with the achievement of this "honorary" white designation, more than a few Africans understandably sought and relished their make-believe whiteness. Colonialists exacted a heavy price for the "whiteness" they dispensed. These "white" Africans either had to fight against their own people's best interests alongside their white "brethren," or, at the least, they had to passively accept foreign conquest and exploitative economic domination.

Observing French colonialism, Albert Memmi concluded that when indigenous peoples accept a status bestowed by colonizers, they acquiesce to colonialism:

> Now, every ideology of combat includes as an integral part of itself a conception of the adversary. By agreeing to this ideology, the dominated classes practically confirm the role assigned to them. This explains, *inter alia*, the relative stability of societies; oppression is tolerated willy-nilly by the oppressed themselves. In colonial relationships, domination is imposed by people upon people but the pattern remains the same. The characterization and role of the colonized occupies a choice place in colonialist ideology; a characterization which is neither true to life, or in itself incoherent, but necessary and inseparable within that ideology. It is one in which the colonized gives his troubled and partial but undeniable, assent.[4]

Therefore, colonialism itself was "an ideology of combat." The metropole's propaganda, symbols, and myth-making were as crucial as bullets in the effort to pacify the colony. The ideology of combat was a weapon fired into the brains of colonial peoples by conquering armies as a complement to bullets.

Victory in war depends on attacking the enemy's forces, resources, and will to fight.[5] Of these three factors, defeating the will to fight was the key to colonial conquest and pacification. It meant controlling the public opinion of conquered peoples. Without a fighting morale, no matter what forces and resources the indigenous had at their disposal, their defeat and conquest were inevitable. When the colonized assented to colonialism, no matter how "troubled" or "partial" their assent, they were defeated. Kwame Nkrumah's first task as a nationalist leader was thus to restore his people's "will to fight." He accomplished this feat by countering the British Empire's ideology of combat with nationalist counterpropaganda, anticolonial symbols, and revolutionary myths.

Mohandas Gandhi's nonviolent campaign against the British for Indian nationhood greatly impressed Nkrumah. This strategy won India independence in 1947. Similar tactics would win Ghana freedom a decade later. However, one important difference between Nkrumah and Gandhi was the former's insistence that nonviolent tactics could only be successful if they were backed up by strong political organization.[6] Sovereignty alone would not free Ghana. African minds had to gain freedom from the colonial mentality. In addition to political organization, it was necessary to supplant the omnipresent colonial ideology with a combat ideology espousing the free, strong, confident, and independent African Personality.

Nkrumah built his ideology of combat on foundations laid by nineteenth-century anticolonial warriors. As early as 1868 some chiefs had formed a confederation to fight both foreign encroachments and their corrupted Ashanti relatives.[7] This split in consciousness between liberation fighters and collaborators, which proved so important to Ghana's and Nkrumah's future, was fully evident in the nineteenth century. Western historians customarily highlight the diasporic nature of the rise of Africans' early Pan-Africanist consciousness as an ideology of combat. It is true that most Africans did not see themselves in the nineteenth and early twentieth centuries as "Africans." Like "Europeans," they saw themselves as members of their own particular linguistic, ethnic, historical, and regional polities. The unifying constructions "African" and "European" were still in their infancy. This often blurs the fact that Africa itself put forward indigenous thinkers who constructed ideologies to combat colonialism within their subnationalist political units, while Edward Wilmot Blyden, Marcus Garvey, and W. E. B. Du Bois were pioneering Pan-Africanist thought in the diaspora.

The Maori historian Linda Tuhiwai Smith writes from the vantage point of the indigenous people of New Zealand. The British invaded and never left her country. The British permanently annexed the Maoris' land to the metropole as a dominion of their worldwide financial, political, and cultural empire. That empire was formerly called the British Commonwealth, but is now simply referred to as the Commonwealth. In her book *Decolonizing Methodologies: Research and Indigenous Peoples,* Smith exposed the research errors shared by some of the most well-meaning scholars in the West. Research into formerly colonized countries that does not strive to bring to the foreground indigenous voices can itself be regarded as a continuation of colonial binaries of scholar and "Other." As Smith notes:

> The term "research" is inextricably linked to European imperialism and colonialism. The word itself, "research", is probably one of the dirtiest words in the indigenous world's vocabulary. When mentioned in many indigenous contexts, it stirs up silence, it conjures up bad memories, it raises a smile that is knowing and distrustful. It is so powerful that indigenous people even write poetry about research . . . It galls us that Western researchers and intellectuals can assume to know all that it is possible to know of us, on the basis of their brief encounters with some of us.[8]

When the African subject of this "research" resisted white supremacy and fought colonial domination, then their distorted depictions by Western scholars became the rule and not the exception. This reason alone calls for reinterpreting and rewriting the biographies of nationalist rebels like Nkrumah.

This study of Nkrumah's life strives to avoid the errors of previous research that failed to foreground unheard voices. These voices are crucial to acquiring more than a superficial impression of Nkrumah. The African American and other voices from the diaspora that helped to shape Nkrumah's consciousness can also be considered indigenous. Without care, however, "diasporic" can become a distancing mechanism between the researchers and the researched. It can deprive the indigenous of recognition as co-agents of liberating ideologies with their brothers and sisters in the diaspora. "Diasporic" can replicate the colonialists' hierarchy. They posed Africans who had been "civilized". (i.e., educated) in the diaspora as superior to the "uncivilized" indigenes.

Nkrumah was an indigenous African who became a diasporic personality. Indigene and diaspora interplayed in his consciousness from 1935, when he arrived in the United States, until his death in Conakry, Guinea, in 1972. Nkrumah himself assigned to the diaspora the rank of its relationship with the indigene that this study fully embraces:

> [I]t would take ten years in America and two-and-a-half years in England, living almost in an exile, to prepare for the struggle that has

so far engaged me. . . . Those years in America and England were years
of sorrow and loneliness, poverty and hard work. But I have never
regretted them because the background that they provided has helped
me to formulate my philosophy of life and politics. At the end of my
student days in America I was offered lectureships in several Negro universities, including Lincoln. . . But I could not dismiss from my mind . . .
the flame of nationalism that had been fanned and kept alight for over
ten years.[9]

The indigenous African arrived in the West with the fires of nationalism already burning inside him. The diaspora intensified that flame
and pointed it, like a lamp, toward the knowledge that would best
prepare him for his future role of leadership.

Nkrumah's nationalist and Pan-Africanist consciousness blossomed
in the diaspora. He found in the Black Atlantic the means to utilize
many indigenous methods to counter the metropole's colonizing mental imagery with myths, propaganda, and symbols that exalted
Africans rather than degrading them. Foremost among his associates
in the ten years he spent in the United States were indigenous Africans,
African Americans, and Afro-Caribbeans who had, with proud defiance, shucked off the denigration of neo-slave consciousness to exude
a robust black pride.

Opposing colonialism required Nkrumah first to break the ideological coupling of colonizer and colonized. His unique innovation
was to synergize the African indigenous and the diasporic Black
Atlantic to formulate an ideology of combat that led to Ghana becoming the first sub-Saharan country to gain independence from European
colonialism after World War II. Mental decolonization required
undermining the value of the past and future visions of colonialism
and asserting the African's inherent humanity as complete, equal, and
even superior to the colonized "honorary white" person that was the
metropole's ideal African. Nkrumah was first of all a decolonizer. The
veracity of any presentation of his life depends on the degree to which
this fact receives primary attention. Nkrumah's critics from both the
political right and left have routinely overlooked this basic fact: before
and after Ghana's independence, Nkrumah's success or failure as a
decolonizer hinged on his abilities to supplant Britain's colonial ideological superstructure with decolonizing myths, propaganda, and symbols. He aimed each of his books, essays, speeches, gestures, and
cultural affectations at the goals of anti-colonial, then decolonizing,
and later anti-neocolonizing Pan-African unity.

When the Ghanaian military overthrew Nkrumah in February 1966, it marked the defeat of two strategies that Nkrumah employed to stay in power and to legitimize his authority. Nkrumah projected these two strategies toward his two constituencies. The first constituency was the 77 percent of Africans in Britain's Gold Coast colony that was preliterate.[10] Their primarily agricultural and village existence made abstract Western ideologies such as Marxism irrelevant. For this vast mass of the Ghanaian people, much of the precolonial culture had survived modernism brought by colonization and Western missionaries. The premodern ways and precolonial gods still held sway in their daily lives. They were often hidden, however, beneath the surface of the subjugating ideology of the missionaries' Christianity.

For this constituency Nkrumah fabricated a cultural and political approach. He tapped into the hidden Africanity that flowed out of their history. As their leader, Nkrumah personified the messianic, divinely driven, warrior/trickster. He became the modern personification of all that was heroic in the African epic. In his twentieth-century epic, this spirit-guided hero who was victorious against all foes—this *Osagyefo*, in the vernacular of the Akan—would catalyze the preliterate majority's support for the anticolonial movement. Then they would win Ghana's freedom. The divine *Osagyefo* would next lead Ghana and all of Africa to an Afrotopian Promised Land. This Pan-African paradise would offer its peoples socialist egalitarianism. Nkrumah would symbolize the unprecedented Pan-African unity. A United States of Africa would give Nkrumah great power on the world stage to challenge Western capitalism and its neocolonialist and imperialist schemes. Nkrumah's preliterate constituency could understand his significance as the cultural symbol and hero of Africa's glorious past and its future.

Nkrumah's second constituency, the Pan-Africanist intellectuals, was both domestic and international. Their materialist modernism was the polar opposite of the grassroots constituency's premodernism. Taking control of Ghana's independence movement catapulted Nkrumah into their leadership. They were the elite of the international Black Revolution. In the 1940s Nkrumah had been the adoring student of such radical luminaries as W. E. B. Du Bois, C. L. R. James, and George Padmore. In the 1950s his leading Africa's freedom struggle turned the tables and made him the recipient of their adoration.

Nkrumah established himself among this second constituency as a revolutionary philosopher through his prolific writings. His ideas were the basis of his power. This violated the Leninist dictum that political dominance could be won only through the agency of a vanguard party. Lenin's party became the instrument of the working classes, carrying out their causal destiny to overthrow the ruling class. As a *nonatheistic materialist,* Nkrumah accepted Lenin's principles only up to the point where they would not interfere with his ability to communicate effectively with his dual constituencies. Nkrumah's nonatheistic materialism fitted in neatly with the philosophy of the Akans: the material world has primacy over the events of history up to the point when metaphysical realities intervene.

Nkrumah's appeal to these two constituencies also reflected his recognition of the duality of interests driving their respective outlooks. For the preliterate many, Nkrumah brought a renewal of all they had lost spiritually and culturally to the white conqueror. For the literate and elite revolutionary few, Nkrumah's pursuit of modernism for Ghana answered their craving to westernize. They wanted to modernize as quickly as possible. Nkrumah's genius lay in balancing these two conflicting structures of thought and action. He understood the importance of calling on Africa's past to serve its future.

Tracing Nkrumah's biographical path from birth to his overthrow and exile is to see how throughout his life these two forces—Africa's indigenous past and revolutionary Africa's present—interplay both in his consciousness and in his interactions with his traditional and modernist constituencies. Nkrumah's life story, *Ghana: The Autobiography of Kwame Nkrumah,* reveals this bifurcated approach. *Ghana* is as much an epic as are the stories of all the ancient kings with which griots and African wordsmiths regale each new generation. But Nkrumah did not write *Ghana* merely to glorify the past. He wrote his life story as an epic that is a discursive structure in which historical knowledge is systematically marshaled and conveyed to appeal to his two constituencies to support his radical vision.

Nkrumah's autobiography serves as a chronology of his epic heroism from birth until the cusp of Ghana's independence in 1956. It is a metanarrative of African epic history brought into modernity. Both his detractors and his defenders use this book to prove contradictory points, as if he represented two clashing personas. Their writings reflect Nkrumah's personification of the fullness of his Akan culture and the revolutionary diaspora as a culture hero. He wove his personal life within this narrative of historical events. He depicted it as an interplay of opposing forces. He never presents false imagery of monolithic people and ideals.

Most writings about Nkrumah's life inescapably rely on his auto-biography among their sources. None of these works, however, has noticed the revealing sleight-of-hand that Nkrumah engineered with a Walt Whitman poem. On the page before his preface, Nkrumah used Whitman's "Wherever You Are Holding Me Now in Hand." In effect, he restructured the meaning of the poem to introduce his life story as a heroic epic. Nkrumah used Whitman's poem to announce his ascension to quasi-divinity. This poem defined the obedient devotion of those Africans who would follow his charismatic authority. Nkrumah omitted stanzas and actually revised the text in one line so that the meaning of the poem better served his political purposes rather than Whitman's homoeroticism. These alterations made the meaning of the poem more Nkrumah's creation than Whitman's. Nevertheless, the trickster's hand still wrote Whitman's name at the bottom as the author. Nkrumah's omissions (underlined below) and his revisions completely change the meaning of the poem.

Whoever you are, holding me now in hand,
Without one thing, all will be useless,
I give you fair warning, before you attempt me further,
I am not what you supposed, but far different.

Who is he that would become my follower?
Who would sign himself a candidate for my affections?

The way is suspicious—the result uncertain, perhaps destructive;
You would have to give up all else—I alone would expect
[Whitman actually wrote here: **to be your God, sole and exclusive**]
to be your sole and exclusive standard,
Your novitiate would even then be long and exhausting,
The whole past theory of your life, and all conformity to the lives
around you, would have to be abandon'd;
Therefore release me now, before troubling yourself any further—Let
go your hand from my shoulders,
Put me down, and depart on your way.
Or else, by stealth, in some wood, for trial,
Or back of a rock, in the open air,
(For in any roof'd room of a house I emerge not—nor in company,
And in libraries I lie as one dumb, a gawk, or unborn, or dead,)
But just possibly with you on a high hill—first watching lest any
person, for miles around, approach unawares,
Or possibly with you sailing at sea, or on the beach of the sea, or
some quiet island,

Here to put your lips upon mine I permit you,
With the comrade's long-dwelling kiss, or the new husband's kiss,
For I am the new husband, and I am the comrade.

Or, if you will, thrusting me beneath your clothing,
Where I may feel the throbs of your heart, or rest upon your hip,
Carry me when you go forth over land or sea;
For thus, merely touching you, is enough—is best,
And thus, touching you, would I silently sleep and be carried
eternally.

But these leaves conning, you con at peril,
For these leaves, and me, you will not understand,
They will elude you at first, and still more afterward—I will
certainly elude you,
Even while you should think you had unquestionably caught me,
behold!
Already you see I have escaped from you.

For it is not for what I have put into it that I have written this
book,
Nor is it by reading it you will acquire it,
Nor do those know me best who admire me, and vauntingly praise me,
Nor will the candidates for my love, (unless at most a very few,)
prove victorious,
Nor will my poems do good only—they will do just as much evil,
perhaps more;
For all is useless without that which you may guess at many times and
not hit—that which I hinted at;
Therefore release me, and depart on your way.

Nkrumah had challenged and changed powerful realities such as
colonialism and imperialism. Why should he not change a gay love
poem into a verse of combat ideology to serve Ghana's revolution?
The African epic hero does not come into the world with an attitude
of acceptance toward what came before. He does not submit to the
compulsion of established precedent. Remolding this poem, as he did
reality, announced that his autobiography would be an instrument to
bond his people to his revolutionary purposes. To follow him,
Africans too would have to renounce *the whole past theory of your
life, and all conformity to the lives around you.* They would have to
give up all else. Nkrumah alone would *be your sole and exclusive
standard.*

Genoveva Marais, one of his most trusted female confidants, wrote about the Kwame Nkrumah whom she personally knew. According to a postcoup article in the Ghanaian newspaper, *Daily Gazette,* she admitted to being one of his "numerous girlfriends."[11] For years she was in intimate contact with him. What she wrote about Nkrumah's expectations of his followers explains his alterations of Whitman's poem:

> He expected admiration, respect, possibly even fear—fear being a form of respect and acquiescence to his desires. These desires being for his nation and his people, they must be carried out and fulfilled. If they could not be achieved through other means, they must be achieved through fear of consequences of disobedience. This was not necessarily the ruthless dictator's dictum, as his enemies tried later to make out, but a necessary part of his Credo—to get his people on the road to achievement and unity. . .
>
> He felt everybody owed him loyalty. That he might be loved as a person, for himself alone rather than for his vision, never entered his mind. . . . He was totally involved in his politics.[12]

Nkrumah did not live in a cocoon but interacted with the world during the time that he wrote his life script. He knew that his portrayal of the past could shape the present and the future and this influenced what he scripted into his life. By his transmuting power as a trickster he turned the past into a tool of his revolution.

Nkrumah had already decided that the manner in which Ghanaians viewed the past would be their bridge to their renascent future. Africans would be the subjects of history and not the objects. To that end he wrote the following words more than two decades before the term "Afrocentricity" became popular as a combat ideology to challenge the hegemony of Eurocentricity. Here in one paragraph Nkrumah established the importance of history for mental decolonization:

> In the new African renaissance, we place great emphasis on the presentation of history. Our history needs to be written as the history of our society, not as the story of European adventures. African society must be treated as enjoying its own integrity; its history must be a mirror of that society, and the European contact must find its place in this history only as an African experience, even if as a crucial one . . . European contact needs to be assessed and judged from the point of view of the principles animating African society, and from the point of view of the harmony and progress of this society.[13]

Furthermore, Nkrumah built national unity by hybridizing this grassroots discourse with the politics of the economic elite and the nationalist intellectuals. The interchange of premodern and modern politics mirrored the liaison between these two forces within Ghanaian society.

Nkrumah made early pretensions at Marxism, but he was never rigidly orthodox. His Marxism was fluid and creative. His methodologies departed from the policies of the powerful Stalinist strain in world revolutionary thought during the mid-twentieth century. Orthodox Marxists viewed their coming to power as the beginning of a new proletarian revolutionary culture. The workers revolution had to destroy religion and all nonmaterialistic fixations. These were the combat ideologies of the previous capitalist and feudal cultures. During the 1960s Mao Zedong launched China's Great Proletarian Cultural Revolution. He asserted that every generation had to undergo these revolutionary upheavals to avoid a retrenchment of bourgeois culture.

Before Mao, Vladimir Lenin had proclaimed that to be a good communist, one must also be a militant atheist. Religion and the occult had to be supplanted in revolutionary Russia by the new radical faith of Communism. Their revolutions heightened the conflicts between the old and the new. Their solution was to negate everything from the past that they could not force into the procrustean conformity of the dictatorship of the proletariat. Nkrumah, however, projected himself as a cultural symbol of both the past and the future. Within him coexisted the indissoluble synthesis between past history and future change. Neither needed to obliterate the other in his African revolutionary schema. Each was a part of the humanistic approach to social engineering that Nkrumah named *Consciencism*.

The African culture hero cannot succeed in his mission until he vanquishes the demons fate places across his path to oppose his destiny. Colonialism, imperialism, capitalism, racism: these were the demons Nkrumah challenged. These mighty forces had dominated the world for centuries. Nkrumah as an individual was for them a small annoyance. Once in power, however, Prime Minister Osagyefo Kwame Nkrumah's persona itself became a combat ideology that threatened the plans of prospective neocolonizers.

Attempting a behavioral analysis of Nkrumah's life without factoring in the counterrevolutionary plotting of his opponents in the United States and Britain is the same as trying to understand the tides without considering the influence of the moon. Yet this is precisely what many previous authors have done. These detractors filled their depictions of Nkrumah with words like "irrational," "erratic," "emotional," "dictatorial," "autocratic," and "undemocratic." They failed to consider that he was often responding to local enemies whom he had identified as colluders with clandestine agencies of foreign subversion. These were the same Western powers that had collaborated in the murder of his protégé Patrice Lumumba. They had conspired to engineer the overthrow of many of his contemporaries. Nkrumah well recognized the precarious lives of African leaders on a continent still dominated by Western economic interests. As he noted:

> Within six years, between January 1963 and December 1969, twenty-five coups d'état have taken place in Africa. . . . Apart from these there have been innumerable attempted coups and assassinations. Underlying every coup there is a similar basic situation. On the one hand, there are the neocolonialist powers teleguiding and supporting the neocolonialist state and power struggles within the reactionary bourgeois power elites; and on the other hand, there are the awakening African masses revealing the growing strength of the African socialist revolution.[14]

Admittedly, although accurate in many cases, this is a narrow explanation of why some Africans join in conspiracies against their leaders. Plain greed and desperation by poor people is another important factor. Most preindustrial societies have few avenues for financial advancement. Military officers know that a high government position offers possibilities for financially helping themselves and their extended families. The desire to aid the advancement of kinship groups is a powerful impetus in preindustrial societies. The clans and ethnic groups of the coup leaders stand to benefit monetarily from their relative's seizing power. Most of the coup supporters are not members of Nkrumah's "reactionary bourgeois power elites." The proportion of this social class is small in the extended families of most coup leaders. When the coup happens, people who have little opportunity to gain wealth will expect high-paying jobs and money from the corruption of the well-placed family member in the new regime to come their way.

The Cold War caused alarms to sound in the West any time an African mentioned socialism. Yet, what Nkrumah meant by "socialism" was not to emulate the Stalinist state-controlled monstrosities that were part of the Soviet empire. Nkrumah's was a Fabian socialism that resembled European social democracies more than any Soviet or Maoist experiments. He lived in England in 1945 when the Labour

Party came to power. That party failed to advocate freeing Britain's African colonies. But its domestic program of socialism with democracy did not escape Nkrumah's notice. The British Labour Party's policies offered Britons a social safety net out of the common pool of riches. Its democratic socialist ideology did not consider that this was filled with the plunder from colonial exploitation and oppression. Nkrumah's first glimpse of workable collective farms was in religious communities in the United States and not in either Eastern Europe or China.

Finally, three factors interplayed to create the heroic epic of Kwame Nkrumah: a subaltern occult/cultural discourse, a radical modernist ideology, and opposition from the Western powers and their African collaborators. The goal of this study is to reveal the evolution and interplay of these three factors leading up to Nkrumah's overthrow in 1966.

Nkrumah viewed himself as living in both the physical and the metaphysical worlds. His Pan-Africanist intellectual constituency embraced the atheistic tendencies of Marxism and eschewed the occult. His grassroots constituency viewed the occult as a world no less real than the one perceived by their senses. To them it often superseded the laws and prerequisites of the physical world. The use of a people's occult consciousness to arouse resistance and revolution is hardly unique to Nkrumah. The leaders of Haiti's revolution against French imperialism and enslavement utilized so-called voodoo to great effect. Nat Turner recruited soldiers in his rebellion in Southampton, Virginia, by claiming divine guidance. The anti-British Mahdist revolt in the Sudan was an outgrowth of one man's Islamic mysticism. The Ngoni peoples' Maji-Maji uprising against the German invaders in East Africa used indigenous African religion to arouse fearlessness. Throughout history, people resisting a more powerful enemy have gained courage from faith in a metaphysical source of power. Nkrumah knew that religion was not as Karl Marx proclaimed, "the opiate of the masses." He had seen religion stimulate the masses first in Africa and later in black America.

The life of the epic hero is more than a mixture of economics and politics. The epic life is *literature personified*. Nkrumah's daily activities were the book that Ghana's preliterate millions read. For this majority, Nkrumaism was first of all a cultural phenomenon. They understood Nkrumah, and he knew they did, from his embodying their own cultural conceptions. He manipulated the symbols of their triple heritage—Christian, Islamic, and indigenous—because he understood that this mode of communication was his most direct avenue into the African heart and mind. Nkrumah synthesized this triple heritage and incorporated it into consciencism.

A new history of Kwame Nkrumah as a revolutionary must give adequate weight to his associations with indigenous occult and metaphysical phenomena. Historians have concluded that when Nkrumah lived in the United States and England, C. L. R. James, George Padmore, and the left-wing ideologies Nkrumah studied heavily influenced him. What about those metaphysical influences in the West that resonated with his indigenous African self? After all, he was ordained a Christian minister and preached in numerous churches during his years in the United States. Might his experiences in the metaphysical cultures of black America also have influenced his thoughts and deeds when he became the president of Ghana? If cultural forces in Africa *and* in the West influenced Nkrumah's actions, how might a historian know what weight to give these influences when analyzing his life?

Why, for example, did Nkrumah import a *marabout* (Islamic mystic diviner and seer) from Guinea to consult for regular advice, as Hindus consult gurus? Why did he employ bags of so-called "magic powder" to defeat a political adversary in Ghana's parliament? Answers to these and many other questions pinpoint patterns of cultural correlation with political behavior. Throughout Nkrumah's political career these patterns arose from the deepest meanings in him and his people's cultural and occult consciousness. Observers also took shortcuts rather than flesh out the connection between the behavior and politics of Nkrumah and other Ghanaians. Here they also filled the blanks with pejoratives such as "corruption." "Cultural analysis suggests that these problems may be deeply rooted in a group's total way of life, and that their solution requires more than treating them by political means."[15]

The empiricist socio-political methodology does not look at the total way of life. It does, however, provide a sound starting point. A cultural analysis that looks at recurring patterns of cultural correlation adds another component. Finally, this study utilizes an important point by Jurgen Habermas to complete its methodology. Habermas concluded that kinship groupings defined by language and codes have power as influential as labor and production in determining history.[16] Not social class but kinship groupings often compelled Nkrumah's choices for patronage offices in government and in the Convention People's Party. In Africa, persons who achieve status are often obliged to support members the extended family, clan, or ethnic group. Despite knowing that this was part of the Akan way of life, members of the Ghanaian Opposition still denounced Nkrumah for nepotism and corruption. Nkrumah lamented the obligations of his culture when he wrote the following:

> I had to combat not only tribalism but the African tradition that a man's first duty was to his family group and that therefore nepotism was the highest of all virtues. While I believe we had largely eliminated tribalism as an active force, its byproducts and those of the family system were still with us, I could not have chosen my government without some regard to tribal origins, and even, within the Party itself, there was at times a tendency to condemn or recommend some individual on the basis of his tribal or family origin.[17]

Nkrumah admits here that he combated and submitted to this kinship compulsion. Members of the Opposition did likewise when they came to power after the 1966 coup. Evidently their condemnations of Nkrumah arose from their pique that under his rule their own close kin were not favored for patronage positions. To achieve positions of power to help oneself and one's kin is an ignored motivation for this Opposition. Once in power they expanded nepotism and corruption to previously unknown levels. An objective history of post-Nkrumah governments should not rule out this kinship compulsion as a reason why many joined these regimes.

Most historical accounts of Nkrumah's life have focused solely on his political and economic policies in the physical realm. Historians have looked back on the ten years that he spent in the United States (1935–1945), and the two he spent in England (1945–1947) as preparatory for his life as a revolutionary Pan-African socialist. Nkrumah's quest for knowledge in the West was indeed an element of the intellectual foundation of his leadership. Upon his return to Ghana, he immediately joined the leadership of the Ghanaian independence movement. He enjoyed no intermediary preparatory period in Ghana. So it is incontrovertible that the twelve years of work and study in Harlem; Philadelphia, Lincoln, and Chester, Pennsylvania; Washington, D.C., and London were the crucible shaping his later years as Ghana's leader.

All of Nkrumah's biographers view the roots of his ideological radicalization in his sojourn in the West. His experience with Western modernism understandably influenced his appeal to his modernist constituency. None, however, has pinpointed specific influences during those twelve years that honed his skills at galvanizing his preliterate constituency. Nkrumah understood that their profound knowledge of Africa's metaphysical, premodern philosophies and customs adequately compensated for their lack of knowledge of modernist philosophies. In the African American diaspora, he observed examples of how to become the messianic, mystical leader whose charismatic authority he projected as God's divine will for Ghana and Pan-Africa. This process of *mystification* that so influenced later events in Ghana, has remained a lacunae that the present study also will fill.

Concurrently, we must also examine those acquisitions from the West that led to Nkrumah's failures in the light of his overthrow. The shortcomings of the Ghanaian Revolution reflected his shortcomings as its leader and human symbol. Among those shortcomings was a vulnerability to the military coup d'état driven by domestic opponents and hostile foreign coconspirators. The African epic hero proves his heroism only when he overcomes the obstacles that fate and temporal opponents thrust between him and his divine destiny. Nkrumah believed that his ultimate destiny was to lead a Union of African States. We must examine his failure to achieve that goal in any behavioral analysis of him as a culture hero and revolutionary.

Nkrumah and his supporters vanquished the powerful system of British colonialism. They won Ghana's freedom. The Black Atlantic accordingly heaped deserved adulation onto the movement's leader. But just as a hero's reputation grows with every victory over a foe, so does his reputation diminish when neither divine favor nor his trickster's ingenuity overcomes greater foes. This happened during the Cold War when he challenged with socialist revolutionary zeal the powerful proponents of Western capitalism. He failed to rescue Congo's Patrice Lumumba from the Western plots to eliminate him and, by eliminating his key country, the West ended the possibility of a unified Africa. Nkrumah did not learn crucial lessons from the overthrow of Patrice Lumumba. He failed to study the science of the coup d'état . Therefore he could not foresee and forestall the 1966 military takeover of Ghana. This coup was a defeat for African peoples everywhere. The science of the coup d'état as it relates to Nkrumah's downfall undergoes dissection in the final chapter of this study. Declassified U.S. government documents make it further possible to piece together the shortcomings of the hero and the strengths of his opponents.

From the beginning of the anticolonial movement Nkrumah led after World War II to his overthrow in the 1966 coup d'état to his death in Guinea in 1972, at no point did Nkrumah enjoy the leisure of a "loyal opposition." Of necessity, his persona needed to adjust to the character of the challenges he faced. The exposes and declassified documents that detail the machinations of Accra's CIA station chief, Howard T. Banes, and the Assistant Secretary of State for African Affairs, G. Mennen Williams, were a continuous counterpoint to those ideals and myths that Nkrumah personified.

The term "overlapping Diasporas" refers to the ideas that traversed the Black Atlantic.[18] The White Atlantic also had overlapping diasporas. European, and later U.S., economic and political interests used both force and discourse to maintain dominance. While promoting the ideals of "democracy" and "free enterprise" and the "rule of law," the U.S. State Department's declassified documents reveal the secret collusion with undemocratic forces in Ghana to subvert Nkrumah's ideals and policies. They detail overlapping common interests between opposition forces in Ghana and the opponents of Nkrumah in the U.S. government.

In fact, Nkrumah's failure as a trickster, playing the West off against the East in the great Cold War game, could summarize his downfall. These declassified documents, from the State Department and the Central Intelligence Agency (CIA), describe, in chronological detail, official U.S. duplicity. It displayed to his face a duplicitous friendliness that, in effect, matched Nkrumah's duplicity and turned the tables on Nkrumah as trickster and in the end defeated him at his own game.

Nkrumah returned to Africa carrying on his shoulders the dreams of all Africa and her diaspora. Colonialists had conquered Africa in both the physical and the metaphysical realms. Only a hero with skills in both modernist revolutionary ideology and premodern occultism could topple these twin pillars of settler white supremacy. The accurate historical narrative of Nkrumah's life must also methodologically reflect the interplay between the conflicting and complimentary forces. They drove him personally and politically. Nkrumah lived an epic that ushered in a new epoch. As during times of other great social upheavals, epic and epoch were inextricably intertwined.[19] African epics arrange in sequence important *packages of events* leading inexorably toward the epochal ending.[20] Following are these packages of events in the epic of Osagyefo Kwame Nkrumah.

1

The Call and Preparation of the Hero

Certain fundamental factors are common in African epics and myths. The coming of the hero is marked by mystery, a portentous event, a childhood that sets him apart from other common children, and/or a fantastical occurrence during his youth that inspires awe, veneration, and even a tale of terror. The birth itself is an event of wonderment.[1]

The Mandingo hero, Sundiata of Mali, remained unborn in his mother's womb for seven years. Another Mandingo hero, Dugo Kambili, would leave his mother's womb at night, walk about, and return to the womb in the morning.[2] In the Mwindo epic in the Congo, the warrior Mwindo "was born laughing, speaking, and walking, holding a conga-scepter in his right hand and an ax in his left."[3] These supernatural feats established that the heroes were not constrained by the forces that subdued normal mortals. In these African epics, the hero's ability to counter and overcome forces stronger than himself begins at birth. Not even the hegemonic power of nature can subdue the hero as a child. Hence, no hegemonic power will be able to resist his force when he reaches full manhood. His birth is as inexorable. In the words of the psychologist Otto Rank, "The new born hero is the young sun rising from the waters, first confronted by lowering clouds, but finally triumphing over all obstacles."[4]

Nkrumah's autobiography presented his youth in this pre-heroic mode. He portrayed himself, from the first moment of life, as an extraordinary being who could overcome forces that would have prevailed over persons who were not gifted with special divine favor. Like Africa's previous epic heroes, his birth was extraordinary. He was born on the day of the festive funeral celebrations of his paternal grandmother. Postpartum, he would neither breathe nor cry. He had been out of the womb for so many minutes without breathing that his mother gave him up for dead. His female relatives reluctantly left the funeral festivities and stuffed a banana into his mouth to try to induce coughing. The banana and the women's loud banging of cymbals and other instruments finally convinced the baby to join the world of the living.[5]

At this initial stage of the Nkrumah epic, two noteworthy proce-dures essential to the hero brought him to life. The banana was the sweet fruit of Ghana's soil. It transferred to Nkrumah the power of the earth itself, without which he would not have lived. Nkrumah received this special mystical connection to the land that launched a lifetime of his repaying the debt of life that he owed to Ghana and all of Africa.

No African's loyalty and love for Ghana would be greater than Nkrumah's. The language Nkrumah used to describe his affection for his country often exhibited a connection that was beyond politics. He shared a personal, even romantic, relationship with the soil that had given him life. We hear this fervor in his urging Ghanaians to emulate his enthusiasm: "Love Ghana with a passionate love that can offer the highest sacrifice without demur."[6] He spread this love over the lands of continental Africa and sought the continent's unity and empower-ment as if Pan-Africanism were a personal obsession rather than a political strategy. This personalism would continue in Nkrumah's life-long fervor for indigenous African culture.

When the women left the funeral celebration of Nkrumah's grand-mother to assist his mother in giving birth, their instruments and music reflected the miraculous, life-giving power of African culture itself in the life of the hero on his quest. In Nkrumah's autobiography, each instrument would reverberate with deeper meaning in the Akan mind. Moreover, the Akans are matrilineal; family lineage is traced only through the mother. In the Akan worldview, the child's blood comes from the mother's side of the family; the spirit comes from the father's.[7] There were no men in the room during the critical minutes when the stillborn child came alive and began his epic march from an exceptional birth to an exceptional life. The presence of only women during this supernatural birth pointed toward some special factor in Nkrumah's blood. Long after his miraculous birth, it would continue to give occult legitimacy to his leadership. "The answer to our long suffering was to be found in a boy born of humble parentage forty-nine years ago in a little dilapidated muddy structure in the little vil-lage of Nkroful in Nzimaland."[8] The parallels with the divine birth of Jesus continued when considering that Nkrumah never had an earthly father and his mother bore the title "Mother of Ghana."[9]

In the first six years of an Nzima boy's life, he would not go to any formal school. Adults would encourage him to learn through obser-vation. They would organize the child's play for educational purposes. Elders would also teach the child through stories that conveyed the traditions and myths of their people.[10]

Like other epic heroes, Nkrumah, as a child, set himself apart from other children. Having a childhood that contained marked differences from other children adds to the mystique of the hero as an adult. At this youthful stage in the hero's life, African myths lay foundations of the wunderkind, precociously wielding terror that nourishes "the heroic song."[11] According to the Ghanaian merchant Kojo Atta, one of the principal informants of this study, it was during Nkrumah's youth that his power as a mighty sorcerer first appeared. An Akan would read Nkrumah's autobiography differently than a Westerner. "We would know that Nkrumah was telling us that he was born with special powers and that he was stronger than the white man, even as a child."[12]

Nkrumah wrote about his youthful preference for being alone with nature and animals as opposed to playing with other children.[13] Other African epic heroes encountered "ghosts" and supernatural spirits during their youths. Following this heroic tradition, Nkrumah did not flee in fear of occult communions with the dead. Instead, ghost stories made him long for death so that he could join those beings he referred to as "privileged souls."[14]

Nkrumah yearned for the supernatural. He stated that he did not know whether this longing meant that he had been blessed with psychic power. Even so, his own mother confirmed his occult precocity. During his childhood, his mother frequently told him of an incident that occurred during his early years. She was wading across a river with Nkrumah strapped on her back when suddenly he exclaimed that she was standing on a fish. To her surprise, she discovered that she actually had trapped a fish under her foot. The incident convinced his mother of Nkrumah's special psychic gifts.

Knowing the value that Africans placed on such stories of the supernatural, and the esteem in which the Akan matrilineal clans hold the mother, Nkrumah knew how to present his youth in the epic heroic mode. He did not have to say in his autobiography that he personally believed that the fish incident set him apart as a medium of the supernatural. All he had to do was tell the story and relate that his mother believed it.

Isidore Okpewho, the Nigerian novelist and critic, stated a universal truth about African epics and the supernatural that this study regards as directly relevant to the life of Nkrumah:

> We cannot, in fact, fully appreciate the heroic personality without examining its supernatural dimensions. We are unlikely to find many traditions of the oral epic in which the hero achieves his amazing feats

by sheer force or naked human strength. And considering that, in some of these epic tales, the denizens of the supernatural world are treated as dramatic characters—gods and spirits participating in the action of the tale—rather than simply as metaphors, it becomes hard to accept any definition of "true heroism" that underrates the influence of the supernatural on the personality and circumstances of the hero.[15]

Okpewho's observation is especially applicable to the daily life of the Akans of Ghana. They take for granted the omnipresence of supernatural occult forces in daily life. Communion with the supernatural was one of Nkrumah's daily practices.

Precocious Terror and Witchcraft

The West African epic hero also precociously inspires terror. The Songhay hero, Askia Muhammad, was a Soninke descended from the medieval empire of Ghana. His epic is directly relevant to the epic of Nkrumah, the hero of modern Ghana. The griot Nouhou Malio recited that during the childhood of Askia Muhammad:

> He unslung his lance, and pierced his uncle with it until the
> Lance touched the prayer skin.
> Until the spear went all the way to the prayer skin . . .
> They took away the body, and [Askia] came to sit down on the
> Prayer skin of his uncle.
> They prayed.
> They took away the body to bury it.
> This is how [Askia] took the chieftaincy.[16]

Askia's homicidal disposal of his domineering uncle, Si, established his chieftainship of the Songhay peoples. His illustrious rule began during his childhood, not from an act of virtue but from one of murderous terror.

As a child, Nkrumah terrified two grown men into running away from him. When describing this event, Nkrumah wrote about himself in the third person, as if he were a griot telling his own story: "Few would have believed that the small boy who kept to himself . . . or who would make himself scarce for hours on end, could, when roused, spit fire like a machine gun and use every limb and fingernail in defending his idea of justice."[17] Nkrumah here employed the praise-song metaphoric style, common in African epics, to describe his own terrifying abilities even in his youth.

The way Nkrumah related this tale revealed more than what he explicitly stated. The first man to flee in terror was a policeman whom Nkrumah attacked with sand to force him to release his half brother. The second man was a suitor of Nkrumah's half sister. Nkrumah recalled that he kicked at him and "yelled and screamed like one possessed." This behavior caused the second grown man also to run off in fear. When examined through a "Western" lens, the problem with Nkrumah's explanation is the lack of connection between the child's act and the grownups' responses. Mere infantile impertinence appears insufficient to cause the terror that Nkrumah said he induced. The flight of two frightened adults, one a policeman and the other an ardent suitor, required a greater threat.

Nkrumah's words "like one possessed" suggest a deeper explanation, one that Akan people would readily recognize. A child behaving strangely—staying away from other children for long hours, longing for the world of the dead and seeking supernatural presences, and becoming the subject of stories about his extraordinary psychic powers—would generate respectful regard as a witch or sorcerer-in-the-making among the Nzima, the subclan that was most famous for these powers. The only logical explanation for how a young boy could terrorize two grown men is if the two men were afraid of something other than the tangible. Nkrumah's odd childhood behavior would have already been interpreted through the African lens as having occult connotations. Fear of this power more plausibly explains why two grown men would flee from a child acting furious and "possessed."

Other Akans commonly directed fear of witchcraft toward Nkrumah's Nzima people. Until this author learned of this fear, an encounter with a market woman in the Ashanti capital, Kumasi, was inexplicable. When asked about the "great Kwame Nkrumah," instead of smiles and honorific poetry, she spat forcefully on the ground and proclaimed him an *obayifo*. This word translates as "witch," and, in this context, "damned witch!"[18]

As a teenager, the Ghanaian restaurateur Sam Nyako was a member of the Young Pioneers, a pro-Nkrumah youth organization. "Everybody in Ghana knows the Nzima are witches," said Nyako. "Nkrumah was Nzima, so he was a witch. Only people who were uneducated in the villages put a lot of weight on that witchcraft stuff though."[19]

How many Ghanaians were uneducated and lived in the villages during Nkrumah's rule? "Most," Nyako replied. Then, reflecting further, he concluded, "But so long as things are good, it could not be a problem. In the villages, witchcraft is bad only when something goes wrong. That's why everybody loved Nkrumah, until money went bad. Everybody knew he was Nzima. They've got witch powers. We know it. That's how he overcame the British and brought independence."

Nyako, a member of the Gaa ethnic group, was not among those uneducated rural people whom he said took Nkrumah's occult powers seriously, yet he also took these powers seriously.[20] His self-contradictory comments reflect the ambivalence toward indigenous occultism that exists in Ghana. Born-again Christians, orthodox Muslims, and Western-educated secular intellectuals still pour libations and offer sacrifices to the ancestors and the indigenous spirits.

Ghana's 1960 census classified 77 percent of its population as living in rural areas. The census officials based this percentage on a standard that named localities with less than 5,000 people as "rural". The Ghanaian census also classified 77 percent of the population as "illiterate."[21] These statistics place three quarters of Ghana's population in Nyako's category of persons most likely to believe in the Nzima prime minister's powers as a sorcerer. This popular belief was the foundation of Nkrumah's charismatic authority.

Belief in Nzima sorcery extends into the twenty-first century. Its retention gives further evidence of Ghanaians' attitudes during Nkrumah's era. James Owusu is an Ashanti from Accra who lives and works in Baltimore, Maryland. He has a graduate degree in biology and a theoretical foundation in Western science. But he holds firmly to traditional occult beliefs about the Nzima. "The Nzima have the strongest magic. The Nzima are tight. Their magic is so strong outsiders cannot break through," he said gravely. Owusu further explained that people think that this is mere superstition, but he had first-hand knowledge that confirmed that fears of Nzima witchcraft were well placed. He referred to his scientific background to affirm that he was not expressing ignorant superstitions. His opinion resulted from facts that he knew with scientific certainty. [22]

Writing for Accra's Presbyterian missionary publishing house in 1961, during Nkrumah's presidency, Hans. W. Debrunner produced a book entitled, *Witchcraft in Ghana*. According to Debrunner, "The reputation of mystery with which popular superstition surrounds Nzima . . . strengthens the belief current in Ghana that all Nzima are witches."[23] Debrunner found it unnecessary to mention at the time that the president of Ghana was an Nzima and, therefore, was included in the "all."

George P. Hagan, in his assessment of Nkrumah's leadership style, wrote: "The African mystical notions associated with him arose out of the fact that Nkrumah was an Nzema [sic].[24] The Nzema are famed for witchcraft. In the mind of the average Gold Coaster [i.e., Ghanaian], Nzema witchcraft, besides being powerful—perhaps, the most powerful witchcraft power anywhere—was reputed to be capable of being used for good ends."[25]

Nkrumah promoted his visionary socialist economics as a modernizing vehicle for Ghana and all of Africa. Ghanaian intellectuals who had studied Marxism and who understood Nkrumah's Western theories, judged them by multiple factors during the Cold War within mentalities of modernism. Nkrumah's approach was premodernist for the 77 percent of Ghanaians who were preliterate. According to the Ghanaian street vendor Kofi Ogra, "In Kumasi the Ashanti say, 'If you want money, go see an Nzima.' People believe that the Nzima are able to get money without working. We Ashanti are known for being warriors and the Nzima are known for their sorcery."[26] Ogra's comment evidences an indigenous, premodern criterion for assessing Nkrumah's economics, which has previously eluded the analytical eye of historians. Subsistence farmers, market women, goldfield workers, and cocoa plantation laborers would find the Nzima leader's divine gift for acquiring wealth for himself and, by extension, for Ghana, as more understandable than Marxian rhetoric.

Nzima witchcraft recurs as an important source of charismatic authority in Nkrumah's political life. So some definitions distinguishing witchcraft from sorcery and magic are appropriate at this point. Hagan's comment on Nzima witchcraft as a potential vehicle for good separates it from some of the predominant anthropological and sociological analyses of African witchcraft. One of the best attempts to define and categorize African occult beliefs was made by T. O. Beidelman. He studied the Kagaru people of Tanzania. The Kagarus are matrilineal like the Akans. Beidelman distinguished between magic, sorcery, and witchcraft.

Magic

The manipulation of persons and things through the use of objects, words, and acts to give one access to supernatural powers for either good or evil purpose.

Sorcery

The supernatural power to cause another person or that person's possessions harm through the use of various substances or acts. The efficacy of sorcery depends upon the nature of the acts performed rather than upon the moral character of the practitioner.

Witchcraft

The power to exert supernatural harm upon another person or his possessions, that power depending upon inherent evil qualities in the evil person (witch) himself/herself.[27]

Only Beidelman's definitions of magic and sorcery apply to the Nzima in general and to Kwame Nkrumah in particular. Witchcraft in Beidelman's schema, however, is always negative. But in Nzima culture witches are capable of using their powers for both good and evil. In his quest toward his epic destiny, Kwame Nkrumah utilized magic, sorcery, and witchcraft in his leadership of Ghanaian nationalism.

Historically, as crucial to the African epic hero having supernatural abilities is the belief of his people that he has them. In Max Weber's classic formula, the leader's charisma receives validation from his subjects' recognition of it.[28] However, Weber's formula is too simplistic for application to Nkrumah's Ghana. It requires an addendum. In the Ghanaian dialectic between the leader and the led, Weber's formula invests too much value in the subjectivity of the led. Unlike Weber's European examples, charismatic heroes in Africa's epics seek validation from the occult. These occult forces grant to African heroes amazing powers to determine their own destinies and the destinies of others.

Weber took his ideas on charisma from his analysis of religion and transferred them to politics.[29] Weber then underestimated how much political charisma retained its religious character. In the context of African divine kingship and heroic epics, occult forces ultimately determine the success or failure of the hero. The hero is heroic because he overcomes greater obstacles than an ordinary "unheroic" person is capable of overcoming. Should the hero depart from the path that the supernatural has predestined, should he ignore the divine advisers, only then does he forfeit divine favor. This loss in the spiritual realm precipitates the hero's loss of popular favor; not, as Weber's formula would describe, the reverse process of the loss of popular favor precipitating his downfall.[30]

The Hero's First Challenge

Nkrumah's paramount reliance upon the divine favor of Africa's gods recurs throughout his heroic quest. He first displayed this trait in his encounter with the Roman Catholic Church. Nkrumah's mother had converted to Catholicism. She then apparently arranged for Father

George Fischer, a Roman Catholic priest from Germany, to baptize
Nkrumah and guide him toward a serious adherence to Catholicism.
Here begins Nkrumah's first episode—although apolitical—of criti-
cally thinking outside the hegemonic discourse of colonialism.
Nkrumah did not mention that at this point he had heard or held any
negative attitude toward colonialism. Yet, the young hero bristled
under the dominating dogma of the colonialists' powerful institutionalized religion:

> As I grew older, the strict discipline of Roman Catholicism stifled me. It
> was not that I became any less religious but rather that I sought free-
> dom in the worship of and communion with my God, for my God is a
> very personal God and can only be reached direct. I do not find the need
> of, in fact I resent the intervention of a third party in such a personal
> matter.[31]

We must, throughout this study, keep in mind that Nkrumah wrote
his autobiography to influence Ghana and Africa contemporarily and
in the future. He projected himself as a symbol of the collective
Ghanaian and Pan-African nation. The leader seeks by this means to
collectivize his individual example. For the heroic myth to have an
impact on contemporary events, it must be internalized by the masses.
Success is gauged by how many partisans the leader produces as repli-
cations of himself.[32]

Nkrumah declined to submit to the domination of the doctrines of
the Roman Catholic Church. Like Sundiata and many other African
epic heroes before him, he had met God personally. He would not
allow any mortal to sway him from the divine path of his spirit-quest.
Nkrumah's encounter with the power of the Catholic Church had
placed him in jeopardy of forsaking his divine mission. But forces
drawn from within him led him triumphantly past Catholic doctrinal
hegemony to continue on the heroic path.

The epic context of this rejection of the domination of the colonizer's spiritual system is that heroes face and fight powerful forces,
fearlessly descending into great jeopardy and arising in heroic victory.
The more vulnerable and weaker the heroes than the powers they challenge, the greater their heroic stature after victory. Edward Wilmot
Blyden described in 1878 the awesome power of the psy-ops program
that Nkrumah defied by rejecting Christian orthodoxy. Blyden
observed that along with the "Christian teaching, [the African] and his
children received lessons of their utter and permanent inferiority and

subordination to their instructors . . . All tendencies to independent individuality were repressed and destroyed. Their ideas and aspirations could be expressed only in conformity with the views and tastes of those who held rule over them. All avenues to intellectual improvement were closed against them, and they were doomed to perpetual ignorance."[33]

Nkrumah matched his personal Nzima magic, his personal relationship with his God, against the daily magic of Catholic priests. The powerful Catholic magic of transubstantiation would have awed every African believer in the occult. This was the feat during the Holy Communion during which priests transformed bread and wine into Christ's flesh and blood.

The *Catholic Dictionary* defines transubstantiation as "the complete change of the substance of bread and wine into the substance of Christ's body and blood by a validly ordained priest during the consecration at Mass, so that only the accidents of bread and wine remain."[34] Only priestly sorcery could transform the unseen flesh and blood of the crucified Savior into substances that Africa's black converts devoured. In the African mind, the occult significance of this magic would naturally be intertwined with the superior military, economic, technological, and scientific prowess that also accompanied the conquering colonialists. Africans would have to believe in a comparable or superior magic to reduce the intimidating power of Catholic magic. They would, one day, have to believe that a leader possessed this superior magic to transfer to him the awe and reverence that they had directed to the colonial conqueror's spiritual powers.

Catholic and Protestant missionary doctrines were central to the colonial "civilizing mission" in Africa. Nkrumah's *Autobiography* described his childhood encounter with the Catholic Church as one in which he confronted and defeated this powerful occult institution. The hero won his first victory over Western forces. This would be the beginning of many victories that would lower the esteem and awe of these Western institutions in African eyes. By this means Nkrumah commences Africa's mental decolonization.

We must accurately assess the power of the "civilizing mission," as an intrinsic feature of colonial domination, to know the magnitude of the victory that Nkrumah's telling of the story conveyed to Africans. The legitimacy of the colonialists required the colonized to internalize their own inferiority. After the colonized saw all of their tribal gods smashed by the invader's mightier power, both colonized and colonizer recognized that God was not on the side of the defeated. The legitimacy and value of all that was indigenous was undermined. Every fashion and belief system that came ashore with the colonial conquerors had an aura of victory and superiority. The colonizer then created his antipode in the person of the inferior colonized. Colonizer and colonized were then locked in a dialectical unity of opposites.[35]

Blyden stated, furthermore, that Africans were very negatively impacted by the pervasive white Christian iconography and religious paintings because in their minds the highest moral and intellectual qualities could be found only in a person with white skin.[36] In these pictures the Holy Family was white, like Africa's conquerors, but Africans were black, the opposite of white, the opposite of holiness and superiority.

This iconography of whiteness is very prominent in the Catholic faith.[37] Hence Nkrumah's victory stands as an even greater achievement. Blyden's description of African Christians as being without independent individuality and being slow and unprogressive makes Nkrumah's fierce individuality and his struggle for personal and national independence all the more heroic.[38]

The poet Aimé Césaire, a keen observer of colonialism in his home island, Martinique, as well as in Africa, reduced the whole project of mental colonization to a simple equation that was force-fed to the colonized: Christianity, with its white Holy Family, equaled civilization; indigenous religions (always called "paganism," "witch doctoring," etc.) equaled savagery.[39]

Resistance by Ghana's people to European colonialism and spiritual encroachments was centuries old. Collaboration by Ghana's elites first with European slave traders and later with colonialists was equally old. By the turn of the twentieth century, British military, missionaries, and merchants had vanquished the last vestiges of indigenous resistance in the Gold Coast colony.

An obscure anthropological study by colonial Britain's Institute of Race Relations captured the negative picture of the Ghanaian mentality before independence. This study accentuated the magnitude of Nkrumah's victory in the realm of the supernatural. The title of the book that resulted from the study is *White Man*. The subtitle describes the book as *A Study of the Attitudes of Africans to Europeans in Ghana before Independence*. Colonialists periodically made these studies to stay aware of the mentalities of their subject peoples.

The research in *White Man* concluded that Ghanaians regarded European power as based in the supernatural. The author, Gustav Jahoda, wrote that the illiterate Africans believed Europeans to be possessors of "extraordinary, even magical or supernatural powers."[40] Jagoda next quoted a 1941 study by M. J. Field that stated that Ghanaians regarded Europeans as "not far from Gods themselves."[41] As further proof of their divine status in African eyes, Jagoda described an incident in rural Ghana during which a "fetish priest" asked him to lay his white hands on a black woman whom he was witch-cleansing. "The priest explained that the power of the white man would make the rite particularly effective." The priest indignantly rejected his explanations that Europeans lacked special magical powers.[42]

The history of dubious colonialist anthropological research into the attitudes of colonized peoples raises questions of credibility. Nevertheless, the consistency of Jagoda's study with the observations of Blyden and numerous African observers makes his recollections plausible.[43] In colonial Africa, the colonizers' technological supremacy had penetrated the spirit-realm and caused the Africans to believe that they were spiritually inferior.

Nkrumah had already triumphed over death during his birth. Next he had displayed occult prowess to vanquish two grown men. Finally, he heroically triumphed over this psychological and spiritual hegemony of the Europeans that had afflicted the majority of his people with complexes of cultural and spiritual inferiority. This latter victory exhibited that as a mere child he had begun to decolonize his own mind. Later in his life, more important for preliterate Ghanaians than Nkrumah's modernist ideologies that they could not see, was that Nkrumah's Nzima witchcraft was stronger than the "witchcraft" of the white colonialists, whose powers they regularly saw.

In the Ghanaian mind, Nkrumah's coming from the Akan clan that all Ghanaians regarded as the most powerful masters of the occult, was as crucial in his defeating colonialism as were any of his ideological treatises. His superior Nzima sorcery could exorcise white supremacy from his mind and from the minds of the Ghanaian nation.

In his autobiography, Nkrumah portrayed himself to the people of Ghana, who believed in European spiritual supremacy, as a leader who had met Europeans on metaphysical ground and had come away independently African. Unlike Max Weber's sociological skepticism, and the cynical view expressed in Robert H. Jackson and Carl G. Rosberg's *Personal Rule in Black Africa*, this study asserts that Nkrumah's charisma was indeed that of a uniquely special human being. Whether it derived from "On High" is a theological issue that is too problematical for analytical detection.

What is detectable is that this young hero continually confronted mighty powers and came away spiritually and intellectually independent and victorious. This independence was the foundation of his life. It served as a nationalist template for Africa's independence. Each of Nkrumah's victories raised his standard higher in his own eyes and in the eyes of the persons he met during his quest and whose destinies were intertwined with his own. Each victory and his own personal dynamism increased his charismatic authority.

Aggrey, the Sage of Achimota

The African epic hero does not grow into manhood like a bull, lolling in the fields, eating and drinking among cows until he comes of age. The hero matures while steadily facing challenges and obstacles, and inexorably advancing toward his destiny. As he advances, he encounters forces that aid and guide his quest as well as forces that attempt to deflect and hinder him from his epic destiny. These helpful spirit-guides (genies, sages) usually emit an aura of the exceptional about themselves. By accepting the assistance of the guides, recognizing them as helpers, and overcoming the obstacles placed before him, the hero's legendary status grows.

The Mandingo heroes Samori Toure and Sundiata Kieta both enjoyed the tactical guidance of genies.[44] Those spirit-guides helped each leader at crucial times in their quests. As is evident from the epic of Samori Toure, spiritual guidance does not necessarily insure perpetual success. This lesson bears close observation, considering the known denouement of the Nkrumah epic.

Especially instructive in understanding the Nkrumah epic is the epic of Sonsan of Kaarta. The hero Sonsan meets his spirit-guide on the outskirts of his hometown.[45] The guide is known as *Jinna Mansa*, or genie king. He and his genie wife protect a sacred grove where the local spirits reside. The hero Sonsan walks near this grove. The genie then speaks to his wife about Sonsan:

> His destiny, his fame, and his life
> They are all contained in the earth of this grove.[46]

Sonsan's protonationalism begins with his spirit-guide prophesying that the destiny of this hero and the sacred soil are inseparable. The grove is the home of ancestral spirits who demand the genies' protection. The genies permit no one to defecate in the grove, cut chewing sticks from it, or enter it with an axe.[47] But now the very same spirits, for whom the husband and wife genies protect the grove, command the genies to have Sonsan destroy it. The female genie tells Sonsan:

> Do you see that grove of trees?
> You must return and cut it down to clear the field.
> That is how you will gain your destiny, your fame, and your life
> All of this you will find in the earth of that place, oh Bamana man.

The Bamana hero must destroy whatever has grown upon the earth before he can build a new life for himself and his people. Structures on top of the soil were never sacred; it was only the soil itself. The soil was the home of the holy spirits of the Bamana. But on the top of the soil were growths that were no longer conducive to popular progress. The hero must destroy the growths and then build upon the soil to achieve his personal extraordinary destiny.

Sonsan saw no inconsistency or contradiction in following the prescriptions both of Islam and of traditional African religion when he fulfilled the divine command. As we have already seen, a similar syncretism between monotheism (albeit Christian) and African pantheism was a hallmark of Nkrumah's own guidance from the spirit-realm.[48] Such was the epic prototype into which Nkrumah's heroism matured. At least, this was the way that he portrayed himself in his autobiography.

In the African epic, each spirit-guide that the hero encounters is like a step on a ladder that he climbs toward his fate. The first spirit-guide Nkrumah encountered on his quest was his mother. Even though it was she who brought him into the Catholic faith, she also instructed him always to remember his ancestors. This important advice solidified his relationships with those spiritual forces of the dead that Akans believe effect change and have power among the living. These ancestral spirits were analogous to the jinns who guided the Mandingo heroes, Sundiata Keita and Samori Toure.

Nkrumah's second spirit-guide was the sage Dr. James Emman Kwegyir Aggrey (1875–1927). He was the assistant vice principal of the Prince of Wales College at Achimota. The British colonial governor, Gordon Guggisberg, established this college to train the African elite to serve British interests in colonial Africa. Aggrey was the first black faculty member.

The spirit-guide cannot be an ordinary person, for ordinary sages do not produce extraordinary heroes. Aggrey was the "greatest African since St. Augustine," according to one biographer.[49] In some parts of Africa people literally heralded his coming to speak to them as that of the Messiah. White observers pronounced Aggrey a saint. Nkrumah declared Aggrey the most remarkable man he had ever met.[50] One biographer recalled an elderly African saying, "The good book says there is no man perfect, no, not one, but I reckon Professor Aggrey came as near perfection as any man that ever lived."[51] This was the spirit-guide that Nkrumah credited with setting him firmly onto the path of African nationalism and racial pride.[52]

During the 1920s, Aggrey was arguably the most famous indigenous African in all of Africa. He had received his Ph.D. from Columbia University. While still in New York, the philanthropic Phelps-Stokes Fund recruited him to tour Africa in 1920, under the supervision of white patrons, to survey the social, economic, and educational conditions of Africa. Aggrey performed so well for the Phelps-Stokes African Education Commission that he was asked to return for a second tour in 1924.

On his visits to different African cities, Aggrey spoke with an eloquence that swelled his reputation and fame. Aggrey's fierce pride in his blackness was legendary. The following illustrates this pride:

> If I went to heaven, and God said Aggrey, I am going to send you back, would you like to go as a white man? I should reply, No, send me back as a black man, yes, completely black. And if God should ask why? I would reply, because I have a work to do as a black man that no white man can do. Please send me back as black as you can make me.[53]

As a spirit-guide, Aggrey's divine mission was to teach Nkrumah to oppose the hegemonic discourse of colonialism in the arenas of racial pride and cultural integrity. This Aggrey achieved without equivocation:

> Too often the African was taught that everything African was heathen, wrong, ungodly. Our very names were designated as pagan and we were given European or American names. Our dances were all tabooed, our games dropped, our customs discarded and all that was best in our system was forgotten with baneful results.[54]

Aggrey's most famous speech was his parable of the eagle. Very possibly Aggrey had heard a version of this parable at church when he was a student in the United States.[55] An eagle is raised as a chicken and comes to believe that it is in fact a chicken. Aggrey says: "Eagle, thou are an eagle; thou doest belong to the sky and not to this earth; stretch forth thy wings and fly." After the eagle at last takes flight, Aggrey continued, "My people of Africa we were created in the image of God, but men have made us think that we are chickens, and we still think we are; but we are eagles. Stretch forth your wings and fly! Don't be content with the food of chickens!"[56]

The eagle parable spoke in the universal language of the mythic fairy tale. In its Hindu version, Indra, the king of the gods, forgot his true lofty nature when he became a pig. Spirit-guides had to awaken him to his divinity, which restored him to his rulership. Then "he began to laugh when he realized what a hideous dream he had; he, the king of the gods, to have become a pig and to think that pig life is the only life."[57]

In what direction will Aggrey's eagle fly? He refrained from concretizing the abstraction by saying that the eagle flew toward independence. The eagle did not fly over a future Ghana and look down to see an end to British military occupation and economic exploitation. Aggrey's speeches would go no farther than to advocate cultural nationalism; he did not speak for anticolonialist African nationalism.

Nkrumah wrote that Aggrey disagreed with his own identification with Marcus Garvey and that he believed in an African future of harmonious brotherhood between whites and blacks.

> I could not, even at that time, accept this idea of Aggrey's as being practicable, for I maintained that such harmony can only exist when the black race is treated as equal to the white race; that only a free and independent people—a people with a government of their own—can claim equality, racial or otherwise, with another people.[58]

Nkrumah did not mention the extent of Aggrey's subservience to British colonial interests. Nor did he mention that Aggrey was a pacifier for the British. Aggrey's urging passivity during colonialism and his oratory against black nationalism made him a trusted underling of the colonial masters.

Chief Albert Luthuli, the late president of the African National Congress of South Africa, starkly depicted Aggrey's collaboration in his memoir. One day in the 1920s, Aggrey visited Luthuli's segregated Adams College in South Africa. Aggrey told the assembled youths, "Take what you are given, even if it is only half a loaf. Only when you've used up the entire half-loaf should you ask for more."[59]

Luthuli wrote that he thought following Aggrey's advice was unwise when the Boers of South Africa did not give bread but stones. In South Africa's Transkei region, one African stated bluntly that Aggrey promoted their cooperating with and loving their enemies because he had been bought by the whites.[60]

Aggrey lived in New York during the rise of Garveyism and when W. E. B. Du Bois's magazine *Crisis* grew in popularity among the educated black elite. Nevertheless, his advice to the Africans to passively accept half of a nonexistent loaf parallels the equally conservative admonition of Booker T. Washington to black Americans to "cast down your buckets where you are." Aggrey, in fact, preached accommodationism in the Booker T. Washington tradition as opposed to the agitation of W. E. B. Du Bois. This was not an accident because the plan of the Phelps-Stokes African Education Commission was to replicate the Tuskegee model in Africa.[61] The Aggreyism that Luthuli and other South Africans heard was essentially Marcus Garvey's race pride, detached from Garvey's black nationalist activism by Booker T. Washington's conservatism and Bible-based pacifism.

The British censored and suppressed anticolonialist persons and ideas in their colonies. Had Aggrey not accommodated himself to colonialism, it is highly doubtful that the conservative Phelps-Stokes Commission would have selected him as their African co-worker. Neither would the British have given Aggrey a free rein to speak throughout Africa, nor would he have been appointed assistant vice principal on the founding day of Achimota College.[62]

Aggrey's Achimota was as racist an institution as any other produced by British colonialism. It was like an exclusive club for white British colonial educators. African scholars like Dr. J. B. Danquah, Kobina Peters, and G. N. Alema—who were more academically qualified than white staff members—never got the opportunity to teach there.

Nkrumah's friend, the future president of Nigeria, Nnamdi Azikiwe (1904–1966), still felt the insult more than forty years later when he recorded his first-hand impressions of Achimota. Moreover, Azikiwe revealed that Aggrey's appointment as Achimota's lone black employee might itself be viewed as a kind of British deception of Africans. Aggrey was actually not the vice principal that people thought he was. He was merely an *assistant* vice principal. Azikiwe asked why the British colonials with lesser academic credentials and abilities than Aggrey had "pulled the wool over the eyes of Africans by appointing him on the staff as a figurehead to be admired by liberal-minded humanitarians and spurned by small-minded snobs." [63]

Even though Nkrumah came to viscerally despise neocolonialists and other Africans who collaborated with European colonialism, he never revised his praise for Aggrey. This inconsistency deserves analysis because in it is a key to understanding this stage of Nkrumah's intellectual history.

Both Aggrey and Nkrumah had an attachment to and love for indigenous African culture. As an Akan, Aggrey was as aware as Nkrumah of the craftiness of the trickster Ananse the spider, the Akan symbol of human ingenuity. The most plausible explanation of Nkrumah's tolerance of Aggrey's blatant collaboration with colonialism is his knowledge that Aggrey was himself a trickster. Evidence suggests that Nkrumah knew that only by playing the role of a subservient colonial subject could Aggrey introduce his students to the words of Marcus Garvey and W. E. B. Du Bois. Aggrey knew that not he but his students would liberate Africa from the colonial masters he outwardly served.

Very much in the mold of the trickster, Aggrey exhibited "doubleness." He introduced Garvey's and Du Bois's powerful ideas of national liberation to the brightest minds of a colonized people. Then he stepped back and told them and the British that he really did not believe in those ideas. He believed that whites and blacks must amicably share the future of Africa the way the white and black keys on the piano make music harmoniously.[64] Surely a man who was as brilliant and perceptive as both white and black observers stated would know the impact of the nationalistic ideas he propagated.

None of the biographies and hagiographic articles about Aggrey reinforces this analysis, perhaps because these authors either did not read or undervalued a letter that Aggrey wrote to W. E. B. Du Bois in 1913. This letter does not appear in any of the writings about Aggrey, yet what it reveals is indispensable for appreciating the powerful impact of Du Bois on Aggrey as Nkrumah's spirit-guide. This letter establishes a fifty-year continuum of Du Bois's influence on Ghana's future, from 1913 until his death in Ghana in 1963.

In Africa, Aggrey's true political feelings were concealed behind the pacifist and accomodationist mask he presented to European colonial power. In this ten-page letter that Aggrey wrote while serving as the financial secretary and registrar of Livingstone College in North Carolina, he unmasked himself and revealed a totally different person.

Aggrey dated his letter July 1, 1913, with a postmark from Salisbury, North Carolina. This date is significant because it shows that he wrote the letter when Booker T. Washington's influence was diminishing and W. E. B. Du Bois's was rising. The year 1913 brought Woodrow Wilson to the presidency of the United States. Wilson's administration proceeded to resegregate the federal workforce and to dismiss those black officeholders who owed their positions to Washington's influence. This further weakened Washington's power and prestige in comparison to Du Bois's.[65] Moreover, the racist atmosphere fostered by Wilson's policies left many black Americans distraught and incensed. Wilson's praise in 1915 for the pro-Ku Klux Klan film, "The Birth of Nation," later deepened their distress. The National Association for the Advancement of Colored People (NAACP) and Du Bois's *Crisis* magazine articles were constants of courage and challenge during these times. In 1913, the NAACP also launched its own legal department to fight in the courts for black people's civil rights. When Aggrey wrote his letter to Du Bois, few black Americans could still have retained faith in the white benevolence that Washington had relied upon but that was plainly nonexistent at the highest levels of government. There was growing support for the NAACP's approach of agitation and protest, as opposed to Washington's accommodationism.

Aggrey started his letter by telling Du Bois that he wanted from him three things: (1) he wanted to get to know the African American sage on a personal basis and to be known by him, (2) he wanted to come to New York and study under Du Bois, and (3) he wanted to "identify myself with the NAACP."[66] Aggrey went on to tell Du Bois that he knew him already through reading his books, including his literary work and his sociological research. "I use your 'Souls of Black Folk' every year in my literature classes. There seems to me a consciousness of kind between us, hence I would like to know you more. I am a student and you a master."[67]

Du Bois's *Souls of Black Folk* contains a sharply critical essay about Booker T. Washington and the Tuskegee model of industrial education. If Aggrey had a "consciousness of kind" with Du Bois, then why was he traveling in Africa for the Phelps-Stokes Commission spreading the Tuskegee gospel? He obviously held a far more critical view of Booker T. Washington and the Tuskegee model than his trickster's mask revealed. Aggrey next presented his activist credentials to Du Bois, the master activist:

> When the native Kings, chiefs and people of the Gold Coast were fighting Joe Chamberlain in the nineties about the Lands' Bill, I as secretary of the Gold Coast Aborigines Rights protection Society with the assistance of Sarbah of Cape Coast, and Bertram & Co of London, retained

Asquith, then Q.C., now Premier, as our Counsel. We won our case. This will give you some ideas about me, and why I should like to study under you, the Moses of us along this line.[68]

Why this activist side of the young Aggrey in Africa, before he departed to America, has not been mentioned in his biographies is puzzling. Aggrey continued his letter by asking to be able to spend the summer studying the "ins and outs" of the NAACP. He further identified himself with Du Bois's ideology by telling him that a young woman who was his dearest friend had heard Du Bois lecture on Africa. This woman returned to Aggrey and told him that Du Bois had corroborated everything that Aggrey had already told her.

Aggrey climaxed his letter by listing seventeen books that he had read. He apparently believed that this list would further emphasize to Du Bois the commonality of their points of view. These books relate the intellectual structure behind the mask of this man, whom Nkrumah described as the most remarkable he had ever met.

One book, Edward Wilmot Blyden's *Christianity, Islam and the Negro Race*, seems especially out of place in Aggrey's library. This is because biographers have repeatedly described Aggrey as a saint who was devoutly, even fanatically, Christian. Blyden's *Christianity, Islam and the Negro Race* was very critical of what he called the "slavishness" of black Christians. Aggrey's listing Blyden's book evidences a critical and nuanced perspective on Christianity that he concealed behind his mask of uncritical devotion. Nkrumah would in the future present himself behind a similar mask. His own courageous (even bull-headed) character and strong personality, however, would not permit him to maintain the false front with the unflinching perseverance of Aggrey.

Aggrey also listed a book by an African American trickster, the former slave William Wells Brown, entitled *Three Years in Europe or, Places I have Seen and People I have Met*. This book, like Brown's slave narrative, is a practical manual of trickiness. In the tradition of the black American trickster, Brown routinely used his wits to subvert the intentions of established and stronger powers. In one illustrative incident, a destitute Brown sought employment in Monroe, Michigan, from a barber. The barber refused to hire him, so Brown secured financing to open his own shop across the street. Brown then had a sign painted that announced that he was a *"Fashionable Hairdresser from New York, Emperor of the West."*

Brown wrote, "Of course, I had to tell all who came in that my neighbour on the opposite side did not keep clean towels, that his razors were dull, and, above all, he had never been to New York to see the fashions. Neither had I. In a few weeks I had the entire business of the town, to the great discomfiture of the other barber."[69]

Brown's picaresque tricks were a perfect complement to the machinations of the Akan trickster. Aggrey showed how impressed he was by Brown by placing this book among the other books he mentioned to Du Bois. He would have, unavoidably, seen the parallels between the underdog situations overcome by the wits of this black freedman in America in the 1850s, and the similar disadvantages to be overcome by a black colonial subject in the Gold Coast in the early twentieth century.

Aggrey also listed J. E. Caseley-Hayford's books about the Gold Coast. Caseley-Hayford was one of the fathers of Ghanaian nationalism. He wrote an important and revolutionary book that a British publisher surprisingly placed into print in 1903. He was an attorney and was well aware of British sedition laws, so he first introduced his criticisms of the colonialists by stating that they were intended to bring to British attention points that could improve their relations with their colonial subjects. The title of his book illustrates his caution—*Gold Coast Native Institutions, with Thoughts upon a Healthy Imperial Policy for the Gold Coast and Ashanti*. His text went to the heart of Britain's disturbingly unhealthy imperial policies toward his people He condemned British economic unfairness, employment discrimination, forced labor, and their cultural degradation of African manhood. He did not address the British as a colonial subject but as an African liberator with a free mind:

> We notice with aching hearts . . . that in your haste to fill the colonial exchequer, little regard is paid to what will work for the material advancement of the Aborigines; whose mites help mostly to fill these coffers. . . .
>
> If you earnestly sought the material advancement of the people, you would remove obstacles from their line of progress. . . .
>
> If [the African does not labor for the Europeans] he will be driven, if needs be, into labour compounds, and made to work, as the Israelites of old were made to work for their masters . . . It does not matter if, in the process, he exchanges all the finer manly qualities, which agriculture fosters, for the common-place dram-drinking,—the cursing and the devilment of the mining camp. It does not matter to some that the best manhood of the country is being drained for this sort of work, while the ancient farms lie neglected and unattended to, and food gets scarce, and yet more scarce, in some districts. Gold! gold! gold! That is what the white man wants; and gold he must have at any price.[70]

Nkrumah would repeat Casely-Hayford's arguments forty years later. He would again compare his people to the Israelites. This time, however, the Israelites would not toil leaderless in their bondage. Nkrumah would be their Moses.

Through just these books, Aggrey presented an altogether different impression of himself than appears in the writings of any of his black or white admirers. This Aggrey who sought to join the NAACP and agitate for racial progress is not the same Aggrey that black South Africans heckled for preaching accommodationism in 1921 and 1924.[71] Nor was his pacifist message the one that he would deliver as a channel for Du Bois's ideas in Africa. Being Du Bois's conduit was clearly his intention when he wrote to him, "You can be of very much help to me, and through me to a thousand others."[72]

Finally, there were Du Bois's own writings in the *Crisis* magazine in 1913. These were militant attacks on white supremacy and affirmations of black humanity. That Aggrey identified himself with them speaks volumes about himself. It also speaks volumes about the hidden intellectual history of Kwame Nkrumah. Du Bois launched the New Year with an article titled, "A Philosophy for 1913." Du Bois's words sound presciently like a description of Aggrey at Achimota:

> Boldly and without flinching, I will face the hard fact that in this, my fatherland, I must expect insult and discrimination from persons who call themselves philanthropists and Christians and gentlemen. I do not wish to meet this despicable attitude by blows; sometimes I cannot even protest by words; but may God forget me and mine if in time or eternity I ever weakly admit to myself or the world that wrong is not wrong, that insult is not insult, or that color discrimination anything but an inhuman and damnable shame.[73]

Despite his outward advocacy of passivity before colonialism, Aggrey was a trickster at war with white colonial hegemony. Aggrey knew that he was a symbol of Africa's future through education. Only by giving innocuous speeches and teaching in parables, like Jesus, could he travel throughout Africa serving as a human beacon of African optimism and expectation. Aggrey knew the subversive double meanings of his parables. He did not state that the eagle in his allegory ever looked sharp-eyed over an Africa free of European colonialism. Nevertheless, the eagle in the actual biblical parable symbolized the omniscient God who sees all.[74] Aggrey's eagle flew above colonialism and occupied a superior vantage point.

A letter that Aggrey wrote to his wife on February 9, 1924, contained further evidence of his doubleness. He wrote it following his tour of Abyssinia for the Phelps-Stokes Commission. To everybody else he was neither a nationalist nor an advocate of Ghanaian independence from Britain. But to his wife, he wrote, "You [should feel] free and proud that you are a Negro in Abyssinia. You ought to see how the whites bow and do obeisance to the Negro rulers."[75] The difference between the Gold Coast and Abyssinia was that the former was a British colony and the latter was independent. "There are about twelve million Negroes in Abyssinia. There are a few thousand whites there but they don't rule—the Abyssinians do the ruling." This letter reveals his strong admiration for the effects of independence on the people of one of black Africa's two independent nations (Liberia was the other). Africans acting free and independent made him feel free and proud. He relished seeing whites submit to black power. He had not seen this anywhere else in the world. This is not the outer milquetoast Aggrey, who dreamed only of black/white brotherhood and equality in the future Africa. This is the inner, concealed nationalist, firebrand Aggrey, who looked to the day when in his own country the black majority would rule. He obviously yearned for Ghanaian independence, when white settlers would bow and do obeisance before Ghana's black citizens as they did before Abyssinians.

Like the sages who taught great heroes before him, Aggrey conveyed to Nkrumah an inspiring prophecy of a great awakening. He received his prophetic vision during his travels through Africa. Aggrey was the eagle whose vision swept over the continent:

> As we went we found a lot of restlessness. It was vocal in the British Colonies, subdued in the other colonies. I thank God for that restlessness. You talk about Youth Movement in other countries. There is a Youth Movement coming to Africa that some day may startle the world. This restlessness all over Africa stands for self-discovery and self-realization. It tells of power just breaking through. The great continent has been asleep for a long time. It is now waking up. This Niagara, if allowed to sweep through the land, may deluge and inundate cities and towns and bring forth rivers. If under God it can be harnessed, it will turn a dynamo and generate electricity that will illuminate that great continent, chase out the utter darkness and bring a new Africa into being.[76]

Aggrey used the American term "Niagara" exactly as Du Bois had used it to describe the hoped-for impact of the Niagara Movement that was the precursor of the NAACP. Twenty-five years later Nkrumah would lead this continental restlessness. He would echo Aggrey's prophecies in numerous speeches about Africa's self-realization. Aggrey's prediction would come true when Nkrumah's harnessing of this Niagara would manifest itself in a gigantic project on the Volta River. The Volta Dam would generate electricity to illuminate Ghana and her neighbors. Like Nkrumah, many of Aggrey's African students and admirers went on to lead and participate in independence movements in British colonial Africa. These include Malawi's first president, Hastings Banda, and Nigeria's first prime minister, Nnamdi Azikiwe. Aggrey's students' nationalistic dedication confirms that for Aggrey the trickster, the side of him that promoted racial pride and African cultural awareness proved predominant.[77]

Aggrey would be Nkrumah's first sage to deliver moderating advice. He set an example for Nkrumah by utilizing one trickster technique for dealing with stronger powers: he wore a subservient Booker T. Washington mask to conceal an activist W. E. B. Du Bois mentality.

On the inexorable quest toward his epic destiny, the hero always has the free will to accept or reject the advice of his spirit-guides. When the hero chooses not to follow divine advice, he alters his destiny. Heroic strength and intelligence can be gauged by how he handles the negative consequences of his own fateful choices. As will become evident below, Nkrumah's refusal to follow Aggrey's example altered his destiny disastrously.

Nnamdi "Zik" Azikiwe

From the restless youthful energy for self-discovery and self-realization that Aggrey observed arose an articulate voice in the writings of the Nigerian nationalist, Nnamdi Azikiwe. He became Nkrumah's next spirit-guide. This Ibo from Onitsha, Nigeria, had studied in the United States and received a degree from the country's first historically black college—Lincoln University. He returned to Africa a fervent nationalist. Nkrumah regularly read the column that Azikiwe wrote for the *African Morning Post* in Accra. In the 1920s and 1930s, Azikiwe captured the spirit of the ferment among Africa's youth and articulated their dreams and aspirations for a new Africa.[78]

Genies and sages impact the hero's decisions and influence the direction of his epic at crucial moments. Nkrumah noted in his autobiography how Azikiwe's writings impacted him. After Nkrumah taught for two years at a Catholic seminary near Elmina, he seriously considered taking priestly vows so that he could become a Jesuit. A rekindled yearning to study in America suppressed his desire for the priesthood, and reading Azikiwe's articles renewed his nationalist fervor.[79]

Azikiwe imparted to Nkrumah the courage to sharply critique and defy colonialism. He set the example for Africa's nationalists to speak the truth to the imperialist power and suffer the consequences. In 1936, as editor of the *African Morning Post*, Azikiwe published an article that brought on him and its author, Sierra Leonean Wallace Johnson, a charge of sedition. Following this incident, Azikiwe and Wallace left Ghana and returned to their respective countries. The offending article struck directly at Europeans' spiritual integrity. The Europeans' white god had become the preeminent deity for many Africans. As noted earlier, Africans associated the white conquerors' military and technological supremacy with their also having a god superior to Africans. The article attacked the god of white supremacy in one of the early battles against black inferiority. These words illustrate that the hero, Nkrumah, had in Azikiwe an extraordinary genie at this point in his life:

> Personally, I believe the European has a god in whom he believes and whom he is representing in his churches all over Africa. He believes in the god whose name is spelt Deceit. He believes in the god whose law is "Ye strong, you must weaken the weak. Ye 'civilised' Europeans, you must 'civilise' the 'barbarous' Africans with machine guns. Ye Christian Europeans, you must 'Christianise' the pagan Africans with bombs, poison gases, etc.!"
>
> In the Colonies the Europeans believe in the god that commands "Ye Administrators, make Sedition Bill to keep the African gagged, make Deportation Ordinance to send the African to exile whenever they dare to question your authority."
>
> Make an Ordinance to grab his money so that he cannot stand economically. Make Levy Bill to force him to pay taxes for the importation of unemployed Europeans to serve as Stool Treasurers. Send detectives to stay around the house of any African who is nationally conscious and who is agitating for national independence and if possible round him up in "criminal frame up" so that he could be kept behind the bars.[80]

The article also sliced through the carefully propagated moral superiority of Europeans that was a pillar supporting the legitimacy of colonialism. In this sense, legitimacy means the colonized people's acceptance of colonial authority without opposition. Wallace's seditious words were striking for their blunt force. Azikiwe's risking the British colonial power's wrath by publishing them indicates uncommon courage for an educated member of Africa's elite.

Azikiwe published his own series of articles in 1937 in the book *Renascent Africa*. This book quickly became a manual for budding nationalists in anglophone Africa. It also fed the mythic image of black America as a positive counterpoint to all that was negative on the continent of Africa. In *Renascent Africa*, Azikiwe urged, "Come now, Renascent Africa, believe in yourself." The examples of African genius that Azikiwe listed were all achievements of African Americans. A black man had actually invented the cotton gin. Norbert Rillieux had invented the evaporating pan for refining sugar. Henry Blair invented two corn huskers. Jan E. Matzelliger invented the lasting machine for mass producing boots. These achievements could only feed the mythic proportions of black America's potentialities in any African mind.[81]

Azikiwe did not distinguish between Africans in the diaspora and Africans on the continent in this 1937 work. Each branch was equally African. Azikiwe's writings (known as Zikism) show that this philosophical and cultural Pan-Africanism had firmly taken root in the minds of at least his progressive segment of the West African educated elite. Here and in the articulated dreams of Marcus Garvey were the foundations of Nkrumah's ideals. Here lies the genesis of Nkrumah's linking of philosophical and cultural Pan-Africanism to political Pan-Africanism via the movement he labeled "Positive Action."[82]

Nkrumah credited Azikiwe with encouraging him to attend Lincoln University in Pennsylvania. Azikiwe influenced Nkrumah's tricksterism regarding Nkrumah's admission to Lincoln and his departure from Africa. Moreover, Azikiwe demonstrated that among his own Ibo people, the trickster is as prominent a cultural icon for emulation as he is among Nkrumah's Nzima. The letter that Azikiwe advised Nkrumah to write for admission to Lincoln University was a masterpiece of deception.[83]

In the letter, Nkrumah identified the quote "So much to do so little done" as coming from Cecil Rhodes.[84] Cecil Rhodes was the founder of the two British colonies, Southern and Northern Rhodesia, which he named after himself. These encompassed all of modern Zambia and Zimbabwe. His orders to his subordinates were to confiscate the land and cattle of the indigenous people and proceed as if the land were unoccupied. His monopoly on control of the diamond mines in South Africa led to a cruel and lethal forced-labor system

Each NEW student must pay a $5 matriculation fee; also a deposit of $5 is required of each stu   t at entrance to cover general damage to University property.

In the Science Department, laboratory fees are charged at the rate of $3.00 a semester for ea h credit hour, and in the Department of Chemistry a breakage deposit of $5.00 is required each year

Remittance should be made by Money Order, Draft, or Cashier's Check.

Who assumes responsibility for the payment of your college bill?

Name   Chief Kwamina Adadie

Address   Nsuem via Discove

In the space below, write, as a specimen of your English composition, a brief story of your life, giving the main facts of your school record and your reasons for desiring to attend Lincoln University. (If space below is insufficient, finish on last page.)

   I neither know where to begin nor where to end; because I that the story of my life has not been one of achievements. Furthermore, I have not been anxious to tell people of what may have been accomplished by me. In truth, the burden of my life can be summarized into a single line in "The Memorian" quoted by Cecil Rhodes "So much to do so little done." Notwithstanding I shall endeavour to write few words to throw a dim light on the life that has hitherto been led by me.

   To begin with, I was born on the 21st of September 1909 in a little hamlet called Nkroful via Axim in Nzima — a country generally known to Europeans as Apolonia, in The Gold Coast. My father went with his family and stayed at Half Assinie now about forty miles from Axim, during which sojourn I was born.

   At the age of six I was sent to an elementary school in that town. Having successfully passed the Standard VII Examination of the Board of Education of that Colony, I was appointed a pupil teacher in the very school. After a year's experience in teaching I was further sent to the Teachers' Training College at Achimota for a four years' course. On leaving college, I was appointed Head Teacher of the Elmina Catholic Junior School. This was in the earlier part of 1931. After a year's work, I was transferred

Date   1st March 1935   Sign your Name   F. Nyakofi Nkrumah

When this blank is returned properly filled out, if you appear to be eligible for admission we shall send to your principal for your school record and notify you that we have done so. If your school record is not received within a reasonable time, after it has been sent for, we shall notify you. After it is received you will be informed what action has been taken regarding your admission.

UNDER NO CONDITION SHOULD A STUDENT PRESENT HIMSELF AT THE UNIVERSITY FOR ENTRANCE UNTIL HE HAS BEEN DEFINITELY INSTRUCTED BY US TO DO SO.

Address all correspondence concerning entrance to the Registrar of the College, Lincoln University, Penna.

Figure 1   Nkrumah's Lincoln University Letter of Application.

that he spread to his personal colonies. This system was in many cases worse than slavery, because a slave was owned and the owners had a material interest in the survival of their property. Forced laborers could be worked to exhaustion, beaten, starved, and killed without a property loss. The overseers then coerced replacements from the vast reserves of Africa's population.

It is difficult to imagine an African nationalist in an anglophone colony being unfamiliar with Cecil Rhodes's reputation for rabid racism. By quoting Rhodes to gain entry into Lincoln University, Nkrumah meant that he also knew about Lincoln's conservative legacy. The Presbyterian minister James Dickey founded the Ashmun Institute (the precursor to Lincoln University) as part of the "civilizing mission" of the American Colonization Society. It was named after James Ashmun, the first governor of Liberia.[85] Dickey was influenced by the conservative so-called old-school Presbyterianism not to oppose slavery because Christ had not opposed it. This denomination advocated humane treatment for the slaves and for their Christianization to precede their emancipation. Freed slaves would then cross the Atlantic to civilize and Christianize those whom their Presbyterian benefactors called "the degraded sons of Africa."[85] Slavery would then be turned into an ultimate good.

In 1935, the all-white administrators of Lincoln University were not the type of persons who would have granted admission to Nkrumah had he expressed Garveyite race pride or Azikiwe's nationalism. However, Cecil Rhodes would resonate with Lincoln's officers as a fellow bearer of the "white man's burden." By citing Rhodes, Nkrumah misinformed the admissions committee about his true political leanings. This was the trickster's self-interested duplicity.

In all likelihood, Azikiwe's experiences with the conservatism and paternalism of Lincoln's administration led him to advise Nkrumah of what trickster techniques to employ in the application process. Whatever the source of this advice, it proved successful, and Nkrumah left Africa in 1935 for Lincoln, Pennsylvania.

As Nkrumah departed he recalled that Azikiwe had urged young Africans to return from the United States with the Golden Fleece.[86] His remembering the meaning of the Greek myth of Jason and the Argonauts pursuing the Golden Fleece is evidence that Nkrumah had, even at the beginning, dreamed of returning to Africa as a nationalist leader. In the story of the Golden Fleece, the Greek hero Jason, deprived of the rulership of his kingdom, could regain his birthright only after a heroic quest. He sails away on the ship *Argo* and undergoes numerous trials and hardships before returning with the Golden Fleece and reclaiming his birthright. For Nkrumah, the ship he sailed on toward a new life in the West was his *Argo*. For the next twelve years he would undergo repeated hardships and trials to win the "Golden Fleece." With it he would regain for all Africans their stolen birthrights.

The Early Stages of the Hero's Quest

In 1935 Nkrumah relocated from the mainly agrarian Gold Coast colony, moving at a slower pace, to the driving industrial pace of the United States. When he left his transport ship at New York harbor, he stepped into new realms of modernity and cultural practices that innumerable immigrants have described as disorienting. Like other immigrants he would have immediately felt the bewilderment of being decentered from a way of life that was familiar and comforting.

The psychologist Jean Piaget has proposed some useful analytic tools for understanding orientation. They assist in comprehending Nkrumah during his early years in the United States. According to Piaget, humans strive to orient themselves within their reality in three fundamental ways: first, *centers,* places where the subject senses life that was familiar and comforting; second, a *direction* toward which that person perceives his life moving rather than its being static and sedentary; and third, *domain,* that is, an individualized place.

The activist/scholar Gloria House study of spatial politics in America elaborated on Piaget's three points of orientation:

> Another way of talking about these spatial reference points or schemata is to say we need a sense of our being in-the-world or identity (center), of our capacity for movement in and engagement with the environment (direction), and the ability to come to rest, to feel rooted, even protected in a place (enclosure).[1]

The black America that Nkrumah entered in 1935 was a place where Africans back home on the continent had deposited many liberatory hopes and fantasies. Africans expected imminent relief from colonialism and forced labor to arrive from the diaspora. This expectation began in the nineteenth century. That is when both Africans and African Americans began voicing their expectation that great fleets of ships owned and operated by blacks would carry the descendants of slaves back to Africa. These courageous returnees would bring Africa salvation, unity, and uplift.

The first dream ships were wooden sailing vessels. Next were steamships, which were the most advanced technology for traversing the Atlantic in the nineteenth century. As transportation technology advanced, the myth kept pace. In the first decade of the twentieth century, steel-hulled ships would bring the long-awaited African American saviors. After World War I, in South Africa, Wellington Buthelezi preached that a mighty fleet of warplanes piloted by African Americans would free Africans from white settler oppression.

James Aggrey, Nkrumah's mentor, recounted that when he traveled throughout Africa in the 1920s for the Phelps-Stokes Commission, he frequently encountered this peculiar expectation. "Everywhere I have gone they have asked me about the fleet that is coming from America. I told them that I know those two ships and one of them is leaking."[2] Aggrey alluded to the two ships in Marcus Garvey's ill-fated Black Star Shipping Line.

Nnamdi Azikiwe's casting of Nkrumah's quest to the United States in the mythical mold was consistent with this mythical image of black America in the African mind. There, in that magic land, black people could attend college and receive degrees as doctors and lawyers. They could pursue a myriad of other occupations that were out of reach for hundreds of millions of Africans. Only in the United States could this miraculous change in status occur.

Nkrumah had seen those changes. Aggrey had spent more than twenty years in the West and returned to continental renown. Azikiwe had returned from the United States to become the editor of the foremost nationalist newspaper in anglophone Africa. Nkrumah had observed that a colonial subject's key to prestige and power was to spend years in the West. He would have naturally commenced his journey across the Atlantic with his mind oriented toward these expectations.

When the African hero is receiving his call, a chance encounter with an unexpected spirit-guide, which at the time seems unimportant, can change the direction of his entire life. According to his autobiography, Nkrumah met his next spirit-guide by chance on the boat ride from London to New York. He was a Dutchman who was a student at the Harvard Divinity School. Nkrumah did not give the Dutchman's name, but the Dutchman played a vital role in Nkrumah's future direction in the United States and in Nkrumah's styles of oratory and leadership when he returned to Ghana.

As noted earlier, the sage usually possesses unusual qualities that distinguish him from other beings. Nkrumah revealed the unusualness of the Dutchman in his description of their visit to Harlem's famous Abyssinian Baptist Church, which was and is known simply as the Abyssinian. In 1935 the Abyssinian's pastor and assistant pastor, respectively, were the Reverends Adam Clayton Powell Sr. and Jr., Nkrumah did not record the date that he attended the Abyssinian, so church records could not state definitively which of these ministers held the pulpit that day. However, Adam Clayton Powell Sr. retired in 1936 and his son became the full-time minister.[3] In his autobiography Powell Jr. remembered Nkrumah's appearance at the Abyssinian. He referred to Nkrumah as "my old friend."[4] His sermons are likely the ones that influenced Nkrumah.

The day that Nkrumah and the Dutchman attended Abyssinian, the preacher evoked fervent shouting and dramatic weeping in the pews. This emotionalism embarrassed Nkrumah, because he thought that the Dutchman would draw from it a negative conclusion about black Christianity. Nkrumah's religious orientation in Ghana was toward the quiet solemnity of missionary worship services. He apologized to the Dutchman for the "undignified" behavior of the African American Christians. Here Nkrumah revealed that despite his heroic portrayal of himself resisting the hegemony of the Catholic Church, his consciousness still bore the religio-cultural stamp of the knowledge/power nexus of British subjugation.

The Dutchman then astonished Nkrumah by stating, "With all sincerity, that it was the most beautiful thing he had seen at any service. If other denominations introduced something like it . . . they might have a greater following."[5] A white man from Holland who was more attuned to the beauty of African American spiritual culture than an indigenous African was a special sage indeed. What is also remarkable is that Nkrumah—future champion of African and African American culture—had the self-effacing temperament to tell the story.

This incident displayed that although black Americans were descendants of Africa, they demonstrated cultural attributes that were distinct from that which Nkrumah had become accustomed to in Christian worship services in Africa. This was Nkrumah's first appreciation of the African diaspora as a space of cultural difference that could be a source of his own discomfort.

Here is also evidence of his seeing the power of the African American style of preaching. Nkrumah knew that he possessed what he called the "gift for gab."[6] He had been a winning debater back in Ghana. But the preaching at the Abyssinian Baptist Church would have immediately informed him that his skills were rudimentary compared to that of the preachers in Harlem. The vocal power to affect an audience so fervently that women cried and swooned and men jumped and shouted would be a valuable skill Nkrumah would acquire during his stay in the United States.

The African American Paradox

Nkrumah began his orientation in the midst of an African American paradox that would confront him continually during his ten years in the United States. In the Abyssinian Baptist Church, Nkrumah entered the paradoxical world of the black American's African historical memory discontinuity and simultaneous African spiritual-culture continuity. Deepening the paradox was Nkrumah's own African historical continuity and African spirit-culture discontinuity. Nkrumah did not mention that the spirit-possessed Christian services were a diasporic transplantation of common indigenous African religious rites.[7] Yet in the rapturous religious frenzy, many of these Afro-Baptists would no longer retain the historical memory to understand their Christianity as being as African as it was Christian. Among some of them, a suggestion that their practices had originated in Africa would likely have met hostility. Although they had forgotten their African roots, these branches swayed to African rhythms in the American breeze.

W. E. B. Du Bois captured this attitude when he stated, "Among Negroes of my generation there is little inherited knowledge of Africa but much distaste."[8] The sociologist E. Franklin Frazier identified Du Bois's social class, but not Du Bois personally, with this disdain for things African. He wrote in the 1920s that the African American elite was "little concerned with African affairs and identified even less with Africa itself."[9] In 1922 Marcus Garvey more directly challenged Du Bois for this attitude.

> One editor and leader went so far as to say at his so-called Pan African Congress that American Negroes could not live in Africa, because the climate was too hot . . . The old time stories of "African fever," "African bad climate," "African mosquitos" [sic], "African savages," have been repeated by brainless intellectuals of ours as a scare against our people in America and the West Indies taking a kindly interest in the new program of building a racial empire of our own in our Motherland.[10]

Du Bois defended himself with writings that extolled Africa and the wondrous beauty of blackness; he could be equally eloquent when claiming that Negro Americans were principally Americans and not Africans. In the 1890s, Du Bois had been one of the first black intellectuals to lay claim to both Africa and America. He wrote that the black people's centuries in America had made them irrevocably American. Even so, the American Negroes were forever tied to their brothers and sisters throughout Africa and the diaspora. He projected this personal ambivalence between his American-ness and his African-ness onto all of black America. He called it "double-consciousness."[11]

Although Du Bois did not apply this bifurcated consciousness to African intellectuals, Nkrumah's response to the fervent services at Abyssinian Baptist Church suggests that an African application would have been accurate. Nkrumah shared Aggrey's and Azikiwe's pride in Africa and Blackness, but in Harlem he was embarrassed to see African culture coming out of African Americans. Nkrumah's missionary upbringing had shifted some of his sensibilities westward. In Africa, indigenous rites of "spirit possession" were severely rebuked as "pagan savagery" by missionaries. That minority of Africans who attended European mission schools were taught an unanimated, "proper" way to worship. Nkrumah responded to the Abyssinians as a westernized African who expected the westernized Africans in the United States to share his religious/cultural sensibilities.

Nkrumah would later recognize the Africanisms present in African American culture. In the discourse between the black sociologist E. Franklin Frazier, who discounted these retentions, and the white historian Melville Herskovits, who championed them, Nkrumah agreed with Herskovits.[12] Many members of the Abyssinian Baptist Church no doubt practiced their African cultural retentions without a historical memory of them, even though their church wore the name of an African country. During his first days of orientation to the United States, Nkrumah credits the Dutchman for interesting him in pursuing a theology degree at Lincoln University.

This decision would prove profoundly fateful. Studying African American preaching styles would arm him with unparalleled tools of communication. Nkrumah was destined to become a circuit preacher in black America. His years of preaching in African American churches would hone his skills to preach nationalism to Africans. At the same time, studying theology would enrich his knowledge of the biblical language of parables, metaphors, and allusions that Africa's Christian converts understood. In this language and in this style, he

Rev. G. Johnson
Dean of the College.

St. Teresa's Seminary
Amisano
via Elmina
Gold Coast
March 1.

Dear Sir

Over half a year ago I wrote to you disclosing my intention of coming to the United States to continue my education at Lincoln University. You accordingly sent to me the Lincoln University Herald and an Application form.

Since then, I have been making serious arrangements towards my coming to the University; and I now feel that I am fully prepared to sail to your end if only a say of hope will come from you.

I here with enclose the Application form filled, with the hope that you will do all that in your power lies toward my admission

I remain
Yours very Sincerely
F. Nyakafi Nkrumah

Figure 2   Nkrumah's application to Rev. Johnson from St. Teresa's Seminary.

could communicate his ideals in a religious vernacular across boundaries of ethnicity and status.

The future independent Ghana would need a leader capable of leading Nzimas, Fantis, Ashantis, Gaas, Gauans, Ewes, and other ethnicities past potentially disruptive internecine score-settling. In the Gold Coast, like in most African colonies, Europeans had created borders without regard for precolonial ethnic boundaries. Throughout Africa, warring ethnic groups with ancient animosities and modern grudges were flung together under one flag. This planted the seeds of the subnational conflicts that would continually stifle the national unity and progress of postcolonial Africa, as the world has seen, with sometimes genocidal results.

LINCOLN UNIVERSITY
Lincoln University, Pa.

APPLICATION FOR ADMISSION
(To be filled out in the applicant's own handwriting)

Name _Francis_ _Nwia-_ _Nyakofi_ _Nkrumah_   Date _1st March 1935_
        (Given name)   (Full middle name)   (Last name)

Home Address _c/o Anthony Kujamah D.c's Office Sekondi_
            (Number)   (Street)   (City)   (State)

Address to which reply should be sent _Amisano Via Elmina   Gold Coast_

Place of Birth _Nkroful_   Date of Birth _21st Sept 1909_   Age _26_

Height _5' 8"_ Weight _———_ General Health _Good_ Defects _None_
        (NOTE: If you have poor health or physical defects, give particulars on page 3.)

Name of Father _Kobina Nkrumah_ Birthplace _Nkroful in Nzima_ Living? _No_
            (Name in full)

Father's Occupation _Gold Smith_
                            (Business Address)

Name of Mother _Kweku Nyaniba_ Birthplace _Nkroful_   Living? _Yes_

Mother's Occupation (if any) _———_   Number of Brothers _None_ Sisters _None_

RECORD OF PREPARATION

Give complete list of all educational institutions, beyond grammar school, attended with dates of entering and leaving, arranged chronologically. Report all such institutions whether or not credit is desired.

Names of Institutions	Location	Date of Entering (Month and year)	Past or Expected Date of Leaving (Month and year)	Were you, or will you be, graduated
Achimota College	Accra	Jan. 1927	Dec. 1930	Completed four years' Teachers' Course

If offered admission, which class do you expect to enter? _Freshman_
                                                    (Freshman, Sophomore, Junior, Senior)

Do you expect to complete the full course at Lincoln University? _Yes_ If not, why not? _———_

What do you plan as your life's work? _Educational and Social work_

Figure 3   Official application for admission to Lincoln University.

The man who would lead the Gold Coast colony to independence as Ghana would have to speak a language that no particular ethnic group could individually claim. That language would prove to be the theological language of Christianity. Centuries of missionary labors had lodged it deeply in the Ghanaian psyche. Neither an African nor an African American convinced Nkrumah to pursue this fateful course. The Dutchman fulfilled the spirit-guide's classic role of directing the hero toward the next stage of his destiny. Nkrumah did not mention him again in any of his published writings.

The Harlem Identity

Piaget stated that decentered persons need first to find a special domain for centering. Professor House's thesis on spatial politics added that this spatial centering is also a form of identity-formation. Before and after Nkrumah reported to Lincoln University for matriculation, he would center himself in Harlem. During his decade in the United States, Harlem's magnetism would continually compel Nkrumah's return. When Nkrumah left America, he would have a Harlem identity. Understanding that identity is a key to understanding the later Nkrumah.

Nkrumah entered Harlem seventy years after slavery when a multiplex of ideas competed for black loyalty. Harlem projected no monolithic black consciousness. After World War I, however, among an influential segment of the black intelligentsia, a militantly proud and politically defiant attitude had arisen. The respective partisans of Du Bois and Garvey represented the two main poles that encompassed the identity of what became known then as the *New Negro*.

The Garveyite pole was nationalistic and working class; the Du Boisian pole encompassed the elite, assimilationist Talented Tenth. This New Negro had initiated cultural renaissances not just in Harlem, but also in Detroit, Chicago, Pittsburgh, Philadelphia, Washington D.C., and by degrees in other cities. The Garveyite New Negro expressed pride in Africa and sought a great dream of African redemption through the infusion into Africa of African American leadership and the eventual expulsion of European colonialists. The Du Boisians showed off black artistry and intellects to a world of awful antiblack stereotypes. The achievements of the Talented Tenth in all fields of endeavor exposed the lie of black inferiority.

The New Negroes were not really new. They had stood up intermittently throughout the nineteenth century.[13] They were numerous during the slavery period. Their numbers refute the pernicious stereotype of the universal "old Negro," who was unassertive, politically unconscious, culturally and historically unaware, or too terrorized and violently repressed to think an independent thought. After the

Civil War, when the majority of black Americans still lived in the South, the Ku Klux Klan viciously enforced the humiliating restrictions of the Black Codes of Jim Crow. These cruelties resulted in a din of black lamentations that drowned out the voices of the New Negro. In the midst of this repression, the optimistic and militant voices of the New Negroes still surfaced. When they did, their ideas sounded strange, as if they were spoken by and to future generations.[14]

Nkrumah entered black America after the New Negro had reclaimed this pride in their black identity. Aggrey and Azikiwe had returned to Ghana as African "New Negroes." During his process of reorientation, Nkrumah naturally gravitated to persons resembling his mentors in America.

Dr. Alain Locke was black America's first Rhodes scholar. He was also a Howard University professor of sociology. In 1925 he was so impressed by the New Negro that he edited a book with that title. Locke's opening essay elaborated on the intellectual world in Harlem between the two poles—Du Bois's leftish black intelligentsia and Garvey's nationalistic masses. This is the Harlem that would shape Nkrumah in the next ten years when he grew to know the black metropolis intimately:

> With the Negro rapidly in process of class differentiation, if it ever was warrantable to regard and treat the Negro *en masse* it is becoming with every day less possible, more unjust and more ridiculous . . .
>
> Take Harlem as an instance of this. Here in Manhattan is not merely the largest Negro community in the world, but the first concentration in history of so many diverse elements of Negro life. It has attracted the African, the West Indian, the Negro America; has brought together the Negro of the North and the Negro of the South; the man from the city and the man from the town and village; the peasant, the student, the business man, the professional man, artist, poet, musician, adventurer and worker, preacher and criminal, exploiter and social outcast.[15]

Professor Locke here describes Harlem as the quintessential African diasporic milieu. Harlem contained the three principal components in the transatlantic triangular trade in black thought: the African, the Afro-Caribbean, and the American Negro. The migrants brought with them class stratifications and inner-group divisions. Clashes between these classes and groups could have sealed Harlem in the perennial disunity that Nkrumah had observed between feuding African ethnicities. To the contrary, as Piaget's *domain* of orientation, Harlem in 1925 displayed a transformative power. The space, itself, and the people who inhabited it were together a single, living organism that could reshape a newcomer's consciousness.

> Each group has come with its own separate motives and for its own special ends, but their greatest experience has been the finding of one another. Proscription and prejudice have thrown these dissimilar elements into a common area of contact and interaction. Within this area, race sympathy and unity have a further fusing of sentiment and experience. So what began in terms of segregation becomes more and more, as its elements mix and react, the laboratory of a great race-wielding.[16]

The hand of Harlem, Piaget's *center,* shaped the disparate elements of Africa and the diaspora into a race with what Piaget labeled *direction.* The *domain* now means not just the space Harlem, but it includes the Harlemites themselves. The Harlemites advance and transform Harlem and are in turn advanced and transformed by Harlem.

> Hitherto it must be admitted that American Negroes have been a race more in name than in fact, or to be exact, more in sentiment than in experience. The chief bond between them has been that of a common condition rather than a common consciousness; a problem in common rather than a life in common. In Harlem, Negro life is seizing upon its first chances for group expression and self-determination. It is—or promises to be—a race capital. Without pretense to their political significance, Harlem has the same role to play for the New Negro as Dublin has had for the New Ireland or Prague for the New Czechoslovakia . . . A transformed and transforming psychology permeates the masses.[17]

Nkrumah arrived in Harlem ten years after Professor Locke's observations. He was but one of many recent arrivals in a flow that continued after Frazier defined Harlem as a race-creating and a race-wielding force. Harlem's orientation process was continuous for all of them. If all classes and ethnicities from Africa and the diaspora could unite as one people under the mystical influence of Harlem, if Harlem could be for the New Negro what Dublin and Prague were for their respective nationalistic struggles, then Harlem could also be the laboratory in which the ideas for a unified Africa itself could receive nourishment. Role models for the techniques of leadership and organization for Nkrumah's future endeavors to unify Africa were to be studied in Harlem. For, like Harlem, the *domain* Africa must one day become a transformative and reorienting *center* that creates a Pan-African people with a revolutionary *direction.*

Lincoln University

K. A. B. Jones-Quartey was Nkrumah's classmate at Lincoln University. He was also Nkrumah's Phi Beta Sigma Fraternity brother. Years later, when he was a professor at Ghana's University of Legon, Jones-Quartey described how Nkrumah comported himself on the

LINCOLN UNIVERSITY
LINCOLN UNIVERSITY, PA.

OFFICE OF THE REGISTRAR

Official Transcript of the Record of_____ FRANCIS NUBA-KOFI NKRUMAH

DESCRIPTIVE TITLE OF COURSE	Course Number In Catalog	FIRST SEMESTER			SECOND SEMESTER		
		Semester Hours		Grade	Semester Hours		Grade
		Rec.	Lab.		Rec.	Lab.	
Year of _1936-37_							
General Chemistry	1	(2	2	4)			
Elem. Economics	1-2	3		2	3		2
Social Psychology	5	3		1			
American Gov't	1	3		3			
Comparative Gov't	3-4	3		2	3		2
French B	3-4	3		2	3		2
Library Methods	15	(1		2)			
Social Pathology	6				3		1
Religious Education					3		1
1937-38							
Old Test. History	3-4	2		1	2		1
French C	5-6	3		1	3		1
Philosophy State	3-4	3		1	3		2
Anthropology	7	3		1			
Sociology	1-2	3		1	3		1
Money & Banking	5	3		2			
History of Economic Theory	5				3		1
Race Relations	8				3		1
Symbolic Logic Seminar					1		1
Statistical Methods (Auditor)							
1938-39							
Botany	11-12	2	1	2	2	1	3
General Biology	1-2	2	2	3	2	2	2
Elem. Greek	1-2	3		1	3		2
German A	1-2	3		2	3		3
Plato's Dialog	9-10	3		1	3		1
Labor Problems	8				3		2

Passing Grades are_____

This transcript issued_____

Requirements for Graduation__**124**__ Semester hours

Total Semester hours secured__**128**__

A semester hour on this transcript indicates either a recitation period of 60 minutes or a laboratory period of 120 minutes per week for 18 weeks.

Registrar

Figure 4   Transcript from Lincoln University.

campus of Lincoln University in a way that is central to understanding Nkrumah's *directions* henceforth: "At Lincoln [Nkrumah] always brooded about Africa's lack of a 'national' symbol or myth." The British had their monarchy and the United States had its flag and constitution. But Africa had none of these nor did it have a rallying cry or a focal point.

It was imperative, Nkrumah insisted, to develop a myth—some national symbol:

> Eventually this symbol turned out to be—Kwame Nkrumah himself, and the whole African case then assumed the form of a pyramid in his own mind. Africa was its base, Ghana was somewhere in the middle, and at the top—Kwame Nkrumah. But I want you to understand that at this point it was to him a question of filling a vacuum which plainly existed. I believe he genuinely could not find this needed symbol and therefore decided to fill the gap with himself.[18]

Nkrumah's reorientation was already toward his messianic call to liberate Africa when he arrived at the historically black university in Pennsylvania in 1935. Contrary to Jones-Quartey's description, in the African epic the hero does not personally decide his calling. Higher forces mark out his destiny before his birth.[19] In liberatory terms, Nkrumah's calling was the collective calling of his generation, personified and concentrated in the life of this single person. His heroism and charismatic authority stemmed from his people recognizing that one among them had been divinely chosen to lead them to the idealized future. The hero might seek to evade his calling because it pushes him toward directions that are not his personal choices. He might also unconsciously miss his predestined opportunities. However, the hero's destiny is a metaphysical direction. Regardless of the hero's personal wishes, metaphysical forces like fate—in the form of coincidences, chance personal encounters, accidents, and divinely sent assistants—will repeatedly push him back onto his divine path.

Becoming the national symbol of Pan-Africa's liberation was a lofty goal for a twenty-six-year-old Nzima. Even loftier was the development of the national myth. This myth had to project an idealized, Afrotopian future for one of the least utopian continents. This myth would project the future Africa as a revitalized and independent power equal to Europe and the United States. Only a powerful quasi-religious Pan-African myth would galvanize the masses to loyally follow a messiah toward this Promised Land that existed only in the messiah's faith in its inevitably.

The preacher of this new faith needed concrete imagery. Nebulous prophecies of future joys were insufficient to inspire repressed Africans to risk death and imprisonment to oppose the colonialists' conscienceless lethality. Instead of boundless bliss and the infinite delights of life after death, Nkrumah's Afrotopia had to project a future that answered Africa's deepest longings. Those longings were specific. Nkrumaism had to undo the indignities and emasculations of colonialism and restore Africa to its precolonial glory. Where the glory did not actually historically exist, Africa needed him to invent it. During his orientation process to his new life in the United States, evidence suggests that the first place that Nkrumah perceived the specifics of his future Afrotopian myth appeared is in the black press of the United States.

Joel A. Rogers, W. E. B. Du Bois, and George Schuyler

During a subject's orientation to a new environment, the subject may attach himself to persons who are already oriented toward a direction that attracts him. Nkrumah naturally sought models for orientation who were in sync with his conscious movements toward his heroic destiny. During his early years at Lincoln University, the most useful models for both personal greatness and Afrotopian myth were published weekly in the *Pittsburgh Courier*. During the mid-1930s, of all black newspapers in the United States, the *Pittsburgh Courier* had the highest circulation. Like the *Chicago Defender* and Harlem's *Amsterdam News,* the *Courier* was a fighting journal of racial uplift and anti-lynching advocacy. For the black residents of Pennsylvania such as Nkrumah, their own *Pittsburgh Courier* had no peer. Three of the *Courier*'s contributors (George Schuyler, Joel Augustus Rogers, and W. E. B. Du Bois) established the high intellectual standards of the newspaper.

On the left side of the *Pittsburgh Courier*'s Saturday features page were the serialized tales by journalist George Schuyler. "The Black Internationale" was Schuyler's first story. It appeared between November 21, 1936 and July 3, 1937. The *Courier* next published Schuyler's "Black Empire," between October 2, 1937 and April 16, 1938.[20]

Printed next to Schuyler's serial, in the middle of the page, was an illustrated feature, "Your History," written by the historian Joel A. Rogers. The illustrations and Rogers's words often spotlighted interesting historical facts about the greatness of the sons and daughters of Africa. Rogers also wrote in-depth history lessons and polemics opposing negative portrayals of black people by ideological adversaries of his New Negro history. In addition to the features page, his lessons and opinion pieces frequently appeared throughout the *Courier.*

Also on the front page in the features section, usually to the right of J. A. Rogers's illustrated feature, was the column "Forum Fact and Opinion" by W. E. B. Du Bois. In these articles Du Bois offered polemics on any issue affecting black America that attracted his considerable intellect. The opinions of other famous African American intellectuals, such as Kelly Miller and Claude McKay, appeared intermittently as well in the *Courier* during these years.

Schuyler, Rogers, and Du Bois presented a collection of brain power and talent without equal in any other African American publication. Nkrumah was an insatiable reader and an obsessive follower of world events. That he would live in Pennsylvania and not read the *Pittsburgh Courier* was extremely improbable.[21] The similarities between Nkrumah's own developing ideas toward the creation of Africa's national myth, and the ideas promoted by Schuyler, Rogers, and Du Bois in the *Courier,* take improbability to impossibility.

The influence on Nkrumah of Joel A. Rogers's depictions of the glories of African peoples is obvious. Rogers portrayed an African past of wonderful greatness. The epigraph next to the title of Rogers's articles reads, "Your history dates back beyond the cotton fields of the South; back thousands of years before Christ." Rogers's illustrated history lessons were instruments to build black pride versus the pervasive negative stereotypes purveyed by Hollywood and the white media. The 1930s was the era of Steppin Fetchit, bug-eyed mammies, slavery-loving black field hands in *Gone with the Wind,* and Tarzan in Africa saving white purity from cannibalistic Sambos. Hollywood invented and mercilessly marketed these stereotypes. Joel A. Rogers contrasted this hideous present with a magnificent past. He regularly proclaimed in the *Courier* that past greatness in science and humanities could be replicated by the current generation. Fallen African civilizations could also rise again.

Rogers consistently asserted that former African civilizations were the equals of the classical civilizations of Greece and Babylon, which were his measures of ancient greatness. He used his interpretations of history to polemicize against those historians who denigrated black people in the twentieth century by demeaning the role of black people in world history. To prove his points he interlaced sources from archeology, anthropology, and history. The comments of Herodotus about the blackness of the ancient Egyptians and Ethiopians were the bedrock of his proof where modern white historiography supplied no such confirmation.

In 1938 Nkrumah followed Rogers's form in one of his first published articles:

> Who are the makers of history but those individuals who caught the torch of inspiration, lit by the fire of the achievements of the makers of their past history? A country or race without knowledge of its past is tantamount to a ship without a pilot.
>
> Thus motivated, I hope to demonstrate in this and subsequent writings the role the Negro has played in past civilizations classical, medieval and modern. I shall resort to evidences from archeological explorations, anthropological researches and classical literature to substantiate the authenticity of the historical traditions and facts that shall be herein envisaged.[22]

Nkrumah here responded to his messianic call and assumed the mission of educating his readers about their African heritage. He was still an undergraduate. Yet he confidently took upon himself the role of correcting the false impressions of the entire Lincoln University community about Africa. This included the several hundred black students and their several score of white professors and their wives and other employees who read the *Lincolnian*. He continued his article with the usual J. A. Rogers's references to classical Western authors such as Herodotus, Josephus, and Diodorus to prove the high status of ancient Africans. He concluded by asking rhetorically whether the modern conception of black people challenged the old one.

On the right side of J. A. Rogers's illustrated articles were the opinion columns of W. E. B. Du Bois. Nkrumah would have immediately been attracted to the weekly opinions of this man to whom his mentor, James Aggrey, had introduced him in the 1920s. Aggrey's own respect and admiration for Du Bois had primed Nkrumah to respect and admire Du Bois.

The serialized stories of George Schuyler were most directly useful to Nkrumah for the production of what Jones-Quartey described as the national myth of Africa. The conventional wisdom of most Nkrumah biographers holds that it was Nkrumah's own studies of Marcus Garvey and of the socialist ideologues that laid the foundations for his later ideals. Nevertheless, the likely role of George Schuyler's serialized writings in the *Pittsburgh Courier* should receive its proper place. At Lincoln, Schuyler's literary Pan-Africanism must have struck Nkrumah as a godsend.

The titles of these two serialized works immediately generate Garveyite imagery: "The Black Internationale" and "Black Empire." Much of Nkrumah's vision for Ghana and Africa is pure Garveyism. Nkrumah stated that of all of the books he read while in the United States, none influenced him more than Marcus Garvey's *Philosophy and Opinions*.[23] In this book Garvey elucidates a racial dream that would be the foundation for the future Pan-African utopias of most black nationalists. "The masses of Negroes in America, the West Indies, South and Central America are in sympathetic accords with the native Africans. We desire to help them build up Africa as a Negro Empire, where every black man, whether he was born in Africa or in the Western world, will have the opportunity to develop on his own lines under the protection of the most favorable democratic institutions."[24]

In Schuyler's "The Black Internationale" and "Black Empire," his fictional "New Africa" brought Garvey's dream to life. Schuyler began with the building blocks of Garvey's generalities and had black heroes cement them with specific programs. Schuyler's serial was Garveyism put into practice. "The Black Internationale" and "Black Empire" present a view into the past when New Negroes harbored a militant, Pan-Africanist dream. Their dream was radically different from the later integrationist dream promoted by civil rights leaders of the next generation.[25]

In 1936 Schuyler introduced a revolutionary Pan-Africanist character named Dr. Henry Belsidus who appears to be the prototype for the later Dr. Nkrumah. Belsidus was a charismatic trickster figure who employed the collective genius of the black world to defeat the combined power of international white supremacy, that is, colonialism and imperialism.

Belsidus's ideals went beyond black diasporacism. He presaged a super Pan-Africanism that is today's black globalism. He did not recognize any borders between Africa and her descendants anywhere on earth. To Belsidus, black people everywhere were equally obligated to liberate and unite Africa. The instrument for Africa's liberation would be the Black Internationale, the vanguard party of the most advanced minds among the race. Though Schuyler's characters did not mention it, the Black Internationale was the worldwide Du Boisian Talented Tenth organized into the epitome of black globalist unity. The goals were the same, no matter on which side of the Atlantic the black intellectual was born. As Dr. Belsidus defined those goals, their similarity to Garveyite dreaming is unambiguous:

> I know every Negro intellectual in the world . . . That is my vocation . . . White world supremacy must be destroyed . . . I, Dr. Henry Belsidus, will destroy it with the aid of my loyal assistants in all parts of the world.[26]

Dr. Belsidus espoused to his followers the counter-hegemonic discourse of the anticolonial revolution:

> We must disobey all laws that hinder our plan, for all laws here are laws of the white man, designed to keep us in subjugation and perpetuate his rule. All the means of education and information, from nursery to college, from newspaper to book, are mobilized to perpetuate white supremacy; to enslave and degrade the darker peoples.[27]
> We are going to out-think and out-scheme the white people, my boy. I have the organization already, Slater, scattered all over the world; young Negroes like yourself: intellectuals, scientists, engineers. They are mentally the equal of the whites. They possess superior energy, superior vitality, they have superior, or perhaps I should say more intense, hatred and resentment, that fuel which operates the juggernaut of conquest.[28]

Dr. Belsidus utilized the collective genius of Africa and the diaspora and masterminded the seizure of Africa back from European colonialism. The Black Internationale could not achieve such a tremendous task without first defeating the military might of worldwide white supremacy. The Black Internationale's attacks upon white power included biological warfare. Belsidus ordered the black air force of super stratospheric planes to release upon Europe by miniature parachutes rats infected with typhus, cholera, yellow fever, and smallpox. Europe then suffered debilitating plagues. The diabolical Belsidus foreshadowed the Nazi gas chambers by having his minions lock European leaders in a great hall and pumping gas into the vacuum.

The Black Internationale moved from strength to greater strength in espionage and through demonstrations of black scientific and technological superiority. Then the final battle for possession of New Africa unfolded near Monrovia, Liberia. Against what appeared to be superior European forces, the Pan-African legions unleashed a

Cyclotron, a new secret weapon. The Cyclotron fired a laser beam of five million volts that annihilated the combined navies and air forces of Italy, France, and England. According to Belsidus, the victory of the Black Internationale would usher in the utopian future that would reclaim all the lost glories of precolonial African kingdoms.

After colonialism, but before Afrotopia, Africa had to purge its human impurities. In 1937, Schuyler presciently placed neocolonialism in the minds of some of his fictional Africans. He described this intellectual impurity in words nearly identical to those Nkrumah would employ against the enemies of the Pan-African revolution twenty-five years later in his book *Neocolonialism: The Last Stage of Imperialism.* Schuyler wrote:

> Of course, we had to use ruthless methods in some places. There were miseducated Negroes who still favored the rule of white men to the rule of black men. There were still Negroes who had been given a few crumbs from the tables of the exploiters, who now tried to help them by stirring counter-revolution against us.[29]

Moreover, in Dr. Belsidus's voice resonates the combination of socialism and nationalism that would be Nkrumah's raison d'être. Nkrumah would later echo these words virtually verbatim:

> Africa is rich. Those riches will remain in Africa. Africa is populous. That populace will remain here and the products of its toil will remain here. From henceforward black men will labor to advance the interests of only black men.
>
> We have the natural resources, the will and the ability to create the greatest civilization the world has seen . . .
>
> We are going to build factories, operate giant collective farms, ranches, mines, mills, become self-sufficient . . .
>
> Together we can build on this, the second largest continent, an empire of black men and women working toward a cooperative civilization unexcelled in this world.[30]

The writings of Rogers, Du Bois, and Schuyler gave Nkrumah part of the template for the national myth that was his obsession at Lincoln University. Nkrumah would construct a mythic Afrotopian past where a noble precolonial people lived in African socialist societies on a par with any nation in Europe. This was vintage J. A. Rogers. Nkrumah would become the polemicist warrior against Africa's enemies, foreign and domestic, emulating Du Bois's polymathic expertise in economics, philosophy, history, and sociology. Finally, Nkrumah's new national myth would create a glorious African future, united, strong, "scientific socialist," militarized, and ruthless in breaking away from colonialist domination. This was George Schuyler's "Black Empire." Nevertheless, Rogers, Du Bois, and, Schuyler left missing pieces in Nkrumah's national myth for postcolonial Africa. Other sages would fill in the lacunae.

Father Divine

Lincoln University stipulated that its students had to vacate the campus during the months of the summer break. This rule forced Nkrumah into black America during his undergraduate years, 1935–1939. Had Nkrumah lived with an American family, he could have remained stationary during the summer. Because he had no such sponsor, he had to fend for himself. This was during the Great Depression when jobs were a very difficult to find for a native-born African American. Being a foreigner, who spoke English with an African accent, could only have made his travails more onerous.

Nevertheless, Nkrumah had to go out and fend for himself in the United States. This compelled him to travel to different African American social milieus. He had to interact with the many different people of the African diaspora. His pursuit of the national myth and the personal tools for bringing about Africa's redemption would receive major assistance during his travels.

Almost weekly, and sometimes daily, the front page of the *Pittsburgh Courier* also featured often-scandalous articles about the man of God whose followers publicly proclaimed that he, in fact, was God. That was Father Major Jealous Divine. Born George Baker in Georgia, or Rockville, Maryland (his several birthplaces and birth dates are disputed). He became Father Divine in answer to his own messianic calling. He started off as a messenger of God and graduated to God in person.[31]

The duality of the nature of genies, spirit-guides, and sages in the African epic needs to be mentioned, lest a false impression leads to expectations of one-dimensional goodness. The following sixteenth-century oracle from the *Epic of Sonsan* touches as much on the duality of the hero as it does the duality of the genie:

> In those days we had good genies,
> But the corruption of man's innocence has spoiled all that.
> At the beginning of their friendship with genies men were good,
> But at the end they turned bad.[32]

This dualism, which augured ill for Kwame Nkrumah, was fully visible in the character of Father Divine. Early in Divine's movement, he and his followers lived in a house in the mostly white town of Sayville, Long Island. From this base, he held court and delivered sumptuous feasts free of charge to scores of hungry believers and seekers during the Depression. So many cars clogged the streets and pedestrians crowded the sidewalks to get to Divine's residence that his white neighbors complained to the police.

The police arrested Divine for disturbing the peace and the prosecutor demanded a trial. At this trial Divine did not butt heads directly with the stronger judicial power, despite repeated disrespectful and racist provocations (the judge ordered the prosecutor to privately interrogate a white female Divine supporter, seeking moral evidence to be used against him). Instead, the trial transcript shows Divine speaking in biblical metaphors and parables.

Despite his flanking behavior, the judge found Divine guilty and sentenced him to a year in jail. The behavior of the judge had been blatantly biased and the sentence was disproportionate and unfair. In the courtroom Divine's supporters shouted that the judge would soon die for opposing the will of God in the person of Father Divine. Three days later, on June 7, 1932, the apparently healthy fifty-six-year-old judge died from a heart attack. The judge's death coming so soon after the pronouncement of Divine's sentence was sufficient to elevate Divine's fame as a man protected by God's wrath. Divine's quick mind added to the glory. When asked about the judge's sudden death, he replied, "I hated to do it."[33]

After he had served just a month of his sentence, another judge released Divine from jail. The throngs that welcomed him proved to him that he was too big for Sayville. He moved to the Negro Mecca—Harlem. That is where Nkrumah encountered his movement, in the course of his hardest times during the Depression.

Nkrumah stated that during these days he attended a lot of black religious gatherings and revivalist meetings. Out of all of them he paid the most attention to the Peace Mission of Father Divine. This was the only religious organization that Nkrumah actually officially joined. Nkrumah allows that it was for strictly material rather than spiritual reasons that he became a member of Divine's Peace Mission.

> I used to go round quite a lot to various Negro religious gatherings and revivalist meetings. The only one that I gave much attention to was a movement headed by Father Divine, and then only because of

the privileges attached to membership. By being a follower of Father Divine I discovered that it was possible to obtain a good chicken meal for half a dollar, instead of the usual two or three dollars charged at other restaurants, and also a hair-cut at a certain barber's shop for only ten cents instead of a dollar. To an impoverished student this was quite enough to attract him to any sort of movement and as long as I could be fed and shorn at cut prices by merely raising my arm above my head and whispering "Peace", I fear I did not concern myself with the motives of Father Divine's group.[34]

Nkrumah only wrote about eating at Divine's restaurants. His laconic description did not capture the awe in which a newly arrived and hungry African would have stood in the midst of Divine's movement's cultural and spiritual dynamism. The late activist-actor Ossie Davis's remembrance more fully described the colorful scene:

Loving Father Divine was as easy as pie. Everybody in Harlem would drop in once in a while . . .
    The faithful would begin to pour into the restaurant in the late afternoon to wait for the arrival of the Father, which was sure to take place before midnight . . .
    There was usually a piano, and most every evening, a different somebody would be there plunking on the keys. Sometimes, a second talent would come in, have dinner, then join the piano player with his clarinet, trumpet, or sax. He'd play for a while and then be on his way to his gig. Men and women were forbidden to dance together, but nobody stopped you if you felt like taking the floor by yourself.
    Often by ten o'clock at night, the place would be jammed. Then suddenly a tremor would run from corner to corner, signaling that Father was close by. Everything and everybody would stop in their tracks. The restaurant would be closed and all attention shifted to the main dining room . . .
    Officers, members, dignitaries, and staff, fluttering like nervous pigeons, would hurry themselves to the doorway. A few minutes more, then a furious joy would find tongue. People would be asked to kindly make way, and Father Divine, accompanied by Mother Divine, a young white woman from Canada whom Father had made his bride, would enter the room. Father would swiftly move to the head of the table, take his seat, and that was the signal for bedlam.[35]

From Mayor Fiorello La Guardia to First Lady Eleanor Roosevelt, any day a celebrity would stop to see the Father. During the worst of the Depression, Father Divine's Peace Mission became even more widely famous for the sumptuous meals it served to Harlem's hungry free of charge. Nkrumah either employed tricksterism to survive during these hard times by feigning allegiance to Divine for the material benefits, or he was so impressed by Divine that he was a true follower. What Nkrumah did not relate is what knowledge he received from his time in Divine's movement. He had attended the famous Abyssinian Baptist Church, where the Reverends Adam Clayton Powell Sr. and Jr. held the pulpit. Surely the art of African American preaching was at its zenith at this Harlem institution. Adam Clayton Powell Jr. was a lyrical genius at turning the biblical phrase and parable to black people's political benefit. Nkrumah would also become renowned for similar skills with the Christian scriptures. But Father Divine was the only African American minister whose name Nkrumah mentioned in his memoir.

Historians of this period of Nkrumah's life have customarily followed his lead and given brief attention to his involvement with Father Divine's Peace Mission. Even the most sympathetic Pan-Africanist historians have minimized Divine's impact on the future leader. And for his Marxist admirers, Nkrumah's adherence to any form of messianic spiritualism is incongruent with their image of him as a revolutionary. Conservative observers, such as Professor Henry Bretton, simply ascribe Nkrumah's spiritualism to superstition. However, in the African epic, the quantity of influence that the hero ascribes to the spirit-guide does not necessarily denote the actual quality of that influence. When Nkrumah's life and the story he wrote of it are viewed as an epic, images become clear and strongly suggest that Harlem's messianic Father Divine deserves a more prominent place in the story of how Nkrumah became Ghana's messianic divine father.

The assessment of this study does not challenge the integrity of Nkrumah's autobiography. It does, however, acknowledge that at no point when seeking to understand Nkrumah should a historian forget that Nkrumah wrote the autobiographical script of his life in the mid-1950s. He was then in the midst of political battles against both a Ghanaian opposition and the British Empire. Neither supported Ghana's total independence. Politics compelled Nkrumah to script his self-image as one that would strengthen his cause and weaken his enemies. For the Nkrumah epic to attribute to Father Divine, an African American of controversial reputation, the credit he was due could undermine the hero's image of purity and infallibility About the influence of Father Divine and other important personal influences, Nkrumah's autobiography serves as a chronological and contextual reference point. It does not always present the objective truth.

When a leader and his supporters are not forthcoming about a particular issue, it is sometimes fruitful to review the words of the leader's enemies. That applies in this case to Father Divine's influence on Nkrumah. Colonel Akwasi A. Afrifa was a principal participant in the military coup d'état that overthrew Nkrumah. In his memoirs, Afrifa repeatedly attacked Nkrumah's character. After over one hundred pages in which he intermittently denounced Nkrumah as everything from an African Hitler to a lunatic Garveyite, Afrifa summarized his denunciations by writing in his postscript, "In all these he saw himself as a kind of Joshua and Father Divine and Cassius Clay rolled into one."[36]

Common familiarity with the biblical Joshua's deeds in making Jericho's walls tumble, and Muhammad Ali's (Cassius Clay's) defiant, anti-imperialist stance, makes the similarity between their epic heroism and that of Nkrumah quickly visible. Why Colonel Afrifa would deem these comparisons with Nkrumah of propaganda value against him identifies the 1966 readership at which Afrifa aimed his book. That readership would not have been most of the people of Africa or the diaspora, for Muhammad Ali's popularity as the people's champ was then at a peak. Comparing Nkrumah to Ali would enhance Nkrumah's image in the black world. So Afrifa did not publish his book in London for a black readership. He wrote it for conservative Britons and other Westerners for whom Ali embodied a resented and despised flamboyant black defiance. One would expect Afrifa to appeal to the Ghanaians. They were the people he claimed he executed the coup to help. Afrifa's own words expose why he did not appeal to Ghanaians or any Africans. They expose the fawning Anglophilia of the mentally neocolonized.[37]

K. A. Busia and Tibor Szamuely, respectively, wrote the preface and introduction for Afrifa. In the preface the scholar Busia, a longtime Nkrumah adversary, gave his blessing to the coup from the safety of St. Anthony's College, Oxford. In a 1953 interview with black American author Richard Wright, Busia revealed how far his own lack of mental decolonization separated him from the ideology and goals of Ghana's nationalists. Busia spoke disparagingly about the nationalists using Ghanaian indigenous customs of oath taking and pouring libations at rallies to bind the masses to Nkrumah's Convention People's Party (CPP). Busia explained his animus toward practicing African culture by telling Wright, "I am a Westerner. I was educated in the West." Richard Wright wrote that he had the feeling Busia loathed this using of Ghana's indigenous culture.[38] When the military permitted an election in 1969, Busia would become the prime minister of Ghana's Second Republic.[39]

Tibor Szamuely was a Russian communist turned anticommunist defector and Cold War propagandist for British Conservatives. He summarized Afrifa's rambling condemnations in a succinct sociological language that Afrifa did not command. Afrifa's book was to be a Cold War weapon that delegitimated socialism and Pan-Africanism by delegitimating their foremost champion. Szamuely's words give a refined and more understandable description of the practices that gave rise to Afrifa's accusation that Nkrumah thought he was Father Divine:

> The justification of his power was essentially irrational: it rested on the assertion that Nkrumah was endowed with qualities lacking in ordinary mortals. These supernatural, Messianic properties of a divine or quasi-divine nature emanated from him and pervaded the State, the party and—as long as they behaved themselves properly—the people. The divine origin of Nkrumah's leadership—his presence on earth as a reincarnation of Jesus Christ–was insisted on literally.[40]

Nkrumah's enemies did not go further and offer examples of parallels between the messianic behavior and philosophies of Nkrumah and Father Divine. The parallels, however, are numerous. Present in these parallels are those patterns of behavior that are necessary to detect a cultural influence on politics. The celibacy that Divine preached struck Nkrumah as a most bizarre philosophy. Nkrumah wrote that he suspected Divine's preaching celibacy might have been an attempt to exterminate black people by stopping procreation.[41] But Nkrumah was both a student and teacher of philosophy. He stated in *Consciencism* that philosophy was the brain and the other branches of knowledge were the arms and legs. He would have approached Divine as, first of all, a teacher whose philosophy put men and women's limbs in motion. Divine would serve as an instructor for how Africa's messiah could enthrall his followers and lead them to redeem Pan-Africa.

In Divine's urban "Heavens" and in his rural collectivist "Promised Lands," Nkrumah witnessed for the first time how philosophy could influence thousands of people, black and white, to totally alter their lives. Divine's followers sacrificed their wealth, personal comforts, individuality, racial identities, and even their sex lives to follow the utopian communal teachings of a man whose propaganda proclaimed him God. Divine's movement was the prototype for Nkrumah's Positive Action, which was Nkrumah's adaptation of Gandhi's methodologies of anticolonialist struggle. In the future, Nkrumah would launch Gandhian Positive Action as a series of protest and boycotts that would make the colony ungovernable and force the British to grant independence. Concurrently, Nkrumah would use Father Divine's techniques to wage spiritual Positive Action to overcome the spiritual/occult supremacy of Africa's conquerors. Equally important to defeating European colonial hegemony in the temporal realm, was to overthrow the legitimacy of white supremacy in the spirit world.

Nkrumah's goal was to capture the Golden Fleece that would gain self-rule for Ghana with himself as the warrior king who, like Jason, regained the kingdom. How could he galvanize millions of Africans to radically alter their lives, to sacrifice their wealth, their personal comforts, and their individuality to follow the messianic teachings of a man who proclaimed the imminent coming of a utopian African future? Father Divine's movement was the only example thus far where Nkrumah had personally witnessed a philosophy successfully implementing this model for social revolution. Despite his increasing admiration for the solutions of Lenin, Nkrumah knew that the Ghanaians were not Russians and would never countenance an atheistic movement leading them.

On this topic the late Kwame Ture (Stokely Carmichael) commented, "Nkrumah told me that he never declared himself an atheist like the doctrinaire Communists because he knew that African people are spiritual by nature. He said that if God wasn't a part of it, then Africans would have nothing to do with it."[42]

Nkrumah would be impressed by Divine's successful techniques of motivation and leadership. The African Americans whom Father Divine motivated were the cultural and spiritual cousins of Ghana's peoples. Nkrumah's enemies were correct in that he did emulate Father Divine. They were wrong in attributing to him selfish motives for this emulation. He did not seek the Golden Fleece for egotistical vainglory. Nkrumah's imitation of Divine's methodology was simply a philosophical tool. It was a means to the ultimate end—to attain Ghanaian independence and the realization of the messianic vision of Pan-African unification.

Even the newspaper articles that Nkrumah's enemies cited disprove personal motivation in Nkrumah's heroic projection of his charisma. An official of Nkrumah's government stated in the *Accra Evening News,* "In our situation the people need a charismatic leadership, a beacon light to look up to in their development . . . Without this charismatic leadership the people are bound to look for leaders and saviors from many other sources."[43] Nkrumah's Ghanaian enemies understood that his charismatic thrust was the foundation of what they called his "dictatorship" and "personality cult." Heroes of African epics commonly cast magic spells from their charismatic authority. Nkrumah's enemies attacked his charisma to break his spell over his people. They had to break it for Ghanaians to seek leadership and salvation away from Nkrumah and toward themselves. They also had to challenge the revolutionary discursive formations scripted into Nkrumah's life, that inspired support for him and his revolution, with counterrevolutionary discursive formations. He had to be pulled down from the mythic throne of the *Ghana* (which in translation means "king") of their country.

The part of Father Divine's philosophy that was most visible in Nkrumah's later behavior was Divine's messianic projection of an idealized utopian vision of the future with himself as the God of this common destiny. Nkrumah was not so much interested in philosophy *qua* philosophy. Nkrumah's interest was in philosophies that he could use to change Africa. In several ways Father Divine's philosophy in practice provided important precursors to Nkrumaism. The later practices of Nkrumah's regime line up symmetrically with Divine's practices. Several authors have compared Nkrumah's social experiments with Marxian models and frequently use terms like "irrational" to explain them. Nkrumah did not measure up to the orthodox standards of their ideas of what a socialist revolutionary should be. They did not consider that Nkrumah's social experiments were carried out more in accord with the teachings of Father Divine than those of Marx or Lenin.

Nkrumah's rationality returns after comparing his charismatic authority and social policies with those of Father Divine: the leader is both Messiah and God. His charisma surpasses that of all other mortal beings. Supporters and opponents must submit to his charismatic authority as they would submit to God. The leader's divinity is reinforced by the belief in his immortality. He simply will never die.

"Nkrumah Never Dies" was a slogan of the Young Pioneers. According to the Ghanaian author Ayi Kwei Armah, Nkrumah's regime tapped into superstitions and cultural propositions associated with the divinity of African kingship. He utilized them to construct in the Ghanaian mind an image of himself that would foster absolute obedience, regardless of how corrupt and unpopular the sycophants who surrounded him were. "He wanted to be a Prophet and for most people he was a Prophet of God. That God was his idea of the future of Africa. But people can't fill their stomachs with prophecies."[44]

Sam Nyako recalled a different meaning of this slogan when he was a Young Pioneer. "I never believed that Nkrumah would literally live forever. What we were taught was that his *ideas* would never die."[45] Nyako did still recall, however, that some young peers so idolized Nkrumah that they actually believed in his physical immortality.

Father Divine's movement was also based on an idealized utopian vision of the future that utilized some of the principles of socialism, but rejected some of the other basic, doctrinal principles. Divine constructed an internal communalism within the Peace Mission and the promotion of a socialistic ideal based on the innate human capacity for utopian goodness. Nkrumah inserted this innate capacity into his concept of the African personality and consciencism.

When Father Divine implemented his philosophy of socialistic pooling of resources for the benefit of humanity, in the early 1930s, he maintained a tenuous alliance with the Communist Party of the United States. The Communists then had a reputation for championing the rights of the Negro.[46] Later, during the Cold War, Divine vocally opposed organized Communism while maintaining his followers in communes in cities and on communal farms. Still, even during his most pro-Communist period, he maintained a doctrinal distance from the Communist Party, whose central committee of leaders was primarily white. Divine did not become what was known in the vernacular of the times as a "Red Uncle Tom." Neither did Nkrumah when he ruled Ghana.

Nkrumah identified himself as a Marxist and a nondenominational Christian. Father Divine set the example of the synthesis of Marxian communalism and unorthodox Christianity. It is the trickster's unorthodox doubleness that is important here. Prior historians have sought to attach a coherent orthodoxy to Nkrumah's Marxism, with Leninism being the most logical suffix. This has led to their overlooking or undervaluing Father Divine as a template for Nkrumah's unorthodoxy.

This ambivalent and ambiguous relationship with official Communism would come to mark Nkrumah's regime. Even though Nkrumah promoted socialist ideals, contrary to his critics, he was no Leninist Czar.[47] One fundamental of Leninism is the workers' vanguard party ruling through its violent crushing of bourgeois ruling-class opposition. Leninism never stated that a socialist revolution could occur without the use of force. The wielders of this force would be the vanguard party of the workers.

While in power, Nkrumah did not form such a party nor did he seek to violently launch an orthodox Marxist-Leninist regime by extirpating his upper-class opponents. Nkrumah was also not a czar in the sense of Russian royalty. His "royalty" was that of an African philosopher-king. To his followers he was a special leader granted divine authority to change Ghana and all of Africa. Nkrumah would emulate Father Divine in attempting to achieve the revolution in the Ghanaian mind by nonviolent persuasion and not by the coercive commands of Leninism. Nkrumah would not abandon this position as long as he held power in Ghana, despite his sometimes labeling himself a Leninist.

Nkrumah received his master's degree from the University of Pennsylvania in philosophy. Moreover, he taught philosophy at Lincoln University. He definitely would know that not nondenominational Christianity but Leninism was the suffix for revolutionary Marxism in 1957 when he published his autobiography. He had made a conscious choice to synthesize two potent philosophies for the spiritual and political revolutions Ghanaians needed. More than this, these philosophies were external manifestations of his inner convictions. "I am convinced that in the interpretation of history and future events, the will of God must be discerned. I believe that if He has any task for me in the future this is the time for thorough preparation. Hence my detest for anything which might thwart this preparation."[48] He would be a Christian *and* a Marxian socialist, despite the orthodox Communist adamancy against this concept as oxymoronic. Had not their belief in their leader and God inspired Father Divine's followers to work on socialist-style collective farms? Nkrumah knew that Divine's lead, and not Marx's and Lenin's, would be more efficacious for the African revolution. Hence he ignored Marxist-Leninist orthodoxy to promote the syncretistic concepts that he would refine in the future into a philosophy that he named consciencism.

Previous historians have nearly unanimously insisted that Nkrumah first heard about collective farms in the Soviet bloc or Communist China. They attribute his enthusiasm to create communes in Ghana to his desire to emulate what he thought were successful operations in the Communist countries.[49] Unnoticed by biographers was Nkrumah's membership in Father Divine's organization and the lauded successes of Divine's communal farms. On Divine's rural New York and Pennsylvania communes every race and social class worked without concern for personal profit. They sought solely to attract the light of their prophet's approval upon themselves. Like Christ's apostles, they owned everything in common and labored unselfishly to sustain and promote his ideals. Whether the ways and means of messianic leadership Nkrumah observed while in Father Divine's movement helped or hindered him cannot be definitively concluded. In the African epic the knowledge or advice of a sage does not guarantee success to the hero. It simply assures that he will not pursue his quest without guidance. Sages in the African epic can be either good or bad. This impression often depends on the subjectivity of the observer. Outcomes caused by those sages can receive multiple interpretations.

There is no record of Nkrumah's communications with Father Divine after his departure from the United States in 1945. Nevertheless, in 1957 the *New York Times* and Divine's official news journal reported that Father Divine sent a contingent of his followers to a demonstration in Harlem celebrating Nkrumah's coming to power. Divine also sent his "Rosebud Choir" to perform for Nkrumah at the outdoor reception.[50]

The Trickster at Work

An initial success of Nkrumah's trickster's mask might be evident in his Federal Bureau of Investigation (FBI) file. It contains the usual blacked-out pages. The FBI states that it does this to protect sources and methods, that is, informers' identities and the various methods (human and electronic) that they employ to collect information. In the Nkrumah file, what was not blacked out indicates either that the FBI was very incompetent in their assessment of Nkrumah or that he had presented to them a face, like his mentor Aggrey, that was not the real he.

In March 1945, the FBI decided to investigate Nkrumah to see whether he was engaging in any "Communistic or subversive activities." The FBI activated an informer at Lincoln University to keep tabs on Nkrumah. Information from this informer caused the FBI file to state that as a student at Lincoln, Nkrumah lacked three qualities that, evidently, would have made him a subversive threat to U.S. security if he had them: the ability to lead, independent initiative, and independent thought.[51]

In 1945 Nkrumah published strongly anti-imperialist articles. Even the college yearbook, the *Lincolnian*, contained a pithy statement that ought to have aroused the paranoia of the FBI Communist-hunters. Yet, despite all evidence to the contrary, the file virtually

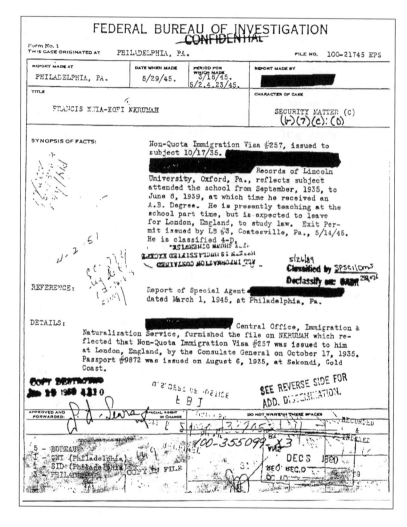

Figure 5   FBI document File no. 100-21745 EPS.

calls this lion a lamb. Did Nkrumah succeed in deceiving agents who routinely labeled as "subversive Communist" the persons exhibiting strongly liberal politics, let alone Nkrumah's growing advocacy of anti-imperialist and anticolonialist ideas? Moreover, Nkrumah's association with left wing activists distinctly marked his behavior. A mere perusal of the college yearbook would have shown Nkrumah's true political focus.

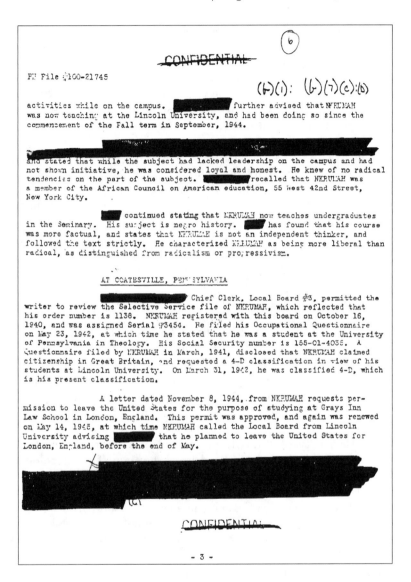

CONFIDENTIAL

FBI File #100-21745

(b)

(b)(1): (b)(7)(c):(b)

activities while on the campus. ████████████ further advised that NKRUMAH was now teaching at the Lincoln University, and had been doing so since the commencement of the Fall term in September, 1944.

██ and stated that while the subject had lacked leadership on the campus and had not shown initiative, he was considered loyal and honest. He knew of no radical tendencies on the part of the subject. ████████ recalled that NKRUMAH was a member of the African Council on American education, 55 West 42nd Street, New York City.

████████ continued stating that NKRUMAH now teaches undergraduates in the Seminary. His subject is negro history. ████ has found that his course was more factual, and states that NKRUMAH is not an independent thinker, and followed the text strictly. He characterized NKRUMAH as being more liberal than radical, as distinguished from radicalism or progressivism.

AT COATESVILLE, PENNSYLVANIA

████████████ Chief Clerk, Local Board #3, permitted the writer to review the Selective Service file of NKRUMAH, which reflected that his order number is 1138. NKRUMAH registered with this board on October 16, 1940, and was assigned Serial #3454. He filed his Occupational Questionnaire on May 23, 1942, at which time he stated that he was a student at the University of Pennsylvania in Theology. His Social Security number is 155-01-4035. A Questionnaire filed by NKRUMAH in March, 1941, disclosed that NKRUMAH claimed citizenship in Great Britain, and requested a 4-D classification in view of his students at Lincoln University. On March 31, 1942, he was classified 4-D, which is his present classification.

A letter dated November 8, 1944, from NKRUMAH requests permission to leave the United States for the purpose of studying at Grays Inn Law School in London, England. This permit was approved, and again was renewed on May 14, 1945, at which time NKRUMAH called the Local Board from Lincoln University advising ████████ that he planned to leave the United States for London, England, before the end of May.

CONFIDENTIAL

- 3 -

Figure 6   FBI document File no. 100-21745 EPS contd.

It is more likely that the FBI penchant for prejudging black subjects caused them to deceive themselves. Evidence of this prejudice is in the FBI's Marcus Garvey file. In 1919 a twenty-six-year-old J. Edgar Hoover stated in a Bureau of Investigation (the precursor of the FBI) memo that Garvey was strongly pro-Communist, even though Garvey had spoken in opposition to Communism, socialism, and even labor unions. He believed that the Communist system would place in power the working-class white man who was the most antiblack and ignorant segment of white America. He feared that Communism would leave black people suffering under worse racial oppression than capitalism.[52]

Garvey stated that Lenin and Trotsky's revolution in Russia brought to power a social class with whom the world's black peasantry had a natural affinity. But in no way did he advocate a Marxian revolution because he was an enthusiastic capitalist. When black people from the diaspora took Africa back from Europe, his examples were not Marxists for Africa's leaders. "Why should Africa not give to the world the black Rockefeller, Rothschild and Henry Ford?"[53] He further stated, "Capitalism is necessary to the progress of the world, and those who unreasonably and wantonly oppose or fight against it are enemies of human advancement."[54]

Despite these clearly articulated conservative views, J. Edgar Hoover classified Garvey as a Communist sympathizer. This false impression was as striking as the FBI classification, in 1945, of Nkrumah as apolitical and lacking leadership abilities.

The evidence of FBI incompetence or self-deception appears stronger when one reviews the paper trail of articles Nkrumah began writing in the 1940s. His 1943 essay, "Education and Nationalism in Africa," offers a striking example of his growing radicalization. He states here his anti-imperialist and anticolonialist views. In the journal of the University of Pennsylvania School of Education, Nkrumah wrote that Africa needed new models of education. The old colonial schools would not meet the needs of the African future. Among the examples he listed for emulation was the "current social, political, technical, and economic ideals now in vogue in progressive schools in America, China, and Russia."[55] It is significant that Nkrumah included Soviet Russia as a model for Africa's future. J. Edgar Hoover's FBI routinely regarded such references as prima facie evidence of pro-Communist sympathies. Nkrumah's use of the word "progressive" would have been viewed as a euphemistic code word for "leftist."

If this statement was insufficient to expose Nkrumah's growing radicalization, the next page should have removed all doubt. The renascent youth of Africa would throw out all imperialistic forces from Africa. Then he issued a warning. If, following the defeat of Germany and Japan, "imperialism and colonialism should be

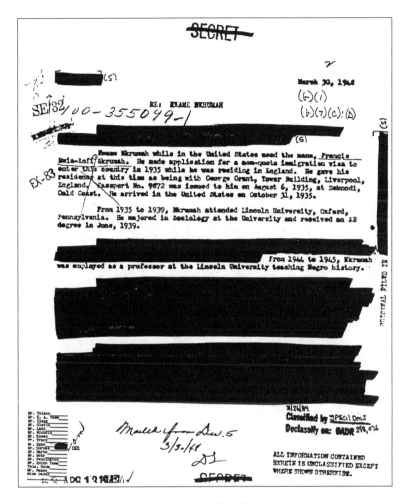

Figure 7   FBI document RE: KWAME NKRUMAH.

restored, we will be sowing the seed not only for another war, but for the greatest revolution the world has ever seen."[56] The FBI documents do not detail the processes of their conclusions. This information is possibly in the blacked-out paragraphs that are still not declassified.

If Nkrumah did in any way trick the FBI into believing he was an apolitical lamb when he was becoming a left wing, anti-imperialist wolf, the first sign of his relaxing this trickster's guile came in a letter from Lincoln University President William Hallock Johnson. This incident set a pattern that differentiated

Nkrumah from, James Aggrey. Unlike Aggrey, Nkrumah had limits after which he would no longer conceal his real opinions to appease white power. Aggrey, on the other hand, displayed an endless capacity to bend so as not to rupture his relations with his white patrons.

Nkrumah's turning point at Lincoln University resulted from an African ceremony that he led at a memorial in honor of Aggrey at Salisbury, North Carolina. Nkrumah's mother was a Christian but she had told him never to forget his ancestors. They were the reservoirs of Akan culture and indigenous deities. It was to them that Nkrumah poured libations three times. Lincoln University had been founded on the white Christian "civilizing" mission to remove the "plague" of animism from Africa. Now Nkrumah, after being ordained as a minister, graduating from college, and teaching philosophy classes at Lincoln, had shown that for all of the Christian civilization that Lincoln had given him, he still retained his Africanity. The dean of Lincoln Seminary, George Johnson, was one of Nkrumah's chief benefactors. He scolded Nkrumah for conducting the biblically "heathen" forbidden ceremony. He had evidently been concealing this part of himself sufficiently to retain the patronage of the executive Johnson and the officers of the university. But the Aggrey memorial received media attention.

Nkrumah's response was even more striking.

He again demonstrated that he was his own man. Just as he had held fast to his Africanity to overcome the dominance of the discursive formations of Catholicism as a child, so he now held to the same to not succumb to the hegemonic discourse of Lincoln's Christian "civilizing mission" to de-Africanize him. He additionally had the effrontery not to admit wrongdoing when chastened back to Eurocentric orthodoxy by his superiors. His relations with Lincoln University were tenuous at best after this letter. The documentation shows that after this his financial troubles increased. The attempts to secure him funding from his Lincoln patrons decreased as well.[57]

At Lincoln, Nkrumah's ideas congealed to the point where he knew that he would create a mythic African past to forge an ideal African future. He would be the unifying king of the new Ghana—the *Osagyefo*. He would be the symbol of Africa's revived greatness.

The Trinidadian Cyril Lionel Robert James (1901–1989) in New York and George Padmore in England. Nkrumah met C. L. R. James in New York in 1941. According to James, he played a greater role

603 N. 39th St.,
Philadelphia, Pa.
April 24, 1943.

My dear Dr. Johnson,

        I must apologize for delaying so long in answering your kind letter. I have the book you sent me; I am making the best use of it and shall let you have it by May 15th.

        With regard to your remarks on the Aggrey Memoria Service which took place at Salisbury N.C. may I say that a letter of explanation will not do me justice. I am therefore trying to find time to visit you at Lincoln in order to talk at length over the issue.

        You seem to have misunderstood me partially and you are right at that if all your reasons are coiled from the report in the Africian Interpreter. May I say however that to meet Christ on the highway of Christian ethics and principles by way of Christian salvation, and turn back, is a spiritual impossibility. The burden of my life is to live in such a way that I may become a living symbol of all that is best both in Christianity and in the laws, customs and beliefs of my people. I am a Christian and will ever remain so but never a blind Christian.

        Wishing you and Mrs. Johnson a very happy Easter.

        Sincerely yours,

        Francis N. Nkrumah

Figure 8   Letter to Dean George Johnson, dated April 24, 1943.

in Nkrumah's life than indicated by the single-sentence reference to him in Nkrumah's autobiography. The only credit Nkrumah gave to James was for teaching him "how an underground movement worked."[58] Why Nkrumah said so little about James is not explained anywhere in Nkrumah's writings. Nkrumah did not give James credit for connecting him with George Padmore, yet James's letter to Padmore introducing Nkrumah is among Padmore's papers.

When viewed in isolation, Nkrumah's lack of mention of the influence of James on his life looks like a personal slight. When viewed within the worldwide political context of revolutionary Marxism in 1957, when Nkrumah published his autobiography, the reason for Nkrumah's disregarding James becomes clear. Nkrumah likely distanced himself from James because James was a Trotskyist.

At the twentieth congress of the Soviet Communist Party on February 26, 1956, Soviet Premier Nikita Kruschev made his famous speech denouncing Stalin and exposing decades of Stalin's incompetence and murderous crimes. Some of Stalin's victims, loyal Communists all, were beginning to have their reputations rehabilitated, but not Leon Trotsky. Even so, the most prominent Third World revolutionaries continued to promote a Marxian holy trinity of Marx, Lenin, and Stalin. The Marxism-Leninism of the Union of Soviet Socialist Republics (USSR) had forever vanquished Trotskyism in the practical politics of the homeland and the international revolutionary Left. The Asian anticolonial revolutionaries—China's Mao Zedong, Viet Nam's Ho Chi Minh, and Korea's Kim Il Sung—all led Communist parties in which no traces of the Trotskyist heresy openly existed. Orthodox Marxist revolutionaries had branded the Trotskyist schism heretical and pronounced anathema upon Trotsky and his followers.[59] Like religious heretics who stray from the One True Faith, Trotskyites were shunned and sometimes persecuted by the orthodox.

Even in Yugoslavia, when the leader Josip Broz Tito critiqued and ushered out Stalinism, he could never advocate Trotskyism. Tito's critique of the Soviet Union closely resembled Trotsky's. Still, Tito could not embrace Trotsky and maintain credibility within the world of institutionalized socialist revolution. His particular brand of non-Stalinist Marxism became known as Titoism. Similarly Nkrumah's non-Stalinist and non-Leninist Marxism would become known as Nkrumaism.

When C. L. R. James met Nkrumah in 1944, James was already a well-known theorist of Trotskyism and unorthodox, non-Stalinist Marxism. His later critiques of Nkrumah would be an incisive presentation on the pitfalls of the hero who departs from the paths advised by his sages.[60] In 1966, however, James recalled that in his letter to Padmore introducing Nkrumah he had written that Nkrumah "was not very bright but that he was determined to throw the imperialist out of Africa."[61] Furthermore, in James's opinion, Nkrumah was talking a lot of "nonsense" and incompetently using Marxian terminology about imperialism and Leninism. James estimated that Nkrumah "knew nothing about them."[62]

This assessment of Nkrumah brings up the question of whether Nkrumah deliberately gave James a false image of himself. It also raises the possibility that James looked at Nkrumah through ideological lenses that shaded his viewpoint negatively. Nkrumah had taught courses on philosophy at Lincoln University and had a master's degree in western philosophy from the University of Pennsylvania. By 1944 he was already well versed in the radical anti-imperialist philosophies of the day.

Unlike James, other people who met Nkrumah were impressed by his brilliant intelligence. It stands to reason that Nkrumah had concealed from James all of his capacities. Apparently he viewed James as a person who should not know how much he really knew. Disguises are defensive weapons of African tricksters. Another possibility is that James regarded Nkrumah as unintelligent because Nkrumah did not speak in agreement with James's Trotskyist interpretation of Communist ideology. Nkrumah's reserve could have really been his leeriness toward Trotskyism. It was a marginalized and ineffectual force in the world revolution. Nkrumah would have recognized immediately that it was not the Golden Fleece of Ghana's liberation.

Scholar/activist Grace Lee Boggs arranged the first meeting between Nkrumah and James in 1944. She had purposed to get Nkrumah together with James and Raya Dunayevskaya. The latter was the principal theorist of Marxist humanism. Sixty years later, Boggs offered a different interpretation of why James described Nkrumah so negatively. "Yes, I saw James acting condescending and patronizing to Nkrumah. He had a tendency to be that way."[63] She recalled that James and the other black people from the Caribbean in New York viewed themselves as cosmopolitan and sophisticated in contrast to the less well-read and well-traveled Africans.

The scholar Harold Cruse lived in Harlem during those years. Grace Lee Boggs's impression of the Afro-Caribbean attitude toward indigenous Africans was a reiteration of what Cruse stated. "Those West Indian Blacks thought they were better than us."[64] Even though African Americans were as sophisticated as the West Indians, Cruse contended that West Indians carried the attitude that they were always more militant and more intelligent than black people from anywhere else.[65]

In summary, during that meeting, James viewed Nkrumah as a sort of African country hick. Then Nkrumah went to England in 1945. A year later, James read an address by Nkrumah on imperialism and proclaimed it a masterpiece. After a year under the tutelage of

Padmore, James's fellow West Indian, Nkrumah had been transformed into a first-rate revolutionary in theory and practice. The logical conclusion of James's description of the early Nkrumah was that George Padmore had produced the Nkrumah that the world would come to know, and that he was responsible for Nkrumah meeting Padmore. Also challenging James's memories was the fact that when Nkrumah departed the United States for London in 1945, he was already a professional philosopher. He did not need George Padmore to inform him about imperialism or Leninism.

Nkrumah's encounter with the New York leftwing set, particularly with Raya Dunayevskaya, was the most significant contribution to his quest. Dunayevskaya advocated a humanistic approach to revolutionary philosophy that placed people before ideology. Nkrumah explicated an African revolutionary form of this humanism in his philosophy consciencism. As with all the philosophies Nkrumah absorbed during his twelve years in the West, he recast Marxist humanism in the mold of the necessities of Africa's revolution. "The idea of the original value of man imposes duties of a socialist kind upon us. Herein lies the theoretical basis of African communalism."[66] The revolution exists for humanity; humanity does not exist for revolution. This humanism was a distinct and unbridgeable gap between Nkrumaism and Stalinism and homage to Dunayevskaya.

This is not to say that Nkrumah did not benefit from James's sagacity. From James he took back to Africa an unwillingness to use Stalinist methods of repression, even when they would have preserved him in power. James's later critiques of what he deemed Nkrumah's "undemocratic" rule would dispute whether Nkrumah sufficiently learned his anti-Stalinist lessons about democracy. However, Nkrumah's humanistic unwillingness to use Stalin's brutality was James's and Dunayevskaya's most lasting influence on Nkrumah.

This leniency, however, would be the principal personal flaw in his character criticized by his future comrades, Guinea's leader Sekou Toure and Kwame Ture (Stokely Carmichael). Kwame Ture was the founder and chairperson of the All African Peoples Revolutionary Party, which defines itself as "Nkrumahist."

"Sekou Toure told me that revolutionary repression that thwarted the plans of the counterrevolutionaries was all that could secure the revolution in power," said Kwame Ture. "Sekou Toure was a great Stalinist and Nkrumah was overthrown because he was not. Nkrumah wouldn't kill anybody. He didn't order any executions, even of the cats who tried to kill him. Had he done like Sekou, those traitors would have all been hanging some place and he would never have lost power."[67]

When Nkrumah departed the United States for London in 1945, he carried with him the Golden Fleece that Nnamdi Azikiwe had urged him to bring back to Africa. Like the mythical Jason, he never could claim the crown of leadership without this trophy. Nkrumah believed that Africa needed a national myth and a messianic leader to spread it. The Golden Fleece was that entire body of knowledge that he attained in the United States. He was fully aware of the divine nature of his quest. His final sermon at a Presbyterian church in Philadelphia revealed this epic consciousness. He preached on "I saw a new Heaven and a new Earth." As he later recalled, he "reminded the people of how history repeated itself. Just as in the days of the Egyptians, to-day God had ordained that certain among the African race should journey westwards to equip themselves with knowledge and experience for the day when they would be called upon to return to their motherland and to use the learning they had acquired to help improve the lot of their brethren."[68] No person present in that congregation could have doubted that Nkrumah himself was one of those God-ordained Africans. As in the days of the Egyptians, a divinely guided Moses had lived and worked among them. He had sought and received knowledge from them; all the while he nurtured a dream of his people's liberty. Now the time had come for him to depart the shores of the United States. He sailed away fully confident that he had achieved the goal that the Lord had set before him. With God's help, he would make Pharaoh set his people free. Then they would remake Africa into a new heaven and a new earth.

3

Africa's Future in England

The British have a popular saying: the Battle of Britain was won on the playing fields of Eaton. This refers to how intense sports competition between generations of students created the fierce character required for repulsing the Nazis' World War II air assaults. A similar analogy is appropriate with respect to the Anglophone African students in England during the first half of the twentieth century. The battles that they would fight against colonialism and among themselves while achieving the independence of their countries, and after independence, were first adumbrated in their interactions in the living rooms, meeting halls, pubs, and on the streets of England. Nkrumah would encounter his future supporters and opponents in an Afro-Britain that was at once part of the African diaspora, but was at the same time so different from the African American diaspora as to shape characters so different in his fellow Ghanaians and plant the seeds of his future political demise.

Mythical heroes enter worlds between their quests and their returns where successfully passing further trials heightens the power of their heroic authority. The power of this authority derives from heroic action in the face of opposition. This is different from what Max Weber called "charismatic authority," which several authors have stated was the source of Nkrumah's hold over the Ghanaian masses. Charismatic authority derives from the magnetism of the hero's personality. The deeds of heroic authority attract supporters because they answer the needs of a socially compelling moment in history. Charismatic authority is inner; heroic authority is outer. Either one has, historically, projected enough energy to compel social, political, and religious changes in societies. Nkrumah's persona combined both charismatic and heroic authority. This combination first became visible through his fellow expatriates' fog of ideological confusions and disorganized anticolonial banter during his two years in England, from 1945 to 1947.

England presented the greater testing region for Nkrumah. It was here that he began acquiring heroic authority by becoming a living example of what he would later refer to as the African Personality. The cultural heroism of the African Personality is a more serious office than the term "folk hero" implies. Imperialist white England viewed its own culture as superior to all of those in the conquered colonies. Africans living in the belly of the metropole could easily internalize British loathing as their own self-loathing of all that was "primitive" and "backward" about their peoples. Many succumbed, but the culture hero stood up for his culture and his history versus all imperialist onslaughts. Folklorist John W. Roberts' use of the term folk heroism corresponds closely with Nkrumah's cultural heroism:

> Folk heroic creation occurs because groups, at critical moments in time, recognize in the actions of certain figures, which may already be known to them, qualities or behaviors that they have reason to believe would enhance culture-building *(that is, their ability to protect the identity and values of the group in the face of a threat to them)* . . . The type of hero that a group will embrace, depends, first of all, on the nature of the forces responsible for the situation perceived as threatening to culture-building. [1]

The threat of conquest by British culture did not cease, but intensified, when the "natives" left the colony for the metropole. British culture threatened the identities and values of the African patriots who received higher education at its various colleges, because the purpose of that education was to create elite blacks through whom the British could indirectly rule their colonies. England in the 1940s is where we see the powerful influence of space and place on Africa's future. For the deterministic power of not just diaspora, but which *place* in the diaspora shaped the consciousness of the African nationalist, was central to the leaders' future conceptualization and implementation of their countries' liberation.

Many of Nkrumah's initial supporters who studied in England's universities or military academies would later form the Opposition to his government. Whether the Ghanaian patriot studied and developed into manhood in the English or the American part of the diaspora was an important determinant of his future attitude toward Ghana and Africa's *kind* of independence. Some key nationalists and Pan-Africanists from Africa who had studied in U.S. colleges and who grew up in African American communities returned to Africa with radically different attitudes toward African culture, Pan-Africanism, and Africa's future than did their peers who studied in England. Nkrumah's experiences among African Americans had steeled him against the cultural onslaught of England and cemented his future role as a culture hero.

Toward the end of his life, the Tanzanian hero, Mwalimu Julius Nyerere, remembered the dissimilar effects of different parts of Africa's diaspora on Nkrumah and his peers:

> [Kwame Nkrumah and I] differed on how to achieve a United States of Africa. But we both agreed on a United States of Africa as necessary. Kwame went to Lincoln University, a black college in the US . . . Africans who studied in the US like Nkrumah and [Nnamdi] Azikiwe were more aware of the Diaspora and the global African community than those of us who studied in Britain. They were therefore aware of a wider Pan-Africanism. Theirs was the aggressive Pan-Africanism of W.E.B. Du Bois and Marcus Garvey. The colonialists were against this and frightened of it. [2]

Mwalimu Nyerere identified the sources of the different consciousness of Africans educated in the African American as opposed to the British diaspora as Du Bois and Garvey. But they were only two influences amid the myriad sources in the African American diaspora. These influences made Nkrumah into both a political and a cultural hero. The political hero represents the interests of his people against the overwhelming might of oppositional political powers. The culture hero defends and asserts his people's culture against the denigrating projections of foreign cultural supremacy. Colonial cultural hegemony was as important a component of European political hegemony as was the machine gun and the bayonet. The awe and wonderment inspired by European technology alone imbued European culture with an image of superiority. As culture hero as well as political hero, Nkrumah had to become the living embodiment of that culture which white supremacy disparaged.

African Diasporas in Conflict

When Nkrumah arrived in London in May 1945, he joined a society of African nationalists who carried abstract nationalistic dreams. Some of them theorized about a future of gradually shared power with British colonialism. Total independence was not in all of their vernaculars. Some of their names are well known in the annals of African independence, for they would devote their lives to Africa and would adjust to the times as best they could.

Nkrumah quickly joined forces with some of the foremost leaders among the nationalists who were destined to become prime ministers. Kenya's Johnstone (later Jomo) Kenyatta and Malawi's Hastings Banda were among the first. Nkrumah would now also make the acquaintance of his future supporters and his future rivals in Ghana, prominent among them was Joseph Appiah. Later in Ghana, Nkrumah would meet J. B. Danquah and K. A. Busia. Appiah, Danquah, and Busia were all products of British colleges and universities. They were also scions of Ashanti royalty. These two facts would play critical roles in Nkrumah's future relationships with each of them and their interactive roles in Ghana's independence and postindependence.

Some biographers have sought motivations for Nkrumah's actions in psychological analyses of his supposed megalomania and drive for personal rule. Others have zeroed in on his Marxian sympathies. These analytical variables inadequately explain both Nkrumah's behavioral driving forces and the resulting history of Ghana from 1948 when he assumed leadership of its independence movement until his overthrow in 1966. The later contradictions among Ghana's independence leaders (and between Nkrumah and other African leaders) cannot be fully understood without understanding their genesis in the two years Nkrumah spent in England.

Nkrumah had been educated in English missionary schools in Anglophone Africa and received a college education in the West, as did most of the educated leaders of Ghana's independence movement. The difference between Nkrumah's experience and that of his compatriots in England was that England had no historically black colleges where black students and faculty were the majority and where their culture was viewed as positively as European culture. There was no Lincoln University where an all-black student body included Africans like Nkrumah, the poet Langston Hughes, Nigeria's future president Nnamdi Azikiwe, or the future United States Supreme Court Justice Thurgood Marshall. At such U.S. institutions African and African American students could collaborate their dreams for future uplift against the forces of white supremacy. Neither did England have a black brain trust remotely similar to the list of famous scholars teaching at Howard University in the 1940s. At Howard the world's first black Rhodes scholar, Alain Locke, future Nobel Peace Prize winner Ralph Bunche, and eminent sociologist E. Franklin Frazier were living refutations of white intellectual supremacy.[3]

Had Nkrumah's future archenemy, K. A. Busia, seen Howard University as his "spiritual home" and not Oxford, his consciousness in all probability would not have tended toward colluding with Africa's enemies and ultimately betraying the ideals of African liberation. Moreover, Joseph Danquah dedicated one of his books with words that one cannot imagine an African who studied in black America writing. "To The Founders of University College, London who Facilitated the Endeavour of a Raw African to Drink deep of the Pierian Spring."[4] The *Oxford English Dictionary* defines the word "raw" in this context as "uncultivated," "uncivilized," "brutal," "inexperienced," "unskilled," and "untrained." Any new student coming into a college is usually inexperienced, unskilled, and untrained. No British imperialist, however, would miss Danquah's meaning when he followed the word "raw" with "African." For this was the pejorative term of the white colonialist about the charges of the white man's burden. By referring to himself as a "raw African," Danquah meant that he had internalized the denigrating Western terminology for the African whose contact with the West had not yet "civilized" him. Even worse, "raw African" is the language of the British slave trade. It was the slavers' colloquial classification for Africans before the cruel "seasoning" process that conditioned them for chattel slavery.

Danquah's dedication highlighted the key difference between him and Nkrumah—that they drank from different springs. The Pierian Spring in Greek mythology was a spring in Macedonia that was sacred to the Muses and was a source of inspiration. Danquah drew his words from Alexander Pope's poem:

> A little learning is a dang'rous thing;
> Drink deep or taste not the Pierian Spring;
> There shallow draughts largely intoxicate the brain;
> and drinking deeply largely sobers us again.

An African who drank so deeply from a spring polluted by centuries of racism and class oppression would find difficulty developing a consciousness that was compatible with that of Nkrumah. He drank from multiple springs, the deepest being in Harlem, Washington D.C., and Philadelphia. It was these springs that gave rise to the New Negro.

Starting in the 1920s in black America, the New Negro had cast off such denigrating terms as those used by Danquah. The equivalent in the United States of Danquah's using "raw African" in Britain would have been W. E. B. Du Bois's dedicating a book to his professors at Harvard because they took an "uncivilized savage" and made him a scholar. The term played a dual role for Danquah: inwardly denigrating, outwardly ingratiating. This pattern for dealing with the Western powers would hold true beyond England for him. As leader of Nkrumah's political Opposition, Danquah would continually denigrate Nkrumah's efforts toward economic development and Pan-African unity. He would also belittle his fellow Ghanaians who had not been privileged to receive a Western education. At the same time he would successfully ingratiate himself with the Western enemies of Nkrumah's policies.

Neither prewar nor bombed-out wartime London could offer Danquah, Appiah, Busia, and Kenyatta the deep springs of cultural vibrancy of black America. Black cultural renaissances, beginning in Harlem and spreading to other cities, exalted the so-called "raw" African culture that Joseph Appiah discarded as "unchristian," that did not inspire Danquah, and that filled Busia with loathing.

Nkrumah's cohorts came of age in England without resources approaching the power of black America's politically and culturally assertive institutions. Nkrumah had arrived in black America in 1935 after the 1920s concepts of the New Negro had advanced from radical assertions to matter-of-fact acceptance by the avant-garde of the black intelligentsia. He never used the term New Negro probably because of its specifically African American context. Instead, he used the term "African Personality" synonymously with "New Negro." Preeminent among the traits of the African Personality was a dignity that had to be fought for and won in the movement for independence from the demeaning forces of colonial servitude. The advocacy of the African Personality conceptualized the cultural heroism that Nkrumah epitomized and added to his heroic authority.

Appiah, Danquah, and Busia, Nkrumah's supporters who would become his opponents, also had in common a background in Ghana's black petite bourgeoisie and were the equivalent of princes in their respective Ashanti royal families. Their bourgeoisie was "petite" only in comparison to the British bourgeoisie. Compared with other Ghanaians, they were the *le grand bourgeoisie*. When they lived in England, lacking black America's mainstays of political and cultural identity, they identified with the corresponding British social class as opposed to the English working classes who corresponded to the "primitive" and "savage" Africans. They internalized the criteria of the British middle and upper classes for judging themselves politically and culturally. They would be Africa's future leaders. Add the Cold War to these identity issues and Africa's future conflicts are plainly visible in London in the years following World War II. The Malian scholar Manthia Diawara perceptively recorded the influence of the Cold War in also shaping the different identities of Nkrumah and his elite opponents:

> Leaders such as Sekou Toure, Modibo Keita, and Kwame Nkrumah, who were trying to uphold the sovereignty and equality of our nations and to resist the shaping of our identities by the Cold War, were opposed by other Africans who were on the payroll of France, Belgium, the United Kingdom, and their allies. [5]

The following review of the dialectic between Nkrumah and his future opponents reveals underlying cultural differences that made their future antagonisms inevitable. The cultural contradictions in England were but outer manifestations of the as yet concealed political contradictions that would turn them into enemies in Ghana.

West African National Secretariat

In December 1945, Nkrumah helped to start an organization known as the West African National Secretariat (WANS). The South African author Peter Abrahams observed Nkrumah making his move to dominate the Pan-African movement and to place the radical stamp for a socialist West African Union upon the future of the continent. His description of Nkrumah during this phase is surprisingly flattering:

> He was one of the members of the inner circle of the Pan-African movement until he broke away to found his own West African National Secretariat. I thought then, and still think, that he was the most practical politician of the lot of us. We were concerned with ideas, with the enunciation of great principles. He was concerned with one thing only, getting power and getting it quickly. [6]

That a youthful newcomer had seen fit to launch an organization that had not been formed before him by his elders was an implicit criticism of the elders' strategies. Men like Appiah, Danquah, and Busia who believed that leadership of Ghana belonged to them by right of social class, ethnic bloodline, and British education, could not easily accept the upstart. The derisive tone Joseph Appiah used in his auto-biography to describe Nkrumah in their London years is evidence of their pique.

After forming WANS, Nkrumah came to see a need for a vanguard party that would train revolutionary cadres to carry the struggle to any part of Africa.[7] What is likely is that he used WANS as a means to the end of establishing that type of disciplined, frontline organization that he believed was necessary for a successful socialist revolution. This organization was known as THE CIRCLE (Nkrumah's caps).

THE CIRCLE was to begin underground as the revolutionary vanguard of the quest for West African independence and unity. At an opportune time later it would become the public advocate of the "Union of African Socialist Republics."[8] But THE CIRCLE would be a socialist vanguard unlike any other. Its motto, *The Three S's*—Service, Sacrifice, and Suffering—do not appear in Lenin's precepts for the vanguard revolutionary organization.[9] Instead they reflect the philosophy of Nkrumah's Christian ministry in black America. He lifted each of the Three S's from the mission of Jesus described in "Acts" in the Bible.[10]

Initiation into membership in THE CIRCLE required an oath while letting "a few drops of our blood in a bowl." Peter Abrahams recalled that the initiate swore to serve Africa and to follow Nkrumah's leadership.[11] Both Joseph Appiah and Johnstone (Jomo) Kenyatta rejected membership in THE CIRCLE. They were too "sophisticated" for such rituals now. Kenyatta was the more "westernized," and he rejected the ritual out of hand as primitive and childish juju.[12] Appiah's autobiography depicted Nkrumah in this instance as a "bush" African, the continental equivalent of the American country bumpkin. Such "childish" rituals were beneath his Anglophilic dignity. Appiah left out his opinion of the idea of swearing an oath to follow Nkrumah's leadership. Such a prospect must have been especially loathsome to men of the stature of himself and Kenyatta. They viewed themselves as senior to Nkrumah in both nationalist and anticolonial experience and in wisdom. Moreover, back in Africa, Kenyatta was the son of a chief, and Appiah's sister was the wife of royal Ashanti blood. His sister was the wife of the Asantehene, the Ashanti king. Both Kenyatta and Appiah identified with England's royalty, while Nkrumah's socialist ideology put him squarely among the workers and peasants.

K. A. Busia would become Nkrumah's chief opponent and the first prime minister of Ghana after Nkrumah's overthrow in 1966. In 1953 he described to Richard Wright, the African American writer, the implication of these same rituals that Nkrumah was then using at the rallies of his Convention People's Party (CPP):

> It's to bind the masses to the party," he said. "Tribal life is religious through and through. An oath is a great thing to an African. An oath links him with his past, allies him with his ancestors. That's the deepest form of loyalty that the tribal man knows. [13]

Although he was also an Akan, Busia was disgusted with Nkrumah's cultural methodology for appealing to the masses. His laconic explanation of why he would never employ these tactics accentuated why the respective places in the diaspora where he and Nkrumah went to college was crucial to Africa's future. Busia would not engage in African ritualism because, "I'm a Westerner . . . I was educated in the West." [14]

Busia's locating his attitude in the West explains why Appiah and Kenyatta responded similarly when first approached in England to engage in blood oath rituals. The reality was that Busia had been educated in a particular part of the West that promoted this new identity for the Western-educated African elite. He received an education structured to make him an apparatus of British colonialism. He would be sent back to the Gold Coast as a tool through which the infamous British policy of indirect rule controlled its colony. Later, when Britain granted the Gold Coast its inevitable independence, trained minions like Busia would serve as conduits of Britain's replacement of indirect rule with neocolonialist indirect influence.

In 1946, while Nkrumah was still in England, Busia was one of the first two Africans appointed by the British to a new "Africanization" post. As an assistant district commissioner, he was a conscious tool of indirect rule. His definition of indirect rule, however, differed considerably from that of his British masters, not to mention Nkrumah. In his book *Positions of the Chief in the Modern System of Ashanti,* he defined it as "the progressive adaptation of native conditions to modern conditions." Busia's source for this definition was the 1936 book *Native Policies in Africa* by L. P. Mair. [15] That Busia's Oxford education and Ashanti elitism caused his uncritical acceptance of indirect rule as "progressive" augured ill for his future relations with Nkrumah before they had even met. Moreover, the definition reveals the narrowness of the

Oxford indoctrination of Africa's British-trained elite, whom the British still referred to insultingly as "trousered blacks" or as "examination bred."[16]

While at Oxford, had Busia looked a little deeper he would have discovered the English author Geoffrey Gorer's 1936 revelations about the actual diabolical purposes of indirect rule:

> When a village fails to pay its taxes the administration steps in brutally and ruthlessly. When punitive measures are taken, as they frequently are, the administrator himself is never present, and therefore has a complete alibi; he sends his Negro soldiers—naturally always of a different race [meaning ethnic group or "tribe"] to the people they are sent out against . . . The employment of Negroes for the dirty work serves a double aim; *it keeps lively the interracial hatred which is so essential for colonies where the subject races are more numerous than the colonizers,* and it enables the administration to deny forthright the most inhuman practices in which they tacitly acquiesce, or should the facts be irrefutable, to lay the blame on the excessive zeal of their subordinates.[17]

Oxford had "educated" Busia into thinking that Africans submitting to colonial law was progressive. The scholar Asiata Vaai described the impact of European colonial law in Asia as "a sharp sword by the powerful to conquer, and hold subject, the powerless."[18] The law under foreign domination is never a value-free code of service. It is a combat ideology that "has been used to destroy cultures, civilisations, religions and the entire moral fabric of a people."[19] Busia's failure to view European institutions and laws as the pillars holding up colonial conquest put him at odds with Nkrumah and any advocates of full independence.

Richard Wright interviewed Busia when Nkrumah's CPP government had begun disempowering the tribal elites whom the British had used to control and exploit the African majority. Busia had lost his job and with it the hope that the elite he represented would one day serve the British as they had been trained to do.

The interplay between England and Africa, between Nkrumah's present and his future, show his setting a pattern in England to utilize methodologies that drew on his African American experience. The ritual Nkrumah proposed for membership in THE CIRCLE clearly exhibited his continuing to have one foot in Africa and the other in black America. That Nkrumah was, at this early stage, building an organization to unite Africa under his leadership is extremely noteworthy. In the membership ritual of THE CIRCLE, before swearing the official blood oath, the prospective member had to promise to accept and abide by laws, which, in case a prospect was numerologically superstitious, Nkrumah made an auspicious seven in number. These laws reveal Nkrumah's mindset. Far from an exercise in egotistical self-promotion, it is clear that in the document known as THE CIRCLE Nkrumah was already employing a strategy that utilized all that he had learned in Africa and the diaspora:

1. I will irrevocably obey and act upon the orders, commands, instructions and directions of the Grand Council of THE CIRCLE.
2. I will always serve, sacrifice and suffer anything for the cause for which THE CIRCLE stands, and will at all times be ready to go on any mission that I may be called upon to perform.
3. I will always and in all circumstances help a member brother of THE CIRCLE in all things and in all difficulties.
4. I will, except as a last resort, avoid the use of violence.
5. I will make it my aim and duty to foster the cause for which THE CIRCLE stands in any organization that I may become a member.
6. I will on the 21st day of each month fast from sunrise to sunset and will meditate daily on the cause THE CIRCLE stands for.
7. I accept the Leadership of Kwame Nkrumah.[20]

Points six and seven are telling. Fasting had been one of Mohandas Gandhi's disciplines for members of India's independence movement. In Africa fasting and meditation (or prayer) were techniques employed by religious groups. Collective self-denial ritually separates the practitioners from the outsiders who do not fast. It fosters a sense of exclusivity and group unity. Moreover, denying physical desires at the behest of an earthly leader infuses discipline that acknowledges the leader's domain as beyond the physical realm. Meditation is a mental-spiritual discipline that concentrates the mind and builds inner strength. These were the religious prescriptions of other messianic African seers who opposed colonialism, most notably the Mahdi of the Sudan, Al Hajj Umar Tal and Samori Toure in West Africa. Nkrumah's demanding that THE CIRCLE fast and meditate was his first announcement to his followers that his leadership extended into metaphysical realms and was messianic.

Nkrumah's resorting to mysticism, however, runs counter to his writings in the United States. His first seminar paper written for the

University of Pennsylvania in 1942 proclaimed his understanding that Marxian materialism excludes "the idea of the supernatural as an explanation of accidents and so on."[21] In this essay Nkrumah uncritically embraced Marxist dialectical materialism as an advancement in epistemology. By combining materialism with dialectics Marx asserted that social phenomena should be understood as a process of continuous change, which stemmed from material causes and not from otherworldly, metaphysical causes. Dialectical and historical materialism are the bases of Marxian atheism.[22]

Nkrumah's ideological writings had taken on a Marxian orthodoxy since 1942. Nevertheless, when forming THE CIRCLE, his hybrid diasporic consciousness now held Africa and the West in balance. He saw no contradiction in a syncretism between African mysticism and Marxism materialism. At Lincoln University he had incurred the derision of white Christians by engaging in a libations ceremony to African spirits instead of sticking solely to Christian orthodoxy. Now in England he would syncretize philosophies from different sides of the Black Atlantic to promote African independence.

The hero shows his strength of character when he can go his own way even if the world goes in the other direction. The Reverend Dr. Martin Luther King, Jr., once stated that if only a single person is right, then he is a majority of one. This is heroic thinking. In 1945, orthodox Marxism looked like the wave of the future for anticolonial movements. The Chinese Communists were well on their way to conquering their country. The international Communist movement had formed an organization of anticolonial activists known as the Comintern. Nkrumah's discarding Marxism-Leninism for organizing THE CIRCLE went against the grain of world revolutionary movements. This incident of cultural heroism signaled that he would not stray from his messianic mission to walk in Marx's, Lenin's, or Stalin's shadow.

Nkrumah capitalized the word "leadership" in the original document in point seven. A cadre of revolutionaries who had sworn a blood oath to follow his leadership was foremost in his mind. But his leadership was not mortal, lowercase leadership; it was capitalized as if the document were a scripture and his leadership divine.

After initiates accepted these seven principles, they took the Oath of Allegiance. The oath unmistakably reflected the influence upon Nkrumah of his quest in black America. Nkrumah had been initiated into the African American order of Prince Hall Freemasons and was a Freemason of the thirty-second degree throughout his years in

America.[23] Point number six in THE CIRCLE pledge is a Masonic pledge taken by new initiates into the craft.[24]

The Prince Hall Freemasons were the most prominent black fraternal organization in the 1930s and 1940s. Its exclusively black membership included W. E. B. Du Bois who had joined the order in 1910.[25] Booker T. Washington, Duke Ellington, and Arthur Schomberg were also members. When Nkrumah arrived in the United States in 1935, 50 percent of the black men listed in *Who's Who in Colored America* were Prince Hall Masons.[26]

Nkrumah based the Oath of Allegiance of THE CIRCLE upon the Masonic oath. He substituted the words "THE CIRCLE" for the Masonic degree to which the initiate into Freemasonry was swearing to adhere:

> On my life, honour and fortunes, I solemnly pledge and swear that I shall always live up to the aims and aspirations of THE CIRCLE, and shall never under any circumstances divulge any secrets, plans or movements of THE CIRCLE, betray a member brother of THE CIRCLE; and that if I dare to divulge any secrets, plans and movements of THE CIRCLE, or betray a member brother or the cause, or use the influence of the circle for my own personal interests or advertisements, I do so at my own risk and peril. [27]

Nkrumah lifted some words of this oath (such as "solemnly pledge and swear") verbatim from the Masonic oaths for the Entered Apprentice, Fellow Craft, and Master degrees of Masonry. Other words are paraphrases of the oaths.[28]

This revolutionary Pan-Africanist organization would also recognize its members by the famous Masonic secret handshake. They applied thumb pressure to a comrade's knuckle.[29] Finally, for all his Marxist-Leninist leanings, Nkrumah did not use titles like "politburo" or "central committee" to designate the organization's leading authority. The leadership body of THE CIRCLE would be a Grand Council, as it was in Prince Hall Freemasonry.

Nkrumah was part of a continuum of rebels who utilized Masonic methods to cement the organizational loyalty of men for a secret cause. According to Gordon S. Wood in his book *The Radicalism of the American Revolution,* the importance of Freemasonry to the American Revolution cannot be exaggerated:

> It brought people together in new ways and helped fulfill the republican dream of reorganizing social relationships . . . Many of the revolutionary

leaders, including Washington, Franklin, Samuel Adams, John Hancock, Paul Revere, Richard Henry Lee, Madison, and Hamilton, were members of the fraternity. [30]

Voltaire, Montesquieu, and other prominent Enlightenment figures were Freemasons. The most prominent firebrands of the French Revolution like Danton, Robespierre, and Marat were Freemasons. Nkrumah, however, was the first revolutionary to merge Masonic oath-taking rituals, African mysticism, and Marxist ideology to organize a conspiratorial enterprise. When he returned to Ghana, he would have ample cause to put these skills into practice.

In the same chapter of Joseph Appiah's autobiography where he related how he and Jomo Kenyatta rejected THE CIRCLE, and therefore Nkrumah's superior status over them as a leader, he unwittingly described how he had attempted to assert his superiority over Nkrumah. The psychology of individuals in political history is sometimes subsumed in the enormity of their contributions. Both Appiah and Nkrumah were giants in Ghana's quest for independence. That fact can overshadow the psychological peculiarities influencing their deeds. Appiah's class and tribal consciousness were strong driving forces in his behavior. He was a prince in Ghana's largest subnationality, the Ashanti, while Nkrumah was from the relatively miniscule Nzimah. Like Busia, who was a member of Ghana's Wenchi royal family, Appiah's British education had westernized his cultural sensibilities. He, too, had drunk deeply from Britain's Pierian Springs.

For centuries the Ashanti had been the dominant military and economic force among the Akans. How could Appiah, brother-in-law to the king, accept a mere Nzimah as his leader without undergoing the thorough revolution in his consciousness that the great African theoretician Amilcar Cabral described as class suicide? Appiah's refusal to embrace and promote class suicide and his attachment to the micronationalism of elite Ashanti-ness would eventually influence his split with Nkrumah. Their respective attitudes toward African culture also started a crack in their friendship that would one day grow into a chasm.

At this point, Appiah would not challenge Nkrumah on political grounds. Nkrumah's drive and his clear-eyed nationalism had impressed many people including Appiah. They were in political accord. But the memoirs of multiple observers of Nkrumah during these years bear witness that he was a man of destiny. He was obviously headed for high places. Appiah's fellows were known as the

Primrose Gang. They had no control over either Nkrumah's ideas or his actions. Appiah sought to establish control over a man whose charisma was quickly taking him to the head of the movement, past Appiah, although Appiah had lived longer in England and had known the men who promoted Nkrumah more intimately than did Nkrumah. Appiah's method for asserting control would challenge Nkrumah's weaknesses and his strengths. He pushed Nkrumah toward English culture incarnate:

> The gang at Primrose decided that he [Nkrumah] needed a white girl-friend and this for good reasons. We had noticed that during dances and other social activities at the hostel—our real home from home—Nkrumah was reluctant or too shy to talk to white girls or to dance with them or even to get too close to them. In our home at Primrose Gardens the old gang were always receiving white girlfriends and, as was usual, cuddling them while Nkrumah looked on embarrassedly. Besides, as a full-grown normal male he required some female touch after the daily exertion of mind and body. Greater still was the need to break his dread of white women that the United States had instilled in him. [31]

The question of Appiah's motives arises from the fact that women of color from the British colonial world were readily accessible to him and the Primrose Gang. England also had an Afro-British community because of its centuries of involvement with the Black Atlantic. While it is true that colonial policy gave preference to males for education in the metropole, there were women of color in England from the East and West Indies as well as Africa and other parts of the empire.

Why, then, did Appiah not consider that Nkrumah's reluctance to become involved with white women was a reflection of his revolutionary nationalism, rather than a dread caused by the United States? Nkrumah stated his attitude toward African women in a 1942 letter to his Liberian friend, Phillip Brown. He did not denigrate the preferences of black men who chose white women, but instead displayed his already mature understanding of the African woman's role in the future revolution that he would lead. "We need our women in everything we plan. We must train our women to realize the magnitude of their responsibility as mothers, wives, workers and inspirers of the movement." [32]

Nkrumah was also not as sexually innocent as Appiah implied. Appiah did not yet know that Nkrumah had fathered a son while teaching school in the Gold Coast town, Cape Coast, before he departed from Africa in 1935.[33] According to Paa Kwame, Nkrumah later became involved with an African American woman in New York. He left behind a son, Kwabina, when he sailed to England. Paa Kwame knew Kwabina personally and stated that Nkrumah could not have allowed this out-of-wedlock birth to be publicized. Ghanaian Christian moralists could have exploited this as a weakness of character that might have hindered Nkrumah's rise to power.[34]

The black psychiatrist Frantz Fanon incisively analyzed Appiah's malady. Since Fanon himself married a white woman, he obviously did not mean that this problem affected every black man who chose a white woman as a life partner. Fanon declared that love was the paramount reason for his own relationship. He apparently regarded his falling in love with a white woman as an exclusively human relationship, rather than her being a whitening object of hegemonic power. The humanity of their love superseded psychosocial motivations.[35] Nevertheless, Fanon keenly focused on the effects of colonization on the African mind. He devoted a chapter in his classic *Black Skin, White Masks* to "The Man of Color and the White Woman."

In Fanon's schema, the modernistic sensibilities of both Appiah and Kenyatta that rejected Nkrumah's "primitive ju-ju" were linked psychologically to their rejection of African women. Even though they were nationalists, they were not yet free of the harmful affects of colonialism. Fanon explained their problem this way:

> Out of the blackest part of my soul, across the zebra striping of my mind, surges this desire to be suddenly *white*.
> I wish to be acknowledged not as *black* but as *white*.
> Now—and this is a form of recognition that Hegel had not envisaged—who but a white woman can do this for me? By loving me she proves that I am worthy of white love. I am loved like a white man.
> I am a white man.
> Her love takes me onto the noble road that leads to total realization . . .
> I marry white culture, white beauty, white whiteness.
> When my restless hands caress those white breasts, they grasp white civilization and dignity and make them mine." [36]

While useful as a starting point, Fanon's analysis suffers grave limitations. Fanon's first shortcoming was his failure to equally explicate the mind-set of the exception, such as himself. He met his wife as black-human-to-white-human and not as Appiah met his wife: black-human-to-white power/object/symbol. How Appiah introduced his future wife in his autobiography left no doubt of this. His description of her "hefty" figure was the only portrait of her as a human being. From then on, he mentioned only her pedigree: her father, Sir Stafford Cripps, was the Chancellor of the Exchequer. She was the granddaughter of Lord Parmoor. She descended from the great merchants who built up the cotton trade in Manchester and helped build the Canadian Pacific Railway. Her mother was a Swithenbank and granddaughter of the great chemist James Crossley Eno, inventor of Eno's Fruit Salts, famous all around the world.[37]

That Appiah was so impressed by his wife's lineage speaks volumes. The Manchester cotton trade fueled the capture of slaves in Africa and their forced production of cotton in the American South. During the Civil War, the Manchester cotton merchants generally supported the Confederacy because they did not want the cost of the cotton they purchased to be raised by planters having to pay free labor. Why would any African take pride in his wife's belonging to this legacy? Appiah might have been an African nationalist, but he had fully embraced aristocratic Anglo-Saxon culture with its pomp and class snobbery. However, unlike Fanon's schema, he was not screaming, "I have this white women, therefore I am white!" This man of the Ashanti aristocracy was yelling, "I have a woman from the British aristocracy, because (or therefore) I, too, am an aristocrat, which proves that I am not an African savage!"

This supposition is buttressed by Appiah's focus on the women he wrote that he "played" with before meeting his future wife. These included "two countesses, a continental princess, some actresses of repute," and a "fashionable" Parisian lady.[38] He says nothing here about whiteness. Fanon missed that for some members of the African petite bourgeoisie in Europe, their connection to white women was not about whiteness per se, but about attaching themselves to a social class that bestowed upon them a status above native and savage.

Joseph Appiah's future wife, Peggy Cripps, was a good example of the kind of compromising consciousness that Appiah and Kenyatta were associating with and wanted Nkrumah to share. The black American journalist Roi Ottley met Miss Cripps and her aristocratic father, Sir Stafford Cripps, in London in 1944. During the recent elections all British political parties, except the Communists, had neglected to include colonial reform or black civil rights on their platforms.

The position of the left-wingers is especially ludicrous. This was illustrated to me one day while I lunched with Peggy Cripps, daughter of Sir Stafford Cripps. This young lady was manifestly shocked, for example, that Negroes were victims of racial discrimination in the U.S. Her pleasant freckled face lighted up, though, when she spoke of the racial progress made in the Soviet Union, where she had lived while her father was British ambassador. This remark, plus her employment by the Soviet Information Service in London, betrayed me into sharply criticizing the British. [39]

Peggy Cripps expressed exasperation with Ottley's American failure to recognize the complexity of all the problems involving races, religions, and minorities.[40] She sent him to her father to "clarify" his thinking. Sir Stafford then "defended British racial policy as stoutly as any hard-bitten Tory."[41]

Peter Abrahams based his 1956 novel, *A Wreath for Udomo*, on his memories of the lives in London and later in Africa of this cohort of young men who dreamt and worked for their continent's independence. He barely masked the identities of his principal characters with fictitious names as he reconstructed their lives within the social circles in London during the mid-1940s. In Abrahams' novel, Michael Udomo (Nkrumah) is in London at a party when the advice of moderation of Lord Rosslee (Sir Stafford Cripps) angers him. Their exchange is a template for Nkrumah's later clashes with the West over his incendiary speeches and writings.

"Be constructive and responsible when you write or speak. Drop Tom Lanwood's [George Padmore's] violently irresponsible slogans. You people can help us work out a basis for co-operation . . . "

Udomo's anger flares and he responds: "Co-operation!" He glared at the peer. "What kind of co-operation can there be between master and slave?"

"Now that's the old claptrap . . . "

"It is our business to be irresponsible! A slave's business is to get rid of his chains, not to be reasonable! Only the free can afford to be diplomats."

The young peer sighed.

"Too much violent passion, my friend. It won't do . . . It will get you nowhere."

It's useless, Udomo decided. He fought back his mounting rage. The man's drunk and stupid. He felt himself trembling. Drunk and stupid. They understand only one thing. Well, they'll get it. They'll get it all right.

"We'll see if we get nowhere!" [42]

The moderation that the "peer" cautioned for Nkrumah augured the future conflict between Nkrumah's "extremism" and the "moderation" of those fellow Ghanaians who were his allies in London. Under the influence of such elitist leftism, Nkrumah's future opponents apparently hoped that Nkrumah would come to see that Ghana would go through a preparatory transition period, supervised by the Queen's colonial administrators. Then at some distant and undefined time, decided by Ghana's tiny black educated and business elite (mostly Ashantis) and the British, independence would come. England would erase from Nkrumah's mind his messianic mission of building a united and socialist Africa. However, Nkrumah's training in black America did not allow his becoming part of a neocolonial African elite. He could not join the Europeans in enjoying Africa's fruits while spitting the seeds toward the vast and hungry masses.

Kenyatta, Danquah, and Busia, Appiah had been culturally conquered by England. These champions of a new Africa had already been compromised by the conquerors and owners of old Africa. For Kenyatta as Kenya's leader and for Danquah and Busia as leaders of Nkrumah's Opposition, making unethical political and economic compromises with Africa's former owners in the future would, therefore, not be new.

The tone of condescension toward Nkrumah in Appiah's autobiography further foreshadowed Nkrumah's troubles ahead with Ghana's Ashanti elite. Appiah was adamant that Nkrumah had to be compromised similarly by the white women that he and the "Primrose Gang" foisted onto him. The ploy did not work. Nkrumah's experiences with white women stayed, like Fanon's, in the human-to-human category. His molding by the African American diaspora had given him a cultural foundation of pride that immunized him against the mania that afflicted his comrades. After becoming involved with the Marxist daughter of a Russian émigré he wrote: "We were . . . very impressed by the English women. There was a warmth of sincerity and sympathy surrounding them, their hearts were big and what they did for us they did in a quiet and unassuming way and expected neither thanks nor reward."[43]

Nkrumah focused neither on their whiteness nor on their social statuses. He valued these women for their humanity and for their contributions to Africa's independence. Later, as Ghana's prime minister, he would hire a white woman, Erica Powell, as his personal secretary. Nkrumah did not give thought to her color when he hired her. "He seemed blind to race, colour and creed. . . 'I am fighting against a system—the system of colonialism, imperialism and racialism—not against peoples,'" he told her.[44]

Previous analyses of black nationalism in Europe during these years have failed to register that just as humans have different skin colors, ideas also have colors in people's minds. Fanon did not fully explain that colonized people of color could compensate for inferiority complexes by putting on the mask of ideological whiteness. He did not perceive the whiteness of ideas or that Africans could strive to receive validation of their own human worth by assuming white ideas. It was white ideas that would create contradictions within their minds that eventually would alienate them from their African personalities. Seeing English upper-class society as having superior value to the extent that Appiah did was a symptom of ideological whiteness.

Peter Abrahams described the alienating outcome of Jomo Kenyatta's embracing ideological and cultural whiteness when he visited him in Kenya. Kenyatta had become a Western man:

> And then Kenyatta began to speak in a low, bitter voice of his frustration and of the isolated position in which he found himself. He had no friends. There was no one in the tribe who could give him the intellectual companionship that had become so important to him in his years in Europe. The things that were important—consequential conversation . . . the concept of individualism, the inviolability of privacy—all these were alien to the tribesmen in whose midst he lived. So Kenyatta, the western man, was driven in on himself and was forced to assert himself in tribal terms. Only thus would the tribesmen follow him and so give him his position of power and importance as a leader.
>
> To live without roots is to live in hell, and no man chooses voluntarily to live in hell. The people who could answer his needs as a western man had erected a barrier of color against him in spite of the fact that the taproots of their culture had become the taproots of his culture too. By denying him access to those things which complete the life of western man, they had forced him back into the tribalism from which he had so painfully freed himself over the years . . .
>
> He was the victim of tribalism and of westernism gone sick. His heart and mind and body were the battlefield of the ugly violence known as the Mau-Mau revolt long before it broke out in that beautiful land.[45]

In Kenyatta's mind, westernism was white while tribalism was black. He now preferred the "white" idea of individualism versus the "black" concept of communalism. He wanted privacy, not collectivity. Whiteness represented modernity, and he no longer felt comfortable in the Kikuyu world of premodernity. Whiteness and blackness clashed in his mind and made him miserable. Years later he would project his Western individualism upon all of Kenya. After the independence of their respective countries, Uganda's leader Milton Obote and Tanzania's leader Julius Nyerere came to Kenyatta. The three countries share borders. Nyerere recalled he and Obote making this proposal to Kenyatta: "Let's unite our countries and you be our head of state." Kenyatta refused, Nyerere theorized, because he did not want to be put "out of his element as a Kikuyu Elder."[46] The reality is that Kenyatta was applying his Western individualism to his whole nation. He had disliked the encroachments of his indigenous culture upon him as a man. He concurrently could not accept that Kenya would lose its national individuality as a member of an African collectivity.

The mythologist Joseph Campbell defined the call, quest, return sequence of the heroic life as a *monomyth*. A central element of the quest is the unexpected forces that attempt to hinder the hero from achieving his goal.[47] Appiah's attempt to culturally compromise Nkrumah was one of these unexpected forces. An Nkrumah who became a "western man" by succumbing like Kenyatta and Appiah to the enticements of self-alienating nonsavagery could not have returned to Ghana and conducted himself so that his nonwesternized "savage" people instantly recognized him as the long-awaited messiah of African liberation.

The "native" was a construction in the white mind and at its base was the savage. If the native is premodern and the civilized Western person represents modernism, then Nkrumah's ten years in the world headquarters of modernity should have made premodernism just as repulsive to him as it was to Kenyatta, Appiah, et al. Nkrumah had arrived in London with a Lincoln University bachelor's degree that certified him as a minister in what his educators regarded as the civilizing doctrine of Christianity. He also earned a University of Pennsylvania master's degree in Western philosophy. Nkrumah should have behaved as a nonsavage. He instead acted upon impulses from the psychic region that most horrified the Europeans and their African imitators—the region of premodern rituals. There Nkrumah's followers in THE CIRCLE swore oaths of allegiance to him with their blood mixing in a juju bowl.

Nkrumah's rituals of dedication were "childish" to Appiah and Kenyatta, because they had internalized the European doctrine that

Africans who still practiced them were not grown-ups in the linear sense of Western time. Nkrumah's juju was a move backward, from the adulthood of modernity to the childhood of the premodern. Nkrumah had a foot in the old and the new worlds, while Kenyatta and Appiah had cemented both of their feet firmly in the new world. In their world, the main criteria for assessing the worth of any belief, culture, activity, or aspiration were Eurocentric.

Appiah, Danquah, Busia, and Kenyatta would make their peace with their respective Akan and Kikiyu cultures for political expediency. The latter three men would each write a book to explain his culture to a European reading public. Each of them wrote his book during the 1940s when African nationalism reached its boiling point. Yet, nothing in their books could serve as vehicles of cultural nationalism to strengthen their people's political nationalism. They had drunk deeply from European springs. But they had not even taken a sip from the springs of Du Bois, Garvey, Edward Wilmot Blyden, and Joel A. Rogers.

The difference between these men and Nkrumah was the diasporic place that educated and shaped them. Despite their receiving the affections of Englishwomen, England was a solidly racist place with centuries-old prejudices against dark-skinned persons that Englishmen enslaved and now colonized. Rudyard Kipling best described the British attitude toward the black man during his 1891 travels in the United States. "He is a big, black, vain baby and a man rolled into one."[48] An observer in 1931 wrote that the most racially prejudiced white Britons had experience with people of color in Britain's colonies. They could not accept that the inferiors, who had to submissively answer their whims in Africa or India, were somehow transformed into their equals after setting foot in Britain.[49] The Jamaican poet Una Marson was at one time Ethiopian Emperor Haile Selassie's secretary. From 1939 to 1946 she also was a program maker for the British Broadcasting Corporation. She wrote a bitter poem about her experiences among white Londoners during these years. The following three stanzas portray the racial atmosphere of the London in which Nkrumah and his cohorts plotted Africa's future.

> They called me "Nigger,"
> Those little white urchins
> They laughed and shouted
> As I passed along the street.
> They flung it at me:
> "Nigger! Nigger! Nigger!"

What made me go to my room
And sob my heart away
Because white urchins
Called me "Nigger"?
God keep my soul from hating such mean souls
God keep my soul from hating those who preach the Christ
And say with churlish smile
"This place is not for 'Niggers'." [50]

Only Nkrumah addressed British racism as intrinsic to the British colonial enterprise. In England Appiah, Danquah, and Busia had been feted by the English social class that they identified with. Therefore, their writings contain hardly a critical word about the notorious British racism or the exploitation of their countrymen under the system of colonialism. Richard Wright observed and described them: "At Oxford or Cambridge, he is far from the world of 'race.' He is a black gentleman in a graded hierarchy of codes of conduct in which . . . he can rise. He can, even though black, become a Sir . . . The more he learns, the more Africa fades from his mind and the more shameful and bizarre it seems." [51]

For this reason Nkrumah's protégé Ahmed Sekou Toure maintained that "decolonization at the individual level must operate more profoundly upon those who have been trained by the colonial system." [52] The colonial system "depersonalizes" African intellectuals. Separation from their culture and people is the price they must pay for colonial higher education. To *re*personalize themselves and end their alienation from grassroots Africa, they must return to the source of African culture. The source is the "illiterate" millions who are farmers, fishermen, craftsmen, and factory workers. They are men and women who retain their "superstitions." They play talking drums and dance wearing brightly colored cotton garments. They maintain memories of their long traditions of resistance to colonialism, and they still have African personalities. Anticolonial nationalism of necessity had to also carry a cultural nationalist element within it. African culture was simultaneously from the past and toward the future. Eurocentrism attempted to thwart the development of genuine African liberation movements by inserting its cultural values between the African cultural past and future. Once successfully disconnected, the past was an ugly stain upon the African's memory. Instead of being a source of strength to fight for national freedom from colonialism, culture became an embarrassment. Then only the modes of liberation legitimized by the metropole's history would receive the stamp of authenticity from the culturally compromised African. [53]

Nkrumah would return to Africa without the depersonalization and alienation that was Kenyatta's, Appiah's, Danquah's, and Busia's lot. His separation would be from alienated personalities who had put on the mask of "white" ideas such as Anglo-Saxon individualism, capitalist elitism, bourgeois political gradualism, and neocolonialism. They did know during their college days in England that they were being trained to oppose the revolutionary Africa that Nkrumah dreamed of and British imperialists feared.

When Appiah eventually sided with the anti-Nkrumah Opposition, he would reject the revolutionary character of Nkrumah's socialist and Pan-African vision, opting instead for the subnationalist politics of the Ashanti tribal elite.[54] The stamp of his years in England and his marriage into the British aristocracy would permanently split his mind between the thesis of African nationalism and the antithesis of British upper-class liberalism through which he expressed his strongly held Christian sensibilities. Appiah's intellectual and personal synthesis was Ashanti subnationalism.

Joseph Danquah would collaborate with the United States Central Intelligence Agency against Nkrumah and act as a secret pawn of their subversive intrigues.[55] Why he would betray his country for the pay of a foreign power is evident in the description Richard Wright wrote after interviewing him in 1953. Wright noticed immediately that Danquah "had the bearing of an aristocrat." Moreover, "he personified, alas, exactly what England wanted to make every African into."[56] Wright told Danquah that Nkrumah appealed to the "masses," using techniques he had learned mostly in the United States and when organizing nationalists in London. Wright asked Danquah why he did not apply the same methods. Danquah replied, "Masses? I don't believe this thing masses. There are only individuals for me."[57]

As had happened to Kenyatta, years of British education had instilled in Danquah a pathological sense of Western individualism. He was of royal Ashanti blood and decades in London only reinforced his royalist elitism. Also like Kenyatta, his social class and his British education ultimately alienated him from his own people. Danquah had written the superb book *The Akan Doctrine of God*. Something was incongruous about a man who could produce such an excellent explanation of his people's beliefs and possess the demeanor of the British upper class. Wright's meeting with Danquah ended, and he privately regretted that the more education Africans acquired, "the more unfit they seemed to weigh and know the forces that were shaping the modern world."[58] Wright came close to drawing the logical conclusion that Nkrumah behaved differently because his education in black America had impacted his psyche differently. K. A. Busia was Danquah's coleader of the anti-Nkrumah Opposition.[59] He would disgrace himself by making backdoor deals with the brazenly racist white minority government of apartheid South Africa against Africa's general interests. His proven collaboration with South Africa elicits suspicions that he would have had no qualms about working with other anti-Nkrumah Western intelligence agencies.[60]

Nonetheless, living in Kenya forced Kenyatta to act as if he were the person his people needed to lead them to freedom and independence. Kenyatta showed that Frantz Fanon was correct inasmuch that the inferiority complex for which the white woman compensates could be the result of living as a minority in a white-majority country. When Kenyatta came home he became associated with the underground organization of the Kikuyu Central Association. This was the movement that came to be popularly known as the Mau Mau. One major practice of the Mau Mau was the "primitive," "childish," oath-taking juju that Kenyatta had rejected in Nkrumah's organization. It is possible that Kenyatta simply rejected Nkrumah's leadership and the oath was an excuse to stay out of the upstart's organization.[61] But the adamancy of Kenyatta's rejection of the oath as being "primitive," and his later involvement with the Mau Mau, elicits a converse Fanonian theory: if an inferiority complex results from the African's displacement into a culture in which he is a minority, then it can be reversed once he returns to the milieu where he is the majority. Amid his own people, Kenyatta returned to the "primitive" talk of blood in his speeches, promoting Kenyan rebellion against the colonists. But his blood now marked the growing radicalism aroused by living in a majority-black culture. To an audience in Kisumu, Kenya, he stated in 1952, "The tree of freedom is planted. For it to grow it needs the water of human blood."[62] Since Appiah and Kenyatta responded differently to the stimuli of returning to majority African societies, neither direction is an absolute. Their cases simply mean that within the context of Nkrumah's revolutionary nationalism, complexities of consciousness existed in his social stratum that have not been adequately explored by such analysts of the colonial and postcolonial African psyche as Frantz Fanon.

Nkrumah eventually accepted an obvious sexual relationship with a Russian Marxist woman. The fate of the hero is that at each stage of his journey, there are forces that come forward to distract him from his destiny as well as to guide him. Neither Nkrumah nor Appiah stated in his autobiography whether Nkrumah's relationship with this woman caused him to begin attending Communist Party meetings. It might have been during this time that Nkrumah acquired the unsigned British Communist Party membership card that was fated to cause him grief in Ghana. What is noteworthy, however, is that the very woman who Appiah hoped would modify Nkrumah's revolutionary zeal only intensified it by a coordination of ideas with Nkrumah's already strongly Marxian orientation. Nkrumah began to attend meetings of the British Communist Party. Peter Abrahams observed their relationship and named the woman "Lois" in A Wreath for Udomo. The class ideology of Lois was as incompatible as the future Nkrumaism with the liberal elitism of Peggy Cripps and the British and Ashanti aristocracy.

Early Strategies

One month after Nkrumah arrived in London in June 1945, he began working with Peter Abrahams, George Padmore, and T. R. Makonnen to organize the Fifth Pan-African Congress to be held in Manchester. He and Padmore became joint secretaries of the organizing committee. This important post allowed Nkrumah to meet and interact with the leading lights of African nationalism. Nkrumah's true rise to leadership and his recognition by his fellow Ghanaians as a leader occurred during his organizing the Manchester Congress, which met in October 1945. W. E. B. Du Bois was the recognized international president of the Pan-African Congress. In his august presence, the delegates from Africa and the diaspora took stock of the new world situation brought about by the end of the war. The imperial countries had done a great deal of propagandizing about freedom and democracy. Now these revolutionaries, young and aging, would hold them to their words.

Nkrumah delivered a paper, "Imperialism in North and West Africa," at a session chaired by Du Bois on October 16, 1945.[63] Amy Ashwood Garvey (Marcus Garvey's first wife) chaired a session on job discrimination and other ill-treatments meted out to blacks in Britain.[64] Numerous other sessions addressed the pressing issues of Africa and the diaspora.

George Padmore's History of the Manchester Congress related that the very idea of a United States of Africa originated in the diaspora in the West Indies and the United States. Distinct groups of Africans became one people on the plantations of slavery and colonialism. They projected this oneness upon Africa. They logically envisioned that future African unity would be no more impossible than the end of tribalism and subnationalism of blacks in the Western Hemisphere.[65]

Padmore advocated socialism as a tool that African nationalists would use for their economic liberation. He strongly opposed black people being the tools of the fluctuating agendas of Communists. His own experience in the Communist International (Comintern) had steeled his will against placing black people's interests under those of Stalin's internationalism. The Hitler-Stalin Pact (1939–1941) had educated many Communists about the unprincipled international manipulations of the Soviets for their national interests. The pact led to mass resignations of Communists in the United States. Nkrumah would have observed this upheaval. When Nkrumah met Padmore in 1945, Padmore had already become disenchanted with international Communism. He had observed in Moscow how the Soviet Communists viewed Communists outside their country as tools for Soviet foreign policy. Black people who permitted themselves to be used this way were labeled "Red Uncle Toms" by Padmore. His break with the Communist International led Stalin to send assassins after him, just as he had sent killers to Leon Trotsky in Mexico. Anyone who broke with Soviet orthodoxy had to face Stalinist inquisition and repression, lest, as any religion, the whole web of myth and faith would begin to unravel.

Nkrumah's infatuation with Marxist philosophy and his attending meetings of the British Communist Party would have made him susceptible to idealistic illusions painted by the Communist International. The sage Padmore bestowed upon Nkrumah his decades of experience and wisdom concerning international Communism:

> Pan Africanism means politically government of, by and for Africans; economically it means democratic socialism, liberty of the subject and human rights guaranteed by the law . . . Pan-Africanism sets out to fulfil the socio-economic mission of Communism under a libertarian political system. [66]

Nkrumah could not be a true nationalist or a Pan-Africanist if he did not put Africa's interests before those of the Soviet Union or any power outside Africa. He had to be true to his own vision for Africa's future and not be diverted by the propaganda of Soviet and Chinese Communists. This was Padmore's principal lesson. It was one that Nkrumah would never forget.

Spies reported to the British government that Nkrumah joined the British Communist Party while in England in 1945. In his autobiography Nkrumah denied ever joining the Communists. The implementation of his vision for a nationalist organization validated this denial. Nkrumah's actions show that he left the United States with paradigms of organization that he viewed as superior to Leninism for African liberation movements. However, he totally accepted the Marxist premise that subnationalism was a bourgeois construct foisted upon the working masses to keep them divided. African tribalism and nationalism were encumbrances to the future African Union of Socialist States that would unite all nationalities.

Pan-Africanism Reconsidered

When Nkrumah returned to the Gold Coast, he carried with him a Pan-African ideology that would be among his principal motivators for the next twenty-five years. Hindsight has exposed three lethal flaws in Nkrumah's Pan-Africanist ideal. First, slavery had forced upon black people in the diaspora blacks, from disparate African groupings, a common language, religion, and culture. In Africa, for all but an urbanized black elite, traditional religions and indigenous languages still reigned, even after centuries of colonialism. Second, communal plantation slavery and a harsh system of white cultural imposition had erased micronationalistic ("tribal") distinctions in the diaspora. African Americans did not inherit the centuries-old animus between, for example, the Ashanti and the Fanti, the Zulu and the Pondos, the Yoruba and the Ibos, the Tutsis and the Hutus, or any of literally hundreds of disunifying micronationalistic conflicts that continue to wreak death upon Africa. Projecting Pan-Africanist possibilities upon indigenous Africans based upon the singularity of the African American nation was a grossly inapplicable exercise.

Third, Pan-Africanism means continental unification and centralization of government, that is, *macro*nationalism. Throughout Africa, centralization of government has usually meant centralization of resources. One of the recurring causes of micronationalistic wars in Africa has stemmed from the ethnicity in power centralizing the resources—tax money and foreign aid—among their own ethnicity, usually centered around the nation's capital. The Fulani (Peuls) in Guinea clashed with Ahmed Sekou Toure's Mandinka rulership over this issue. The Tauregs of Mali fought a civil war against the Bambara/Mandingo majority because of the centralization of the country's resources away from the Tauregs. A long-simmering insurgency in the Casamance region of Senegal arose because the Diola people of Casamance perceived that the Wolof rulers of the country were discriminating against them. They traveled to the capital city of Dakar and saw the development francs at work in the Wolof officials' luxury cars and mansions while their region remained relatively backward.

Postcolonial Africa needed decentralized resources to promote national unity. Unfortunately, centralized government in the hands of a majority ethnic group has meant centralized resources in the hands of that ethnic group. In his book *Africa Must Unite,* Nkrumah provided a paradigm for the ideal Pan-African future. He did not foresee this problem because he believed that socialist ideology would trump nationalism and subnationalism. He could not foresee that the "fraternal" Chinese and Vietnamese Communists would one day fight a bloody war after Vietnam expelled first the French and then the Americans from their soil. Nor did he see the ethnic divisions that Stalin had suppressed in the Soviet Union. These divisions would one day rise to tear apart Lenin's dream.

So when Nkrumah left England for Ghana, carrying the shining hope that he would soon begin the movement that would culminate in a Union of African Socialist States, he based his hopes on a false impression that had been created by Marxist propaganda. He knew from George Padmore's experiences that the Soviet Union placed the interests of other nations after its own, as did every nation on earth. Nkrumah did not know that within the Soviet Union, the Marxist ideology of ethnic equality could not and would not overcome centuries of ethnic hatreds and fissures. Marx, Lenin, and Nkrumah's grand dream that a workers' government would sweep bourgeois nationalistic rivalries into history's dustbin, had become a Kremlin propaganda poster. Stalin used it to hide his brutal suppression of nationalism in the USSR. Stalin's bloody poster also covered the fact that kinship groupings, and not production brigades, were the primary organizational products of social evolution. Nkrumah would come to discover, to his dismay, that in Africa micronationalism trumped utopian ideologies.

So when Nkrumah sailed to Ghana with the Golden Fleece, he thought that he would unite Ghana and then all of Africa. Thirteen colonies had broken away from British rule before and formed a single nation. Socialism had eliminated nationalistic rivalries in the Soviet Union and had given birth to a state so mighty that it had defeated Nazi Germany almost by itself. Under Father Divine's tutelage Nkrumah had seen every race in the United States live and work selflessly in harmonious and prosperous urban economic and rural agricultural communes. Father Divine had made the denial of racial existence compulsory for membership in his communal "Promised Lands" and "Heavens." Only Divine's charismatic leadership could convince whites, blacks, Asians, and others to renounce and ignore their obvious racial differences for a higher ideal. The physical differences between the Fanti, Nzima, Gaa, and Ewe were not as pronounced as between the races that Father Divine mesmerized. Moreover, he had seen Harlem homogenize the diversity of the Black Atlantic into one people. It is understandable that Nkrumah would extrapolate from his false knowledge of the USSR, and his African experience, the he could build a continental movement unifying all linguistic, religious, and ethnic groups under the mighty banner of Pan Africanism. It is understandable that Nkrumah would extrapolate from his African American experience that he could build a similar unifying movement.

The Hero Returns

Nkrumah set himself on the path to lead Africa's independence movement. He did not know how he would move from London Pan-Africanist notoriety to Ghanaian, and then continental, recognition of his messianic leadership. Nkrumah's friend from Lincoln University, Ako Adjei, had returned to Ghana after receiving a master's degree in journalism at Columbia University. Adjei would serve as the next point of assistance for Nkrumah in his march toward his epic destiny. Joseph Danquah and the other nationalists launched an organization called the United Gold Coast Convention (UGCC) in August 1947 and offered Adjei the position of general secretary. But Adjei had seen from his years in America that Francis Nkrumah was more skilled than he at oratory and organization. Adjei recommended Nkrumah for the leadership of the ineffective, fledgling UGCC. The continual intrusion into the hero's life of this ad hoc guiding figure represents the "benign, protecting power of destiny."[1] Guidance such as that of Adjei and of other sages is evident in Nkrumah's eventually becoming the official, accepted leader of the very persons who provided him with the indispensable help to achieve his destiny. That one's destiny is a living and conscious force that shapes one's future, independent of one's own will, is compatible with the traditional Akan perception of the effects of the metaphysical powers of *Nyame* (God) upon the physical lives of human beings.[2]

The UGCC originated in Ghana's indigenous coastal merchant elite and its indigenous royal families. This caused Nkrumah to hesitate to take its reigns. He described UGCC members as disconnected from the Ghanaian masses because they were all lawyers, doctors, academics, and businessmen.[3] Since Nkrumah himself was an academic who had aspired to be a lawyer, the occupations of the UGCC leaders was not his main concern. Their being capitalists whose ideals of liberation stopped short of his radical Pan-African vision argued against his taking up the post. Nkrumah wavered and sought advice from his

London colleagues. They were as noncommittal as he. Then, he received a letter from Joseph Danquah, who was then one of the elder stalwarts of Gold Coast nationalism. Danquah encouraged him to return to Ghana and take the helm of the UGCC.

Nkrumah finally conferred with George Padmore, members of the West Africa National Secretariat, and THE CIRCLE. They convinced him that this was a position from which he could build the type of movement that Ghana and West Africa needed for profound social and economic change. They had all linked colonialism with capitalism and agreed that the struggle against one must necessarily be a struggle against the other.

This point of view was definitely not in harmony with Danquah's views. Danquah had been practicing law in Ghana since he returned from England in 1927. If there was any single Ghanaian whose prestige and experience virtually mandated that the leadership of an independent Ghana would fall into his hands, that man was Joseph Danquah. Nevertheless, without even meeting Nkrumah in person, he approved the appointment of Nkrumah as UGCC leader on the basis of the reports he had heard about Nkrumah's gifts.

In the life of the epic African hero, the sagacity of his elders does not always guide his future. The hero arrives to change what is past and to establish a new design for living. The African epic hero ultimately accepts metaphysical guidance above all temporal voices. The force of his own destiny compels him forward. The genies and sages along the way are but his helpers. They come to the stage and they exit, while he, the protagonist, remains on stage to play out his role to the final act.

In October 1947, in London, on the eve of his return to the Gold Coast, Nkrumah wrote the most explosive book as yet written by an African nationalist: *Towards Colonial Freedom*. London publishers refused to print it. Nkrumah managed to get a few copies published privately. Mass production came when he and his supporters mimeographed and copied it "by other means and distributed to those actively engaged in the freedom movement of Africa."[4] This book promoted an unequivocal anti-imperialist, anticolonialist, and anticapitalist position. Nobody who read *Towards Colonial Freedom* could confuse Nkrumah's mission with petit bourgeois liberalism. And nobody who read this book could doubt that Nkrumah's ideals for Ghana and Africa were the most clear sighted amid the ideological confusion and conflicting economic and ethnic interests within African nationalism.

When Nkrumah returned to Ghana in 1947, his people were ready for a political prophet. Their sense of expectation had been primed by the periodic emergence of African Christian messiahs among them. These men proclaimed that the Holy Spirit swelled in their hearts and compelled them to announce themselves "anointed" to deliver their people from ancient, indigenous un-Christian ideas and practices. Usually they came as vehicles for the further cultural conquest of their peoples by missionary viewpoints.[5] Nkrumah, however, brought a different kind of messianism: the Spirit had anointed him as culture hero to lead Ghana's resistance to the undermining of its indigenous culture. He would also fight to expel the British conqueror.

Nkrumah portrayed his arrival back on Ghanaian soil in December 1947 as both the return of an epic hero and the coming of the Messiah. Confronted by an immigration officer at the coastal city of Takoradi, Nkrumah expected to be hassled after the officer recognized his name. But the man looked at Nkrumah with amazed eyes protruding from his head. "Then his mouth moved slowly and he whispered softly: 'So you are Kwame Nkrumah!' I nodded . . . He shook my hand enthusiastically and told me how they, the Africans, had heard so much about me, that I was coming back to my country to help them and that they had been waiting anxiously for my arrival day after day."[6] Nkrumah's reputation had already spread throughout Ghana and he returned to a country waiting to hear his voice. When he began speaking, the clarity of his vision and his fearless challenge to the prevailing colonial and tribal elites captivated the young. In January 1948 he spoke to a massive rally attended by thousands of youths in Accra. The radicalism of his words could only have alarmed the British and their African allies, for he identified the enemy of the country's independence as not race but class:

A fierce fight against the economic system is raging. It does not matter whether those who have promoted that economic system are black or white. The Convention is against anybody who identifies himself, be he black or white, with that economic system. The present struggle is a historical one, for down the ages this fight has been raging with unabated intensity and has pointed all along to one goal—complete independence for West Africa.[7]

Nkrumah advocated more than that Britain lose the Gold Coast. His speeches threatened to remove European rule from the whole of the vast and rich colonies of British and French West Africa. His speaking on behalf of the "Convention" started the conflicts between him and the other UGCC leaders. They were profiteers participating in the very system that he denounced. Before Nkrumah's arrival, no record exists of the UGCC advocating a change in the capitalist system in the Gold Coast. No Gold Coast speaker before Nkrumah had traveled the lengths and breadths of the country defining what liberation would mean in the context of world revolution and African unity. Nkrumah's words were like matches tossed on a parched field. The young people at the Accra rally delayed his finishing his speech with the length and enthusiasm of their applause.[8]

Nkrumah next launched an attack upon chieftaincy, which was the foundation of indirect rule. He stated that the chiefs were on the side of the British. They would return to the people when the people became organized and strong. If the chiefs did not return then they would have to leave the country in the company of the fleeing Europeans.[9] His critique of the chiefs focused attention on the centuries-old indigenous hierarchical structures. Some, not all, of the chiefs had collaborated first with the slave trade and last with colonialism. Nkrumah advocated a revolution within indigenous Africa that paralleled the revolution against European conquerors by advocating a change in reactionary chieftaincy. He promoted these revolutionary changes among the workers and the farmers. At the same time, many members of the small black intelligentsia, who would have to implement his revolutionary proposals, were either chiefs, relatives of the chiefs, or closely associated with the men at the top of the hierarchy. From the beginning some of them saw the interests of Nkrumah's revolution as contrary to their interests. This reality complicated Nkrumah's mission.

In early February 1948, Nkrumah spoke to two thousand people who had gathered to welcome him home in the Nzimah community of Aboso. His emphasis then was on organizing. No members of the UGCC had attempted mass organizing. From the initial moments of his return home, he asserted his charismatic and heroic authority over the movement and sought to bend it toward his preconceived goals. He returned to the theme that he had stressed at the Accra rally. "Without organisational strength we are weak; unity is the dynamic force behind any great endeavor."[10] That endeavor was the country's full independence on the timeline not of the colonizers but of the leaders of the colonized peoples.

Joseph Danquah placed his stamp of approval upon Nkrumah by introducing him to a rally in Accra with these words: "If all the leaders of the UGCC fail you, Kwame Nkrumah will never fail you."[11]

This was on February 20, 1948. Nkrumah already stood at the helm of the movement. He actually did not need Danquah's assistance. For when the Ghanaian masses heard his voice, it was as if the long-awaited had arrived at last. Even if they had not viewed Nkrumah in this way, it is certain that from his earliest days in the West seeking the Golden Fleece he had viewed himself this way. His early speeches would become legendary ways to demonstrate the charismatic mantle that was the Golden Fleece to the people of Ghana. His name and fame as a nationalist firebrand would quickly spread by that African telegraph that the European wondered at, for it utilized no wireless or wired communications system, but spread information seemingly with a rapidity rivaling their technology.

In England African nationalists had heard of the Atlantic Charter of Winston Churchill and Franklin Roosevelt. The two leaders had met in August 1941 at Newfoundland, Canada, for a conference projecting the type of world that would follow the end of the war in which Britain, but not yet the United States, was embroiled. The language of their declaration closely resembled the idealistic language of Woodrow Wilson in France in 1919 when he attempted to start a League of Nations that would usher in an era in which all peoples would enjoy the right to self-determination. Article VI of the Atlantic Charter stated that with peace would come a time "which will afford to all nations the means of dwelling in safety within their own boundaries and which will afford assurance that all men in all lands may live out their lives in freedom from fear and want."[12]

Colonized peoples, particularly in India and Africa, drew inspiration from these words. They thought that they were included in the category of "all nations" that would live in freedom. But except for the Philippines, such was not to be the case for the American colonial possessions in Puerto Rico, Hawaii, Guam, the Panama Canal Zone, and numerous other little outposts of American imperialism. Britain's colonial empire was far more extensive and far more valuable. It took up one quarter of the globe and included a quarter of its peoples. Britain's wealth depended on dominating 500 million people of color. Winston Churchill quickly dashed their hopes for postwar liberation. On September 9, 1941, he spoke before the House of Commons and made a stark distinction between those European countries that would be freed from the Nazi yoke and Britain's imperial possessions that, he said, "owe allegiance" to the British Crown. Africa and Asia would have to undergo "progressive evolution of self-governing institutions."[13] The Crown would decide how quickly the evolution would take place. Nkrumah knew that this declaration meant that his country could possibly remain a colony for decades. But unlike his UGCC cohorts, Nkrumah had a plan and a vision that led directly to independence and self-rule.

Danquah and the other UGCC leaders lacked specificity in outlining a path to independence. Since they had been in the country during Nkrumah's years in the West, one would assume them to be more ready to lead the Ghanaian masses than Nkrumah. Since they were not, they left a vacuum of vision and leadership that Nkrumah filled quickly in January 1948 by writing a dynamic program for the organization of Ghana's anticolonial movement. The first part of the program required the UGCC to form a shadow cabinet. This copied the British parliamentary system, where the party out of power was prepared at any time to take office because the members of its government were selected in advance to prepare themselves to fill specific ministries.[14] The program next outlined the organizational work for implementing the UGCC platform that would fall into three periods.

In the first period Nkrumah would organize a United Front by coordinating all of the various Ghanaian organizations under the UGCC.[15] They would establish branches of the UGCC in every town and village and persuade each village chief to be their patron. Finally, every branch would launch a weekend school that would educate the people in self-government.

The second period of Nkrumah's program called for "constant demonstrations throughout the country to test our organizational strength, making use of political crises."[16] Nkrumah slyly stated that these demonstrations would gauge how much power they had gathered organizationally. He did not state, but certainly knew, that these demonstrations would also show this strength to Ghanaians and the British. In such a show of strength lurked dangers of violent responses. Violence and counterviolence would not just make use of political crises but would generate them. This was the most predictably dangerous part of the program, for Nkrumah knew well the pent-up frustrations of Ghana's people. Frustrations marching en masse against the cause of those frustrations would inevitably explode.

The third period called for the Ghanaians to convene a constitutional assembly to write their own constitution.[17] This was a direct challenge to the British colonialists, who had reserved for themselves the right and the power to create a constitution for their colony. The Burns Constitution of 1944 (named after Sir Alan Burns, the British governor) had given the Gold Coast peoples their first positions of advisory power in the colony but stopped far short of self-government.

Challenging the constitution on which a colony is governed is a radical, revolutionary step. Only the governing state power can write a constitution. This part of Nkrumah's UGCC program implied the removal of British authority over Ghana at a time when the British had no intention of leaving so profitable a piece of their empire. Danquah and the other British-trained lawyers and businessmen in the UGCC supported this proposal at their June 28, 1948, meeting. Later, despite their legal expertise, they would claim that they had not known the depths of Nkrumah's radicalism.

Finally, in the third period, Nkrumah proposed to escalate their demonstrations to boycotts and strikes.[18] Nkrumah envisaged a general strike as the main nonviolent force that would compel the British to grant independence. After presenting his program he expected opposition within the UGCC. When he heard none he concluded that the organization's leaders doubted his ability to actually get such a program off the ground.[19] When Nkrumah assumed office, the UGCC had only two defunct branches in the entire country. Six months into Nkrumah's speaking and organizing tour, there were over 500 dues-paying branches. This was the real beginning of Nkrumah's rise to personal power and Ghana's rise to true independence. To succeed in expanding the movement, Nkrumah had to successfully balance three segments of society, either one of which in the beginning could have stopped his progress: (1) the indigenous African masses, (2) the British colonial power, and (3) the black bourgeoisie and their representatives in the leadership of the UGCC.

The Masses

History is replete with examples of two kinds of heroes: heroes of thought and heroes of action. Thus, Aristotle was a hero of thought who prepared Alexander the Great, a hero of action. Marx was the thinker, Lenin the actor. Kwame Nkrumah's program for Gold Coast independence showed him as a hero of both thought and action. Without uncritically resorting to the "Great Man" definition of history, it is important to define the specific quality of Nkrumah's heroism at this point. The character of his heroism changed in different circumstances. He had already shown himself to be both a cultural and political hero of thought. He had built up the UGCC from a nonentity to the point where it could lead a nationalist movement. He had become recognized throughout the colony as the preeminent head of the movement. Now he added a courageous willingness to risk his freedom and his life to lead anticolonial protests that the British had mercilessly suppressed with deadly force in other colonies. History shapes heroes, but the very nature of heroism is that the hero is the shaper of history.

The next series of events moved so quickly that the leaders had to catch up with the masses. This is the time when Nkrumah's *preponderant influence* shaped events toward goals he had nurtured since his college days at Lincoln University. Nkrumah's destiny was now involved with three entities: Danquah and the other UGCC leaders, the British colonial authorities, and the Ghanaian people. Strikingly, each group saw a different Nkrumah, as if Ananse the trickster had been incarnated in three different forms.

Three months after Nkrumah took the helm of Gold Coast nationalism, an insurrection broke out in Accra on the afternoon of February 28, 1948. Protesters comprising many ex-soldiers who had fought in World War II attempted to march on Christiansborg Castle, which was the residence of the British colonial governor in Accra. To stop the march, the police fired into the crowd, killing one man and wounding one other.[20] The protests continued with the looting of businesses and the attacking of a European officer and of Europeans' automobiles in Accra.

The colonial officials in the Gold Coast estimated that the anti-British rioters numbered at least 50,000. Local troops were insufficient to quell such a large mass, so the British ordered more "native" troops from Kumasi and the Northern Territories. Next, they brought in Nigerian troops. The violent demonstrations and looting spread. Ex-soldiers demonstrated in several cities.[21] The British began to blame the UGCC for exacerbating the situation and implied that it was a Communist organization, or at the very least, heavily influenced by Communists.[22]

The colonial administrator hired 500 more policemen and called in additional naval and army forces. It stated that the administration must "consider what action can be taken towards preventing outbreaks by protecting the people from the influences giving rise to them."[23] Principal in this "action" was press censorship and stopping any other means of anticolonial agitation. To prevent the movement from further radicalization, the British spelled out a strategy that would lead to independence. "Government's main preoccupation must invariably be to bring about as rapidly as possible the development of conditions under which the causes of disturbance can be eliminated by ordinary constitutional means. Such conditions do not necessarily stem from a tranquility imposed by restrictions and controls backed by the sanction of the armed forces."[24] The white colonials likened the Ghanaians to psychologically sick patients. They claimed that the "poison of excitement and license" still flowed in their bodies. It must be met by restrictions, but not by actions that actually exacerbated and worsened the problem.[25] A frugal economy of force was necessary for an outnumbered European colonial administration.

Next, the British concluded that the riots were Communist-inspired. They decided that they must surgically remove the offending parties who had been agitating. On March 18, three weeks from the end of the protests, the British identified the instigators and settled upon a single man and a single idea as responsible for the turmoil: Kwame Nkrumah and the Union of African Socialist Republics. The two organizations in which Nkrumah held influence and power were the West African National Secretariat and the UGCC. While the British stopped short of saying that these organizations were Communist-controlled, they concluded that they were both actively Communist-supported. The link between each organization and the recent anticolonial disturbances was Nkrumah. The British wanted to know the underlying caused of the February protests. In April 1948 they appointed a commission led by a lawyer named Aiken Watson. His Watson Report stated that Nkrumah had caused the "subversive elements" to use a "Marxist technique."[26]

The British banned all Communist publications from entering the colony. Previously they had banned just Marxist-Leninist writings. Now they banned all publications from Communist publishing houses, whether they dealt with issues of politics or not. Second, they increased the scrutiny of all British overseas officers cleared for duty in the Gold Coast. They were concerned that British Communists were stirring the natives.[27]

The writer Richard Wright was a former member of the Communist Party USA. He had left the organization and turned anti-Communist. Wright recorded his own eyewitness account of the situation and refuted allegations that Nkrumah was using Communist tactics to heighten and guide his people's nationalism. Wright attended several political rallies with Nkrumah and speculated about Nkrumah's power over the masses:

> How had he conquered them? He held them in the palms of his hands. . . . I had had enough experience in the Communist Party of

the United States to know that what I had seen in Cape Coast had not been Communism. . . . These men were not being so much guided as they were being provoked by elements deep in their own personalities, elements which they could not have ignored even if they had tried. . . . What I had seen was not politics proper; it was politics *plus*. . . . It bordered on religion; it involved a total and basic response to reality; it smacked of the dreamlike, of the stuff of which art and myths are made.[28]

Wright detected very few men around Nkrumah who knew anything about Marxism, and common sense told him that Nkrumah could not possibly have indoctrinated Ghana's preliterate millions so quickly. Not Marxism-Leninism but a keen understanding of how to move his people had propelled Nkrumah into preeminent leadership of a rising insurrection. "Seek ye first the political kingdom, and all else will be added unto you." That was his mantra; it tapped into African spirituality and recast a Christian slogan into a political tool of the revolution.

Also recurrently evident during this period was the role of the diaspora in Nkrumah's actions. Ghanaians shared an understanding of the profound occult significance of his being an Nzimah. In the presence of this collective occult consciousness, Nkrumah began to swish a white handkerchief while traveling throughout his country. Sam D. Nyako was a teenager when he met Nkrumah in person and watched him speak at several political rallies. He recalled what he referred to as Nkrumah's use of "handkerchief magic." He associated this with his knowledge of Nzimah witchcraft. Nkrumah's party members offered secular interpretations of the meaning of the white handkerchief to Nyako and other Ghanaian youths. "They said it symbolized the dreams of the revolution that would come true, and that they were moving forward in the right way for us. And they told us that it symbolized the victories that Nkrumah had already achieved over the enemies of Africa's liberation. But we still thought it was Nzimah magic."[29]

Regardless of Nkrumah's intentions, his handkerchief came to symbolize the mystical might of the Nzimah. He had seen this same handkerchief "magic" used in the African American diaspora. In the 1930s and 1940s, like today, before innumerable pulpits, black preachers swished white handkerchiefs in the air and mopped the sweat dripping off their faces with them for dramatic effect. Some pastors even sold white, green, or other colored handkerchiefs as "prayer cloths." They blessed them with words and rituals of presumed mystical potency. The cloths then reputedly become effective in the hands of the faithful for warding off bad luck and ushering in financial prosperity.

Nkrumah would have also observed the famous jazz trumpeter Louis Armstrong and other musicians in Harlem or Philadelphia holding a white handkerchief while playing their instruments. Armstrong arrived in Accra, Ghana, in May 1956, and played, handkerchief in hand, before a reception hosted by Nkrumah. Armstrong answered Nkrumah's request and sang his melancholy critique of racism, "What did I do to be so black and blue?"[30] Asked why he was in Africa, Armstrong replied, "After all, my ancestors came from here—and I still have African blood in me."[31]

Shakespeare's play *Othello* evidences the long association of handkerchiefs with mysticism in Africa and the diaspora. The entire plot hinges on a handkerchief that the black protagonist, Othello, commands his wife, Desdemona, to bring to him. He states these words to her, detailing the handkerchief's powers:

> That handkerchief
> Did an Egyptian to my mother give;
> She was a charmer, and could almost read
> The thoughts of people: she told her, while
> she kept it,
> 'Twould make her amiable and subdue my father

Desdemona laments losing it and concludes, "Sure, there's some wonder in this handkerchief."[32] Nkrumah's Westernized critics frequently denounced him for using such fetishes. But he was not cynically manipulating his preliterate constituency's superstitions with this fetishistic handkerchief. The handkerchief linked him to the collective occult consciousness of Africa. More potent than a speech, it reinforced the mystical bonds between him and the Ghanaian people. Nkrumah's heroic and charismatic authority further strengthened these bonds.

Sidney Hook explained the necessity for Nkrumah's behavior in his book *The Hero in History: A Study in Limitation and Possibility:*

> Perhaps a more important source of appeal made by the leader to his following lies in the vicarious gratification of their yearnings through his presumed traits and achievements . . . The skillful leader makes

effective use of this, especially in the modern era of nationalism when fetishistic attitudes toward abstractions like the state and nation have been developed. By identifying his struggle for power with these abstractions, the leader effects a transference to himself of emotions previously directed to historic traditions, institutions, symbols, and ideologies. He is then able to change the old and established in the name of the old and established.[33]

Nkrumah would not adhere strictly to Hook's formula. He would use both the old and the new to change the old and established. Gandhi had moved India into a new era of nationalism by appealing to his country's ancient indigenous culture. Nkrumah would follow him only to a point, because Nkrumah viewed culture in a more utilitarian sense than did Gandhi, who lived totally within his culture, even though, as an attorney, he had been educated outside it. To bring real revolutionary change to the old and established, the leader needs to appeal to more than the old and established.

According to the sociologist Max Weber, every charismatic leader marches on a road "from a turbulently emotional life that knows no economic rationality to a slow death by suffocation under the weight of material interests."[34] To the contrary, the African epic hero's success does not depend on the strength of the material forces against him. He succeeds as long as he behaves in harmony with the spirit world. To do this, Nkrumah followed a spiritual and physical regimen that is common among history's mystics.

Nkrumah's intimate friend Genoveva Marais observed his ascetical practices and described them this way:

He disciplined himself so rigorously. For example, he had several days in each month during which he fasted. He also set aside days during which he meditated. . . . During the normal periods, when he was not fasting, he was awake at four in the morning, quite alert, an alertness made more vigorous by the exercise he did. He was particularly keen on the practice of yoga and assured me—and his closest friends—that this was a relaxing art invigorating both mind and body. Meditation was especially important.

"It's a spiritual discipline," he assured us. That he gained enormous benefit from this meditational yoga is proven by the fact that he made sure to practice it most especially when he knew he had a busy day and a full programme before him.[35]

Nkrumah's fasts would last for up to two weeks. During this time he would not shake the hand of a man or a woman. Like mystics and ascetics for millennia, "He wanted to withdraw himself completely from human contact. All his friends had to be 'forgotten,' sent into a sort of oblivion. His female friends must no longer exist."[36] In the thirteenth-century Mali kingdom, when the epic hero Sundiata faced his powerful enemies, he appealed to creatures of the spirit world for their assistance. He had been exiled from his homeland and returned to triumph over his opponents and become king. In the nineteenth century, the Malinke warrior Samori Toure fought many battles with the French to save his empire from colonization. Before crucial encounters with his enemies, he placed himself in a spiritual state to receive assistance from the *jinns,* or genies. Samori's oral epic recorded it this way:

> Almami Samori said, "A slave who depends on Allah is never poor."
> . . . As Almami began to fall into deep sleep,
> Two young female genies came.
> Their home was Takirini.
> At that time Samawurusu . . .
> Samawurusu was the ancestor of all the genies
> Samawurusu sent for all twelve genie families to come at the same time.
> "Let's have a meeting,
> Let's look for one trustworthy person,
> Let's give him the first musket in the blackskin's land."
> It was the genie who authorized Almami to go to war.[37]

Other African warriors had fought the Europeans with indigenous weapons without much success. The jinns sought a special "blackskin" to give the first musket. Samori humbly submitted to divine authority as his ultimate source of strength and wealth. He accepted spiritual power as greater than his own. This made him worthy of the genies' favor. When they gave him the musket, they immediately reduced the technological supremacy of the French.

Nkrumah's periodic fasts, meditation, spiritual retreats, and use of "fetish priests," followed in the traditions of other epic heroes. For him Samori Toure was especially pertinent. Before Ghana achieved full independence, Nkrumah had traveled to Samori's capital, Kan Kan, Guinea. He consulted a local Muslim seer, a *marabout,* who predicted his country's future freedom. After coming to power, Nkrumah brought the marabout to Ghana and conferred with him often. A little-known bond existed between Nkrumah and Ahmed Sekou Toure, Guinea's president. Toure was born in Kan Kan and was the grandson of Samori Toure.[38]

The Samori epic showed that even with the favor of the spirit world, the hero might enjoy victory for only a limited number of years. The jinns that grant favors to the African hero can also take these favors away. Their purposes are mysterious and can never be fully understood by mortals. Nevertheless, in the African epic, secular power alone cannot destroy the hero's dreams. He must first lose the favor of the divine. Prideful arrogance and a refusal to submit to sages, genies, or any divine authority often precede his downfall. But an apparent loss of rulership does not necessarily mean permanent defeat. Like a messiah who dies and rises again, the defeated African epic hero's spirit can rise in future generations to carry on his fight.

5

Resistance and Betrayal

The Wolof epic hero Lat Dior (1842–1886) resisted the French conquest of Senegal battle after battle. After several fluctuations of power and alliances, his fortunes met a gruesome fate. The *guewel* (griot) Bassirou Mbaye recited the story:

> Kayor betrayed him, one man after another.
> Some of his closest men
> Said goodbye.
> Others advised him to go into exile:
> "Lat Dior, why don't you go into exile?
> "Why not go to the Sine Kingdom?" they asked him.
> "I can't go there!
> "What should I do with you?" he asked himself;
> "Anyone who does not want to die should not follow me."
> One cavalryman said goodbye to him on that day.[1]

The great Wolof hero survived and fought until his key generals sided with the French and joined them in attacking him. But Allah had bestowed special blessings (*baraka*) on Lat Dior at birth. Only specially prepared bullets could kill him. So his traitorous enemies used the occult to craft magic bullets of gold, silver, copper, and iron.

> They had prepared two bullets.
> Lat Dior never looked behind him.
> The first bullet hit his horse Maalaw on the white spot on his forehead
> The second bullet cut down Lat Dior,
> Tearing out his right eye.[2]

Many are the epics in which the hero dies amid the happiness of his realized dream. The Epic of Lat Dior shows that the divinely driven African hero can also die courageously without ever achieving his vision. But a future reality that the hero does not live to see is not the ultimate criterion for whether or not his cause succeeds. The eventual triumph of some African epic heroes is not bound by the Western sense of time. It is linked to a future epoch that the hero ushers in. Fate simply does not allow some heroes to live to see more than a mental image of their dream's fruition.

Black America's epic hero, Rev. Dr. Martin Luther King, Jr., spoke in more recent times, on the night before his assassination, and referred to the vision he had seen of a Promised Land. He questioned whether he would ever live to see it, but he had no doubt that his people eventually would.[3] Similarly Mwalimu Julius Nyerere, the late Tanzanian hero, also mentioned the future success of the two dreams he had championed throughout his adult life. In one of his last interviews before his death he said that Christianity and socialism had not failed, because neither had yet been tried.[4] Implicit in his words was his faith in a future when his life mission would bear fruit.

Lat Dior gave his life for his people's independence. He dedicated himself to unifying as many Wolof forces as he could inspire to resist the colonial onslaught. Without this unity, he knew that European wolves would feast on his region of Africa. Sheikh Ahmadou Bamba (1853–1927) was another Senegalese patriot and mystic. He was the founder and leader of the Muslim brotherhood known as the Mourides. They were part of the mystical branch of Islam called sufism. Following the defeat of Lat Dior, Wolof Muslims suffered from a decentered polity and spiritual disorientation. Ahmadou Bamba began to gather them together and gave them a renewed mystical relationship with their spiritual leaders and, through these marabous, to Allah. Bamba's growing popularity frightened the French. They seized him and locked him in chains. As would be the fate of future African heroes, they forced him to exile.

The Senegalese peddler Muhammad Gueye is one of Amadou Bamba's present-day followers. He recounted a popular legend of the Amadou Bamba epic.

> The French put Sheikh Amadou Bamba on a big boat to take him to exile to Gabon [in 1895]. The French captain wouldn't let him pray on the deck of the boat so Sheikh Amadou Bamba spread a prayer rug on top of the ocean and prayed on the rug. By Allah's power he did it! Allah made the waves stop and made the water flat like glass and Sheikh Amadou Bamba put his head down and prayed on the rug. It scared the French because Sheikh Amadou Bamba didn't sink in the water because he called on Allah and Allah heard him. Sheikh Amadou Bamba had very, very, powerful baraka from Allah *Subhanawatala* [the Most High]."[5]

Gueye's animation while narrating this story and that of the children listening to the narration convey how orality continues to shape and propagate the knowledge of Africa's epic heroes.

Sheikh Bamba announced to his followers in 1891 that he had a vision to build a city of God in the town of Touba. His vision included constructing a grand mosque. He shared the destiny of other heroes of Africa and its diaspora when Fate prevented him from seeing his vision realized. Nevertheless, the Grand Mosque in Touba became the jewel of the Mourides, and they became pillars of Senegalese political independence.

Both Lat Dior and Ahmadou Bamba ran afoul of the foreign conquerors when they pursued African unity. The generals who deserted Lat Dior, like the generals who would betray Nkrumah in the following century, had visions that conflicted with those of the epic hero. The generals deserted the heroes because they preferred the comforts of compromise and co-optation to the risks of a united front against foreign domination. Resistance meant risking prison, humiliation, exile, and death. But Africa could never win true independence without her leaders taking these risks.

The next packages of incidents in Nkrumah's life are inseparably linked to his advocating the unity of all of Africa. Dior's and Bamba's micronationalist goal of bringing Islamic ethnic groups together in Senegambia threatened the colonialists' designs. Nkrumah's Pan-Africanism was exponentially more frightening to the colonial powers than any African warrior's micronationalist notions. A Pan-African state would alter the world's centuries-old racial power hierarchy in which the white West always occupied the top. A balkanized and weak Africa could never challenge Western hegemony. An Africa divided into ministates could never control its own resources and regulate its own markets. The bottom line of Africa's value to the West was cheap natural resources, cheap labor, cheap soldiers, and markets they monopolized for their high-priced refined products. Had Africa not offered the West these four assets it would have attracted only scientific attention, like Antarctica. Colonialism locked Africa into an inequitable economic relationship with the West. Following Pan-African unity, Nkrumah wanted a unified African military high command that could defend Africa's interests.

Despite the Afrotopian romanticism of some people in the Black Atlantic that stemmed from Garveyite Africanism, Nkrumah taught that Pan-Africanism was ultimately about economics. He summed up his early speeches and notes on the subject in his pivotal book *Neo-Colonialism: The Last Stage of Imperialism*:

> The foreign firms who exploit our resources long ago saw the strength to be gained by acting on a Pan-African scale. By means of interlocking directorships, cross-share holdings and other devices, groups of apparently different companies have formed, in fact, one enormous capitalist monopoly. The only effective way to challenge this economic empire and to recover possession of our heritage is for us to act on a Pan-African basis through a Union Government.[6]

The West owned and controlled most of Africa's wealth as a unified Pan-African capitalist entity. They worked together for each other's mutual profit. They collaborated to suppress nationalist threats and to maximize their profits. Nkrumah campaigned for a socialist Pan-Africanism as the natural counter to the West's capitalist Pan-Africanism. If he succeeded, then the British Empire would lose far more than the Gold Coast colony. It would also lose Nigeria, Kenya, Tanganyika, Botswana, Uganda, Malawi, Northern and Southern Rhodesia (now Zambia and Zimbabwe, respectively), Togo, Egypt, and the world's richest gold and diamond mines in South Africa and South West Africa (now Namibia).

If the French, Portuguese, Belgians, and Spanish lost their colonies as well, then a unified Africa, a huge and fearsome black giant, would stand menacingly beside Europe's divided and war-depleted whiteness. The Europeans who had lost so much during the recent war were psychologically unprepared for such an epochal change. This black giant would threaten to further lower their standards of living. It could endanger a centuries-old economic relationship that impoverished Africa while enriching the West. It could establish continental cartels that set the prices for its raw materials. Decades later a Pan-Arab alliance would enact Nkrumah's idea by founding the Organization of Petroleum Exporting Countries (OPEC). Pan-Arab unity seized power from the West to set prices for their oil and thereby jumpstarted the development of their economies.

When the de-balkanized Pan-African colossus made bargains and treaties with the West as a single entity, the West could no longer manipulate one African state against another. The black giant would bargain from a position of strength. Wealth that flowed out of one of the world's richest continents, leaving little behind, would turn to the benefit of the tillers of the soil and the tens of millions of miners and laborers whose families often lived on the verge of penury and malnutrition.

Most fearsome to the West, the African giant could potentially make a coalition with the Asian giant. Then Western Europe and the United States would have to adjust to a new and dreaded world epoch. Africa, Asia, and potentially Latin America would encompass five-sixths of the planet's population. Militarily, they would comprise a force that would never again have to submit to Western diktat. International white supremacy has been the underpinning of centuries of international politics. An African-Asian alliance would permanently shift the world's balance of power from the West to the South and East. African unity would be the beginning, Nkrumah insisted in the title of one of his books, *Africa Must Unite*. The West saw the geostrategic changes that such an eventuality could bring and demanded more insistently through its actions that "Africa Must Not Unite!"

As in the epic of Lat Dior, Africa's enemies would seek to thwart Nkrumah's dream of unity by luring his generals away from him. Charisma alone could not maintain Dior's protégés' loyalty, and charisma could not keep Nkrumah's generals from betrayal. Once divided, both heroes and generals were conquered.

The epic heroes followed historical patterns and so did their foreign and domestic enemies. For centuries the collaboration of some (not all) African elites supplied crucial help to foreign settlers and slave traders fighting indigenous resistance. The invaders did not need passive traitors. They knew that in Africa their power originated in the barrel of their guns and ended in the colonized minds of the conquered peoples.

The British were keen practitioners of, first, divide and conquer and, next, divide and rule. Tiny cracks in the unity between Nkrumah and his generals began to show within two months of his assuming leadership of the UGCC. The British would waste little time in detecting and widening them. A Ga subchief from Accra began the chain of events that was one of the divine coincidences that often accompany the life of Africa's epic heroes. This chain of events instigated the split and led directly to Nkrumah's eventually becoming the *Ghana* (literally, "king" or "ruler") of Ghana.

A subchief of the Ga people, Nii Kwabena Bonne, began to campaign for a boycott of European and Arab merchants in October 1947. The colony's African people had expected that the high prices accompanying the recent war would decrease to prewar levels.

However, unrestrained price gouging by the European and mainly Syrian merchants combined with commodity shortages to dash their hopes and filled them with fury. Bonne observed, "We had neither a government-controlled economy with an efficient system of price control and regulation such as existed in England at the time nor a liberal economy with free trade and genuine competition which would have cut down the profits of middle-men and importers and forced them to show real enterprise by taking their goods into the distant villages."[7]

Britain's postwar Labour Party government had established a socialist welfare state to protect the interests of its poorest citizens. The government did not extend the same protections to the poor of the Gold Coast colony. Instead, there was a "gentleman's agreement" between the colonial "government or the Directors of Supply on the one hand and members of the Chamber of Commerce on the other under which traders were allowed a profit of 75 percent."[8] Bonne researched the impact of these discriminatory economic policies in the villages where most Africans lived. The system left people so impoverished that "the poorer classes in the villages could not afford to clothe themselves and the majority went in rags."[9] The inflated price of textiles was understandably one of the main commodities whose prices the boycott would challenge.

Bonne gave the colonial government a deadline to lower the profit margin to a 25 percent maximum. If they did not comply by January 24, 1948, the people would stay away from foreign businesses. The foreign traders responded to Bonne with derision, hush money, and threats. They refused to change their prices and expressed doubts that the Africans could sustain a boycott beyond nine days.[10] Bonne refused to call off the boycott.

When Bonne first launched his campaign, he stated his intent to stay within the boundaries of colonial law. But by New Year's Day, 1948, he began to speak like a revolutionary nationalist. In a message to all his fellow chiefs and the indigenous people, he asked for their support of the Anti-Inflation Campaign and Boycott. He also asked them "to fight and die for the liberty and freedom of your country."[11] He did not elaborate on how a boycott of foreign traders would bring this liberty and freedom. This was a fashionable rhetorical flourish after World War II, when many Africans could still remember Winston Churchill's stirring speeches promoting sacrifice to preserve British liberty and freedom. Bonne's changing of the vocabulary of his movement could have influenced the later cataclysmic events. A boycott is a passive-aggressive act requiring people simply to keep their money in their pockets. Fighting and dying for freedom from a colonial system requires overt action directed against an enemy whom nobody needed Bonne to identify.

The boycott began as scheduled on January 24. Then events took a course that Bonne, evidently, had not expected. Africans began looting and burning foreigners' stores and warehouses. Bonne's call to fight and die made inexplicable to these fighting youths his denunciations of their violent nationalistic outbursts as "irresponsible actions." He wrote that he knew that his people were respectful, law-abiding, nonviolent, and possessed of "almost inexhaustible" patience. He concluded that the looting, burning, and rioting by "unscrupulous, hot-headed Africans" had to be inspired by "foreign influences."[12] Bonne's vacillation and inconsistencies highlighted that he had led a protest in which the people advanced farther than their leader. Despite his using the language of revolutionary nationalism, he had set limited goals at the beginning of the protest. But now history demanded that he move to the front of more far-reaching nationalistic demands. His refusal or inability to obey the compulsions of history exposed the vacuum of nationalistic leadership. After tasting the power of mass action, the colonized people now needed a leader who would not condemn their revolutionary fervor but would work to heighten it. Most important, the year 1948 called for a leader to infuse them with an ideology that directed their energies toward acts most likely to bring the freedom and liberty that Bonne had once espoused.

Nkrumah formally took office as general secretary of the UGCC in early January 1948. Nii Bonne's boycott began on January 24. For over a month, the people stayed away from the foreigners' stores throughout the colony. Nkrumah quickly made sure that the UGCC supported the boycott, but its catapulting him to fame was a divine coincidence. "My arrival in the country, my almost immediate appointment as general secretary of the U.G.C.C. and this boycotting campaign were so synchronized that, although the events were coincidental, it was easy to understand why the Government and my political opponents readily associated me with the campaign. It was generally believed, in fact, that I was its instigator."[13]

Not Nkrumah, but, according to Nii Bonne, none other than Joseph Danquah had tried to recruit him in early February 1948. He offered Bonne a high position in a future independent Ghana, but Bonne rebuffed his proposition.[14] Bonne had not needed the UGCC to launch a boycott that had halted most trade in the colony. Bonne also did not need the UGCC to continue the boycott. So adamantly was

Bonne against any association with the UGCC that when another UGCC member offered him a paramount chieftancy in an independent Ghana, he wrote, "I turned him out of my house and but for the intervention of Agbettor I would have had him flogged."[15] Danquah had contacted Bonne during the weeks when he and Nkrumah were crisscrossing the country promoting the UGCC as the vanguard of the people's independence aspirations. Their work was one factor that was responsible for the high pitch of nationalist language that began to enter the African discourse.

At meetings on February 20 and 21, the colonial secretary's office and Gold Coast business associations—including Indians, Syrians, and Europeans—agreed to bring down the profit margin on textiles to 25 percent. The colonial government also empowered the native courts to suppress profiteering on staples like kerosene, sugar, and milk. Bonne and the other chiefs agreed to end the boycott on February 28.[16] But they had opened gates of popular protest that could not be easily closed. Also on February 28, members of the African Ex-Serviceman's Union in Accra decided to press their grievances against the colonial government. Inflation had made their pensions an insulting pittance. The colonial government had also reneged on giving grants to the older men to start businesses. The ex-soldiers decided to march to Christiansborg Castle to present a petition of their grievances to the colonial governor. The government demanded that they march elsewhere, but they refused. Volleys of police gunfire stopped their advance, killing two men and wounding five others. Widespread rioting and looting in Accra ensued, during which 29 people were killed and 237 injured.[17] Unlike Bonne, Nkrumah did not denounce the violence. He called a meeting of the executive committee of the UGCC to take advantage of the opportunity. The UGCC leaders decided that the rioters had advanced the date of independence. They "sent telegrams to A. Creech Jones, Secretary of State for the Colonies, calling for the sending of a special commissioner to the Gold Coast to hand over the administration to an interim government of chiefs and people, and to witness the immediate calling of a constituent assembly."[18]

The British had agreed to compromise on commodity prices to end Bonne's nonviolent boycott. But they refused to begin the process of granting independence to end violent protests. They quickly identified the subversive character of the UGCC's championing of the protests as anti-British nationalism. Fifty thousand angry Africans now filled the streets of Accra and overwhelmed both the police and the local colonial military.[19] Shortly after Nkrumah and his cohorts sent the telegram, Sir Gerald Creasy, the governor of the Gold Coast, ordered the arrest of Nkrumah, Joseph Danquah, Ofori Atta, Akufu Addo, Ako Adjei, and Obetsebe Lamptey. These men would forevermore in Ghanaian history and politics be known as the "Big Six." It is at this point that Nkrumah's future on the path to exile begins. As in the story of Lat Dior, a chasm opened between Nkrumah and the five other generals of the UGCC. The British, always keen for an opportunity to divide and rule, quickly worked to widen the gap.

During Nkrumah's arrest, the British discovered his unsigned British Communist Party membership card and the document that contained the rules and description of the organization known as THE CIRCLE. The British had already mistakenly labeled Nkrumah the ringleader of the unrest. Now they had proof of his Communist proclivities. Worst of all, they discovered that the members of THE CIRCLE swore personal loyalty to Nkrumah as their leader toward achieving two goals that all European colonialists and settlers feared: first, the self-determination of all of West Africa, and second, a Union of African Socialist Republics. Their discoveries while searching Nkrumah's papers brought the first official British notice of Nkrumah's ultimate goal for Ghana and all of Africa. Less than a month after the colonial police arrested the Big Six, British intelligence zeroed in on Nkrumah as the crux of the problem:

> Information available to the Governor gave him no option but to stop the activities of the six men because of the revolutionary and unconstitutional acts which they clearly proposed to perpetrate. The connexion of this group with the Communist Party abroad was demonstrated by the apprehension of a European emissary. There have been indications that the recent demonstrations were part of a larger plot connected with the overthrow of established authority and the formation of a Union of African Socialist Republics, and that the means to be employed by the movement included some of the most evil of the violent measures adopted elsewhere by the Communists. One of the persons now removed was to have been the acknowledged leader.[20]

The so-called European emissary from the British Communist Party appears to have been a paranoid fabrication. Alarms would still have sounded loudly in the capitals of the colonizing powers if Nkrumah—the "acknowledged leader"—had made plans for a "Union of African *Capitalist* Republics." Whether the union was socialist or capitalist was never the central disturbing feature about a united Africa for

Europeans. It was the word "union" that always reverberated with them as an earth-shattering ideal. China, the giant of Asia, was but one year from Mao Zedong's declaration of its unification as a socialist state. The West looked upon that eventuality with dismay because China had for more than a century writhed under their ruthless and highly profitable hegemony. So despicable was the Chinese fate when divided like Africa by the West into spheres of influence that a popular term for a person's lacking a possibility of success was, "you don't have a Chinaman's chance." Once China was unified, Britain could no longer humiliate its people by forcing them to buy the Queen's opium. The Western allies could not make them pay outrageous indemnities for affronting them by resisting imperial conquest. A unified China would lift up the esteem of Chinese people worldwide.

The French colonies in Indochina, particularly in Vietnam, sought unity and independence. This cheap source of rubber, tungsten, and tin, needed to break free from France to unify. Vietnamese unity would alter the nation's underlying status and assert its people as equals among nations. The prospect of Asian nations achieving independence and unity was so frightening that the West fought it overtly and covertly for decades in Vietnam, Cambodia, Laos, Malaysia, Indonesia, and Korea. Now in Ghana, Nkrumah had stirred up a boycott and a violent protest. He wanted independence *and* to make all of Africa—just as all of Asia was potentially becoming—a unified and independent socialist power bloc.

Moreover, scores of millions of African peoples languished under discrimination and Jim Crow laws throughout the diaspora. From South America to the Caribbean to North America, descendants of slaves would likely respond to a unified Africa with protests against the status quo and even rebellion born of a new sense of African power. In the West, the media had spent years drilling the worst images of Africa into the minds of its black and white citizens. Originally Africa was the "Dark Continent" because Westerners were so deeply in the dark about its geography, ethnography, and history. After the slave trade and colonial conquest, Westerners labeled Africa a dark place because its people lacked the "light" of both Western knowledge and white complexions. Explorers into Africa's "darkness," like Henry Morton Stanley, described Africans as subhumans with the minds of children and the passions of brutes.[21] The relentlessly negative portrayals of Africa bore bitter fruit. For all but the Garveyites and nationalists in the diaspora, Africa was a source of shame and revulsion. A united Africa would change that and potentially unleash a tide of black pride and defiance within white supremacist societies.

In the aftermath of the February 1948 riots, a British official, David R. Rees-William, toured the Gold Coast colony and reported his findings back to the secretary of state for the colonies, Arthur Creech Jones. He found the idea of African independence absurd and told the secretary of state that Africans shared his opinion.

> The responsible elements were horrified at the thought of self-government. The old ones remembered the barbarism of the time before the British arrived in the country and had no wish to return to such a condition, and return it would be. . . . When we consider that only 50 years ago barbarism had full sway it will be seen how thin is the veneer of civilisation.[22]

Deluded by his fear of losing the colony, Rees-William had convinced himself that "responsible" Africans (in his mind, the majority) agreed with him that they were too barbaric and uncivilized for independence. The invention of moving pictures, radio, and television reinforced these stereotypes. The denigration of Africa accompanied the denigration of all African people in the diaspora with the Sambo and mammy caricatures. Africa's "savagery," "cannibalism," "primitivism," and "barbarism" were a vital part of the propaganda of white supremacy. Internalizing this negative image of their African origins was integral to African peoples' submission to white supremacy. Especially in the United States, the slave "seasoning" process continued throughout the twentieth century. The enslavers had separated Africans from their heritage to maintain them in mental and physical bondage. In the same way, the modern media images worked to make Africa so repulsive that her sons and daughters in the diaspora would never identify with her. While the chains of physical bondage were long gone, the psychological self-constraints continued to hold back African Americans from their fullest self-actualization.

A unified, strong, powerful Africa; standing as an equal with all other world powers, with a unified army, navy, and air force, with a centralized government based on principles of both political and economic democracy—this Union of African States would lift the hearts and minds of African peoples everywhere. Africa unified would erase the foundations of the black inferiority complex and help to build a mighty black pride throughout the diaspora. The West opposed the unification of Africa for obvious economic and geostrategic reasons.

Less obvious, but just as important, the continued subservience of black populations in the diaspora was a potent yet never-mentioned factor. The British believed that they had discovered in Nkrumah's belongings documentary evidence that he aspired to lead a movement that would shatter their empire forever. They commenced from that point to wage a covert war against him. They would lure his generals from him as their first strategy toward his destruction.

The Watson Commission and the Coussey Committee

The Big Six shared close quarters in prison. Nkrumah noticed that his comrades began to display a growing hostility toward him. During discussions, the other men usually opposed his points of view. They began to blame him for their arrests and for why they were suffering in prison. Then they let Nkrumah know that they now regretted making him the leader of the UGCC because of what he had got them into.[1]

The British wanted the recommendations of Aiken Watson's Commission on what they should do in response to Watson's findings. The Watson Commission brought the Big Six from jail to Accra for questioning. The commission completed its research and decided that the time had come for the Gold Coast to update its constitution. The new constitution should offer the people more democracy, but it stopped far short of independence. The British decided on a new tack to retain their colony. They would constitutionally grant more rights to the Africans. They also would defuse the Africans' discontent with receiving less than full self-determination by opening a parliamentary talking shop. Nkrumah's arrest and imprisonment as a ringleader made him even more well known and admired throughout the colony. Whatever concessions the British made were attributed to Nkrumah's leadership and sacrifices.

That the people associated their political gains with Nkrumah's return and leadership is understandable, even though his arrival and the protests were coincidental. Watson and his fellow commissioners also believed that Nkrumah was the chief culprit behind the disturbances. Their assessment of Nkrumah would color British dealings with him for the next twenty years. Regardless of what Nkrumah stated, the British held onto the initial findings of the Watson Commission as if they were the definitive and conclusive word on his character and intensions. The commission relied on two source documents to assess Nkrumah.

The first were the minutes of the meetings of the working committee of the UGCC. These were basically the policy discussions of the Big Six. The British captured the organization's minutes when arresting the Big Six. The second was the document known as "THE CIRCLE," which they seized from Nkrumah's papers.

The final and official Watson Commission Report stated that the UGCC did not "really get down to business" until Nkrumah became general secretary. Nkrumah had been educated in Britain and the United States. They believed that he had become a Communist in London, despite his statements to the contrary. He intended to become the leader of a "Union of West African Soviet Socialist Republics." The UGCC working committee minutes showed that the other members arrested with Nkrumah gave him carte blanche to use the UGCC organization as his own. This allowed Nkrumah to become the "real power" in the UGCC. If Nkrumah succeeded, the program that he advocated in THE CIRCLE and the UGCC would end in "Communist enslavement."[2] The commission was silent about whether Nkrumah would make slaves of white colonials, black Africans, or both. The commission repeated in two more paragraphs Nkrumah's advocacy of West African Soviets, even though Nkrumah never used the word "Soviets." The word also was nowhere in THE CIRCLE document.[3] Their insisting that Nkrumah wanted to make Africa into a Soviet Union distinguished him from the five other members of the Big Six. They were all members of the small African mercantile and professional elite and were unlikely Communists. An alarmed Aiken Watson possibly forged the word "Soviet" in Nkrumah's plans to impress on the colonial office the intense danger of the threat that he believed Nkrumah posed.

The British observed the trickster Nkrumah attempt to give them an impression of himself that they knew was deceptive:

> Mr. Nkrumah appears to be a mass orator among Africans of no mean attainments. Nevertheless he appeared before us as a "humble and obedient servant of the Convention," who had subordinated his private political convictions to those publicly expressed by his employers. From the internal evidence we are unable to accept this modest assessment of his position.[4]

The evidence they had in the UGCC minutes and THE CIRCLE document, along with the recent disturbances, refuted Nkrumah's attempt to underplay his importance. The British released the Watson

Report and wasted no time driving Nkrumah's generals away from him. They appointed a committee on constitutional reform led by Justice Henley Coussey. To the Coussey Committee they added six members of the UGCC. Three of them were from the Big Six—Joseph Danquah, Akufu Addo, and Obetsebe Lamptey. Excluding Nkrumah from the group that would write the Gold Coast constitution was classic divide and rule. The British attempted to marginalize Nkrumah during 1949, this crucial year leading toward a new constitution. They knew that a constitution whose formation Nkrumah influenced would have a more radical economic and political framework than one on which the conservative "evolutionists" worked alone. Next, this black elite moved to completely eliminate Nkrumah from the Gold Coast political scene. The leading members of the UGCC asked Nkrumah to resign from their organization. They offered him one hundred pounds for a one-way ticket back to England.[5]

African heroes enhance their heroic stature by challenging and defeating ever-greater foes. Less than one year after Nkrumah returned to his country, the Gold Coast black petite bourgeoisie and the British colonial secretary concluded that they should prevent him from influencing the colony's future. They began to conspire against him. Both foes shared the interest that Nkrumah's dreams should never reach fruition. He must never assume political leadership of the Gold Coast, and he must never lead a united socialist Africa. The first goal, Gold Coast independence, was a prerequisite for the second. Nkrumah showed his tactical genius by overcoming this powerful opposition to achieve this goal. The weak overcoming the powerful through guile is where the folk heroic Akan tricksters like Ananse won their reputation.

Nkrumah knew that a break with the UGCC was inevitable. He used his cunning to maneuver himself to a position of strength after the break. At times he abandoned a trickster's caution and cleverness. At other times he employed a trickster's duplicity. After his release from jail, he felt that the time was ripe to speak forthrightly about his goals directly to the people. Toward that end, he founded the *Accra Evening News,* without the assistance or consent of the UGCC leadership. Again a divine coincidence intervened. On the same day that the working committee of the UGCC asked him to step down from the general secretaryship of the organization, the first edition of his new newspaper hit the streets. The working committee had moved to eliminate Nkrumah's influence. Instead they only succeeded in freeing him completely from the obligations to consult them when he now spoke to the larger audience reached by his editorials.

Meanwhile, the British focused their attention on making sure that the two developing factions stayed permanently split. R. Scott was an administrative officer of the colony. In March 1949 he wrote a secret report to Colonial Secretary Creech Jones concerning the African agitation for self-government. He divided the Africans between "extreme nationalists," whose slogan was "Self Government Now," and those whom he called "evolutionists."[6] The latter, he concluded, should be Britain's allies when they granted the Africans degrees of self-government.

Of course Scott named Nkrumah as the chief extremist. He used excerpts from articles in Nkrumah's *Accra Evening News* to define him to the government in London. The newspaper had announced that the Gold Coast was now in the "era of action politics." But Scott believed that the Coussey Committee had forced the pro-Nkrumah nationalists to revise their timetable for self-government. This gave the British hope that "responsible opinion" (meaning the Joseph Danquah evolutionists) could take advantage of the opportunity to consolidate themselves. Scott noted, however, that Danquah's faction was "not hitherto remarkable for robustness and constancy."[7] They also had "no common platform and no imaginative and constructive plans with which to capture public opinion." Then, with prescience that marked the astuteness of some British intelligence reports, Scott wrote that the "evolutionists" would perform the "right tricks," should they lead a government. But he doubted that such obedience to British interests would win them the hearts of the African people. The right trick was, of course, their obedience to an agenda that was non-threatening toward British interests. Scott's assessment of the lackluster character of Danquah's faction remained uncannily accurate for the remainder of Danquah's life.

Scott continued his appraisal. On the other hand, he wrote, Nkrumah's "extremists . . . are colourful and exciting." Nkrumah had centered on his leadership persons of lesser stature than Danquah and the black elite that Danquah represented. Nkrumah's organizational core consisted of "zealots, partly composed of fanatical 'anti-imperialists' and nationalists, and partly of gangsters."[8] Nkrumah replaced the men he left behind in the UGCC with men and women who were personally loyal to him. But this did not neutralize Danquah and the other departed generals. Their covert backing by the West meant that they could always plot to take power by extralegal means, knowing that their regimes would receive the automatic support of Western money and media.

The way forces came into play in the Gold Coast in 1949 set a pattern for the subversion of Africa's future independence and of possibilities for unification. The "evolutionists" who performed the West's tricks were like bombs that foreigners controlled remotely from Paris, London, Lisbon, Brussels, and Washington D.C. When, despite all bribery attempts and threats, the "extremists," such as Nkrumah, Congo's Patrice Lumumba, Mali's Modibo Kieta, Tanzania's Julius Nyerere, and Guinea's Ahmed Sekou Toure, refused to promote the economic and political interests of the former colonial powers, bombs exploded and bullets whizzed past their heads. Militaries plotted and coups erupted.

In the Western two-party democracies, the internal contradictions between forces inside their societies determine how both parties play out their struggles for electoral power. United States law forbids a political party to accept donations from a foreign government. Foreign money would insert foreign influences into what should essentially be the United States' internal decisions. The Coussey Committee wrote no such restrictions into the colonial constitutional reforms it proposed. The poverty of postcolonial Africa made the money of rich foreign interests extremely subversive of democratic institutions. For this reason the two-party system in Africa is a different institution than in the West. In Africa, where there are two parties, there is one party that foreign enemies of true independence can buy and use to pressure, subvert, and eventually attempt to destroy the opposing party. Losing elections did not end the attempts at power for pro-Western political parties in Africa. Like the Resistencia Nacional Mocambicana (RENAMO) in Mozambique and União Nacional para Independência Total de Angola (UNITA) in Angola, they became vicious, trained pit bulls that attacked their opposition upon Western command. This problem and the Leninist "class struggle" ideology made forming one-party states attractive to African revolutionaries. Moreover, the logic of African village culture promoted one party. Since recorded and oral memory, a village Council of Elders or another communally elected body often resolved disputes and represented the people's interests. There is no history of indigenous African polities having two opposing village councils. Factional disputes were resolved within the council. Hence it was natural for Africans to believe that a single party, like a single village council, could adequately address local and national issues.

The British covert and overt support for the UGCC leaders launched a template that foreign interests would replicate in Africa without end.

Whenever a political leader promoted policies that opposed the economic interests of the West, the Western powers would follow the British example and intervene in the African country's politics by throwing their considerable financial might behind persons willing to do all of the "right tricks." With the support of the Western power, these opposition forces would comprise the single biggest threat to the will of the majority. When they came to power, by legal or extralegal means, they served as neocolonial stooges. If they efficiently promoted Western interests, they remained in power. But not even they were safe. Should they at some point grow a backbone and refuse to assist in the continued plunder of their countries, a European or U.S. bayonet constantly hovered above their heads. African military officers received training at Britain's elite Sandhurst academy or at the various military training forts in the United States.[9] When the Western-backed opposition politicians could not get elected by the people because, as the British said about Danquah's faction, they could not win the people's hearts, the foreigners instigated the soldiers to seize power. Western money and subversion undid the positives of a two-party system in the first decades of postcolonial Africa, just as it would corrupt and distort the democratic basis of the U.S. two-party system if foreigners could buy U.S. politicians. The time would come when Nkrumah would meet this challenge too. His solution would be a one-party state. After subverting Ghana's two-party system, Western denunciations of Nkrumah's "dictatorial" one-party state were the height of hypocrisy.

The split between the Danquah faction and Nkrumah came at a crucial time, and the British expertly and realistically analyzed the situation. They did not yet know which faction would prevail in a power struggle between the "evolutionists" and the "extremists." So they planted deep hooks in the "evolutionists" and bided their time. As the Gold Coast's chief decolonizer, Nkrumah had to free the African mind from colonial history to achieve an independent Ghana and eventually a united Africa. Scott's report to the British colonial secretary next evaluated how Nkrumah utilized Danquah's idea of renaming the colony "Ghanaland." Scott wrote that Nkrumah turned what for Danquah was a "romantic notion" into a "political conception," by rewriting Ghana's history. Scott wrote:

> [Nkrumah] employed a technique which has been successful in the hands of undemocratic leaders elsewhere. A legend has been built up on the foundation of a xenophobic and intolerant nationalization; until 105 years ago, Ghanaland enjoyed idyllic freedom under its own

governance; it was enslaved (although never conquered) by the "imperialists" for their selfish ends; in the intervening period, the "imperialists" have reduced the people to poverty and misery; they intend to keep
the people in that condition and every action which may have a contrary appearance is but an artifice. Anything in restraint of Ghana aspirations is undemocratic and/or criminal. The Ghana African is
essentially superior to the European in all desirable attributes. This doctrine has been persistently and skillfully drilled into the minds of Mr.
Nkrumah's supporters for some months with positiveness, unction and
virulence. The main tenets are daily imported into discussions, reports,
speeches, stories and personal gossip on any matter of topical interest .
. . The suggestion that there is a contrary or even divergent point of
view produces an almost hysterical outburst against "stooges" or "quislings" or "sham excuses," according to circumstances.[10]

Nkrumah used history as a combat ideology to challenge the British
version that the colony was steeped in barbarism and savagery before
they brought civilization. The mass decolonization of the African mind
had begun. The West's denigrating history of Africa had been an
important component in their combat ideology. Nkrumah attacked the
colonialist's version of African history with his own version to demolish the canard of African inferiority. Africans could govern themselves
in the 1950s because they had done it quite well in the 1850s.
    Now began the British strategy of discrediting the vision by dis-
crediting the man. African evolutionists joined them. Nkrumah was
"mischievous," "extremist," "Communist," "socialist," "conceited,"
a "demagogue," a "nuisance," "un-African." He used "imported ideologies." He "double-crossed" his benefactors in the UGCC.
Eventually the Western press would join in the attack, employing the
same tactic each time: ignore Nkrumah's ideals; attack the man. This
was not how they related to the assorted dictators and kleptocrats
who were destined to come to power to perform the West's tricks. For
these murderous and venal rulers, the West ignored mass murder to
support their regimes. Nkrumah's refusal to toe the evolutionist and
gradualist line had made him the enemy of the West. His domestic
enemies had been co-opted into the Coussey Committee and now
openly aligned themselves with the British. The hero faced formidable
obstacles blocking the realization of his epic destiny. Overcoming
them and achieving his vision of an independent Ghana would require
considerable skill. He would continue to rely on the knowledge he
gained from African American genies to triumph over these trials. He
would also receive sage advice from new sources.

The Convention People's Party

Nkrumah stood before a crowd of 60,000 people on June 12, 1949, and decisively broke with the UGCC. Before the largest demonstration in Accra's history, he announced the founding of the Convention People's Party (CPP). This was the country's first political party. It marked a new beginning in the Gold Coast of modernist politics and parliamentary democracy. Political awareness among Africans now coalesced between the two factions, with the British taking the side of the UGCC. Nkrumah accurately assessed the new political landscape:

> This marked the final parting of the ways to right and left of Gold Coast nationalism: from the system of indirect rule promulgated by British imperialism to the new political awareness of the people. From now on the struggle was to be three-sided, made up by the reactionary intellectuals and chiefs, the British Government and the politically awakened masses with their slogan of "Self-Government Now."[11]

During the rally Nkrumah called for the British to immediately turn over to Africans the reins of self-government. The working committee of the UGCC had objected to every institution that Nkrumah had founded to promote independence. These included the founding of a college for students who had been expelled from schools for supporting Bonne's boycott, the *Accra Evening News*, and a Youth Study Group. After this rally, Nkrumah felt that the time had come to launch the next stage of the independence struggle. He called it "Positive Action." This was his application of Mohandas Gandhi's nonviolent tactics of political activism to Ghana's independence movement.

Nkrumah wrote a formal letter of resignation to the UGCC. He spoke in the voice of a warrior about to embark on the battlefield. He stated that he was fully "aware of the dangers" that his stance for independence was about to bring upon him. But his "country's cause comes first." He would "take the step and chance the consequences," because he was "prepared if need be to shed my blood and die if need be, that Ghana might have self-government now."[12]

The Positive Action campaign shook up the British and forced them to come to the realization that they would have to grant Ghana independence one day. Nkrumah's character as a culture hero would not allow him to continue polite half-measures that were full of deference to the queen and loyalty to the empire. These were the decades-old policies of Danquah and the Ghanaian petite bourgeoisie. Nkrumah relied on his superior organizational abilities to launch an uncompromising movement for independence. With organization he could defeat both foreign and domestic foes. The words of encouragement of an *Accra Evening News* editorial make clear his intentions. He wrote them under the title "Organize! Organize!! Organize!!!"

> We must organize in order to be able to break down the chains of Imperialism. The agents of our so-called trustees are busy . . .
>
> Do not be worried about the Chiefs. As Kwame Nkrumah has been saying, if we are well organized and strong, our Chiefs shall know where to stand. Do not be unduly concerned about them; they are with us. They know what we are suffering.
>
> Do not be worried too by the presence of the vicious pro-foreign Government activities of some of our own Africans—the quislings, the stooges and their fellow travelers; they are few and will eventually bow to the organizational strength of the people of this country. There is nothing which Imperialist Governments respect more than this. The strength of the organized masses is invincible.[13]

By 1949 the quislings were some of the men who had initially supported Nkrumah's leadership of the UGCC. The British had blamed Nkrumah and the other top five leaders of the UGCC for the anticolonialist rebellion and locked them in prison. Such hardships were not what Danquah and the other members of Ghana's westernized elite had expected. Nkrumah realized quickly that the gradualist "go slow" policy had been used by the British as a means to "not go." He specifically stated his intentions in 1949.

> There are two ways to achieve self-government: either by armed revolution and violent overthrow of the existing regime, or by constitutional and legitimate non-violent, methods. In other words, either by armed might or by moral pressure. For instance, Britain prevented the two German attempts to enslave her by armed might, while India liquidated British Imperialism there by moral pressure. We believe that we can achieve self-government even now by constitutional means without resort to any violence.[14]

Bloodshed and imprisonments accompanied Gandhi's nonviolent campaign. India celebrated its independence in 1947. By 1949 the British knew that Positive Action could demolish their empire without firing a shot. One particularly mendacious international report from Reuters informed Nkrumah and his comrades that they were in for a dirty war. Despite there not being a grain of truth in these words, the West dutifully disseminated them. The article claimed that local African chiefs had given an ultimatum to Nkrumah, the "Extremist Home-Rule Leader." If he caused trouble after the release of the Coussey Report, did not promise the CPP's loyal cooperation with the colonial government, or refused to accept their royal authority, then they would "Forcibly Eject" him to an internal exile to his birthplace in Nzimaland. The article portrayed Nkrumah as obstinately and unreasonably refusing to promise to cooperate with the colonial government. Instead he wanted to use "Boycott, Strikes and Spiritual Force to carry on the struggle."[15]

That the chiefs never delivered this ultimatum is not the point. This Reuters dispatch reveals the new level of British understanding of the degree of threat that Nkrumah posed. He had become a symbol of the opposite type of African than the one they preferred to eventually negotiate with for self-rule. They knew now that he was an implacable revolutionist, not an evolutionist. He could be neither co-opted nor bought. Undermining him inside Ghana was no longer enough to neutralize his influence. His radically anticapitalist and anticolonialist pamphlet, "Toward Colonial Freedom," was becoming a mainstay of nationalist discussion in Britain and throughout the anglophone colonies including the Caribbean. His fame as a heroic opponent of British imperialism had begun to spread. So in concert with the campaign to undermine his influence in the Gold Coast, the British began to undercut his influence internationally. They wanted to stop his becoming a symbol for emulation for dismantling colonialism.

Other books and articles detailing Nkrumah's political life attribute his eventual fate to such things as his personal shortcomings or his "flawed" economics. The truth is that the ultimate success or failure of Nkrumah cannot be accurately assessed without considering the danger to Western interests of his vision of a united Africa. The British recognized the danger and sought to control and subvert him during the 1950s. The United States agreed with the British and stated flatly that the "Nkrumization" of Africa must never occur.[16] The United States would take over the main role of subverting Nkrumah after 1960.

Nkrumah's foreign adversaries could separate his generals from him only if the generals also opposed his vision. The sum total of Nkrumah's ideology and praxis added up to Pan-Africanism as his ultimate goal. But the hero is heroic only when he overcomes the obstacles fate uses to block his path to his goal of ushering in a New Age. Nkrumah's forces were materially weak in the face of British and later U.S. opposition. The Ghanaian masses' chances of success versus such odds must have seemed very limited in October 1949, when the British released the Coussey Committee Report. Nkrumah and most of the country rejected its half-measures toward constitutional reform. But the UGCC leaders and all the Africans who worked on the Coussey Committee were from the African mercantile, professional, and feudal elite. Their now open league with the British made an even more formidable opponent for Nkrumah's "Self Government Now" forces.

The British opposed Positive Action with the Coussey Report. The reformist and gradualist constitution that Coussey proposed was to be the British answer to all African grievances. Nkrumah disagreed. Only members of the African elite had helped write the report. By leaving out all workers, farmers, miners, and small traders, who comprised the African majority, the Coussey Committee lacked credibility with the people from its inception.[17] After the release of the report, Danquah openly aligned himself with the British-made constitution against Nkrumah. On the eve of Nkrumah's launching his Positive Action campaign, Danquah wrote Nkrumah and urged him, "Kwame don't do it." He later explained, "I conceived that ill-fated 'Direct Action' to be wasteful of life, property and energy."[18] Danquah tied his reputation to a British-made constitution, so that as the constitution went, so went his national popularity.

Danquah and the British had to legitimize the Coussey Report by discrediting Nkrumah's Positive Action campaign and demands for immediate self-government. Hence, their positive portrayals of the report and their negative portrayals of Nkrumah. Danquah wrote:

> The Coussey Constitutional Committee appointed in December 1948, as a constitutional (wholly African) body to recommend the necessary interim measures to carry out the Watson recommendations, had reported in September, 1949, and its recommendations were being rapidly acted on by the Government of the Gold Coast and all the level-headed politicians.[19]

As the leader of Ghana's black mercantile and professional elites, Danquah specifically criticized Nkrumah and his comrades for not being "level-headed." Danquah and his supporters now openly aligned themselves with the British and opposed Nkrumah. These were formidable adversaries for the African hero. Nkrumah turned to the African people for strength. Following the October 1949 publication of the Coussey Report, he called for a People's Representative Assembly to convene on November 20. Representatives of fifty African organizations answered his call. Only two major organizations refused to participate in the massive gathering. They were Danquah's UGCC and the quasi-defunct Aborigines Rights Protection Society.

Nkrumah had called together a rival assembly that suspiciously resembled a shadow government. He had escalated his revolutionary campaign against colonialism beyond a point of no return. He placed himself openly in defiance of the colonial government and its allies' designs for the country's future.

> The Assembly resolved "that the Coussey report and His Majesty's Government's statement thereto are unacceptable to the country as a whole" and declared "that the people of the Gold Coast be granted immediate self-government, that is, full Dominion status within the Commonwealth of Nations based on the Statute of Westminister." They also drew up a memorandum outlining the structure of central and local government which they desired to see incorporated in a new constitution.[20]

Barely a year after his release from prison for opposing British interests, Nkrumah fearlessly placed himself in a position of bold defiance of colonial authority and the black petite bourgeoisie. They had guns, but he had the support of the African majority. He knew that when the British turned down his demands, his Positive Action campaign would pit the unarmed against the well-armed. He knew that a few spontaneous riots do not constitute a revolution. He needed persistent and unwavering support for a protracted struggle to win independence. This is the point where Nkrumah utilized a skill that he had learned in the diaspora. If he were simply an ordinary man, then he and his grassroots supporters could not possibly have overcome the extraordinary might of the colonialists and their domestic collaborators. If Nkrumah only opposed physical force with physical force, then his defeat was certain. Gandhi based his movement in the Hindu philosophy of the spiritual power of nonviolence. He spiritually defeated the greater material forces of colonial oppression. Like Gandhi, Nkrumah had to be a conduit of divine power on earth to win his people's confidence to the point where they would persistently follow him into the teeth of the British bulldog. He and his people would fight for freedom on a physical and a spiritual battlefield. Their spiritual strength would compensate for their military weakness. Nkrumah's opponents would denounce his so-called Marxist tactics, but the salvo he fired at them in the *Accra Evening News* elicits no consciousness of Marxist ideology. Rather, it brings to mind the techniques of his experience as a circuit preacher in the United States.

> Blessed are they who are imprisoned for
> self-government's sake,
> for theirs is the freedom of the land.
> Blessed are ye, when men shall vilify you and
> persecute you, and say all kinds of
> evil against you,
> for Convention People's Party's sake.
> Blessed are they who hunger and thirst because
> of self-government,
> for they shall be satisfied.
> Blessed are they who reject the Coussey report,
> for they shall know freedom.
> Blessed are the parents whose children are
> Political leaders,
> for they shall be thanked.
> Blessed are they who took part in Positive Action,
> For they shall have better rewards.
> Blessed are they who now love CPP,
> for they shall be leaders in the years to come.
> Blessed are they who cry for self-government,
> for their voice shall be heard.[21]

Nkrumah's four radical positions—self-government, rejection of the Coussey Report, Positive Action, and risking safety and comfort to support the policies of Nkrumah's Convention People's Party— received the Holy blessing. Nkrumah likely wrote these beatitudes himself. He founded the *Accra Evening News* as the informational arm of Ghana's independence movement and of Pan-Africanist ideology. Its pages usually contained only articles that he wrote or approved.

Nkrumah coined his most memorable slogan during this phase, paraphrasing the biblical admonition to seek first the Kingdom of Heaven. "Seek ye first the Political Kingdom and all else will be added unto you." Like the Reverend Adam Clayton Power, Jr., and Father Divine, he frequently couched his political language in spiritual terms. The CPP and its followers were weak as a purely political movement against the power of the British and their African collaborators. As a spiritual movement that followed a Messiah, they were strong. Nkrumah gave Ghanaians a new revolutionary moral and spiritual standard whose highest attribute was Pan-Africanism.

He was not the Messiah because of his own needs, but because Africa needed one to get to the Promised Land of unification. For this reason, the calumnies heaped on his motives by his political enemies and by his more scholarly critics were based on inadequate information. Had they witnessed Harlem's Reverend Adam Clayton Powell's magical turning of Gospel phrases into political admonitions to boycott, organize, strike, and strive for political power in the boroughs of New York, they would have known that Nkrumah's means and motives were interconnected. Had they seen Father Divine unifying a diverse following through his "Christhood," they would have understood that Nkrumah was motivating people through their Christian consciousness.

Like Divine, Nkrumah deliberately inserted his "Christhood" into his people's occult consciousness. A story he told in his autobiography showed how consciously he acted to promote this perception of himself. A man interrupted Nkrumah's rest at his home one evening and pleaded with him to help his wife: "We have traveled a hundred and twenty miles to see you and maybe tomorrow will be too late." The man's pregnant wife's delivery was several weeks overdue. "They had come all that way to see me because they knew that I was the only person who could help her . . . 'Don't worry,' I told her, placing my hand gently on her body. 'Your child will be born very shortly and you will have no trouble. Have faith.' " By the next day the woman had given birth to a boy whom they named Kwame Nkrumah.[22] Faith was the key. Father Divine had said, "I ask of you only faith. I take from you nothing. I take your sorrows and give you joy. I take your sickness and give you health. I take your poverty and give you peace and prosperity, for I am the spirit of success and health."[23]

Nkrumah did not write that the couple *believed* that he was the only person who could help them. They *knew* it. Why? Because, like Jesus, Nkrumah had the God-given metaphysical power to heal by the laying on of hands. He did not issue a self-deprecating disclaimer after telling this story, because he meant to depict himself as a miracle-performing faith healer. He deliberately designed this image to gain the unwavering confidence of his people. Few Ghanaian Christians would miss that Nkrumah's healing hands had to be anointed by God to perform this miracle. The Bible verse in Acts 4:30 legitimized Nkrumah's feat with an unmistakable association to the holy word: "While thy stretchest forth thy hand to heal; and that signs and wonders may be done through the name of thy holy Servant Jesus."

Critics, who denounced Nkrumah's so-called blasphemy for incorporating Christianity into his politics, also were unaware of the British intent to use Christianity to keep Ghana in the Western orbit. This is revealed in the following three-page secret communication between British Prime Minister Harold MacMillan and his foreign minister. MacMillan reviewed a Foreign Office study titled "Africa the next ten years." In his comments on the British plans for the continent, he wrote, "More thought ought to be given to the role of Christianity in keeping Africans oriented toward Western ideals."[24] Nkrumah's techniques placed him a step ahead of the British. As a minister of the Gospel, with a degree in theology, his Christianity worked as a decolonizing vehicle to orient Africans away from the West. He continued in this way to counter Western discursive hegemony, just as he had done as a child when he refused to imbibe the strict Catholicism taught by the German priest, but instead settled on a nondenominational, personalized Christianity that was not at war with his African heritage.

First, recall that in his autobiography, Nkrumah altered Walt Whitman's poem to state that his followers would have to give up all else and that he alone would expect to be their sole and exclusive standard. Second, consider the desired effects of the "Veranda Boys" creed of the CPP.

> I believe in the Convention People's Party
> The opportune Savior of Ghana
> And in Kwame Nkrumah its founder and leader
> Who is endowed with the Ghana Spirit
> Born a true Ghanaian for Ghana
> Suffering under victimisations
> Was vilified, threatened with deportation[25]

The stylistic paraphrasing of the Catholic Nicene Creed was inescapably obvious and therefore totally deliberate. Measuring Nkrumah's tactics exclusively with a Western yardstick fails to solve the problem of assessing cultural influences upon Nkrumah without taking the shortcut of pejoratives. When viewed in the context of the African

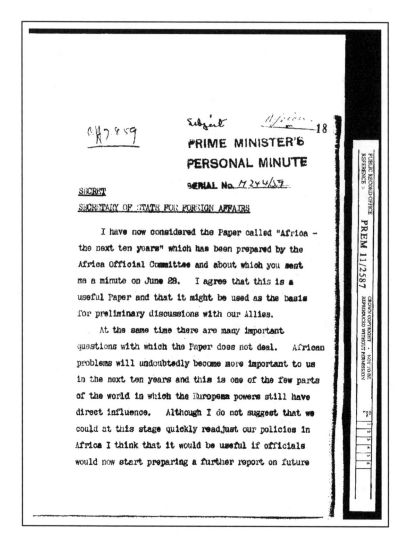

Figure 9   Prime Minister's Personal Minute.

epic, one sees that in Africa griots traditionally recited honorifics to accompany the arrival and departure of kings and heroic warriors. Praise poems preceded the battles of the powerful and more praise followed their victories. The tradition is truly ancient: in Egyptian temples and pyramids, 4,000- to 5,000-year-old hieroglyphics contain lengthy verses glorifying the feats of various pharaohs. Nkrumah's praise poems

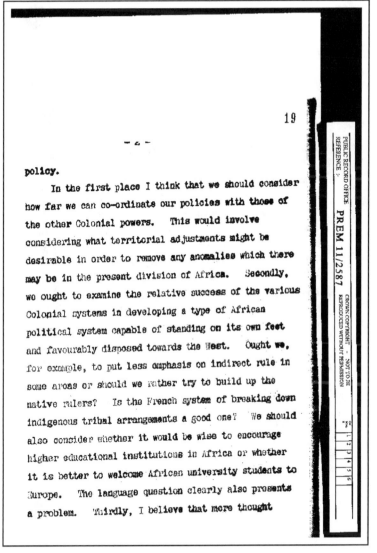

19

— 2 —

policy.

In the first place I think that we should consider how far we can co-ordinate our policies with those of the other Colonial powers. This would involve considering what territorial adjustments might be desirable in order to remove any anomalies which there may be in the present division of Africa. Secondly, we ought to examine the relative success of the various Colonial systems in developing a type of African political system capable of standing on its own feet and favourably disposed towards the West. Ought we, for example, to put less emphasis on indirect rule in some areas or should we rather try to build up the native rulers? Is the French system of breaking down indigenous tribal arrangements a good one? We should also consider whether it would be wise to encourage higher educational institutions in Africa or whether it is better to welcome African university students to Europe. The language question clearly also presents a problem. Thirdly, I believe that more thought

Figure 9   (*Continued*)

were Christian in form because that is the theological language that European missionaries had popularized throughout Ghana. It also was a language containing considerable occult power that was devoid of the potentially negative stigma of African witchcraft.

- 3 -   20

ought to be given to the role of Christianity in keeping
the Africans orientated towards Western ideals.
Finally, as the President of the Board of Trade has
pointed out in his minute of July 2, cooperation in
Africa between the Colonial powers in the economic
field is highly desirable.   We ought to consider how
far this will have to follow economic arrangements in
Europe and whether African problems can be dealt with
separately.   It may indeed be that cooperation in
Africa might help to prevent the economic division of
Europe.

　　　I am sending copies of this minute to the members
of the Africa Committee, the President of the Board of
Trade, and the Secretary of the Cabinet.

HAROLD MACMILLAN

July 3, 1959

Figure 9   (*Continued*)

Decolonization was a millennial movement through which
Nkrumah launched a new epoch. He who would decolonize African
minds had to show himself as more powerful than the settlers who
colonized their minds. Historically, when resistance movements have

opposed more powerful forces in the material world, they have turned to the spirit realm for assistance.[26] Everything that Nkrumah wrote in his autobiographical epic was ultimately for his goal to free Ghana and unite Africa. Nkrumah needed dedicated followers to achieve this goal. The task of overcoming opposition to a unified Africa was Herculean. After World War II, Ethiopia and Liberia were the only independent black-ruled country on the continent.

The most successful black leaders that Nkrumah had seen in the United States had been *called* to leadership. Gifted rhetoric could draw listeners to these men; belief in God's "anointing" on them is what turned listeners into followers. Hence the oath to Nkrumah was neither blasphemy nor a tool of his "megalomaniacal" ego gratification. The function of the Convention People's Party creed was the same as the quasi-Masonic oath that THE CIRCLE recited in London. It was an outer sign of an inner faith in Pan-Africanism. It also marked their commitment to Nkrumah's leadership toward the ultimate goal. Nkrumah viewed each committed follower as another soldier for his life's mission. Cynics routinely condemned these portrayals of his divinity as evidence of his megalomania. They mistakenly conflated their negative opinions of his tactics with his having negative motives. Rather than observe that Nkrumah shaped his behavior for the one central purpose of Ghana's freedom and Pan-African unity, they attributed to him a power-hungry drive to create a personality cult, as if his receiving adulation fulfilled some abnormal psychological drive.

Nevertheless, even Nkrumah's worst enemies recognized that African unity was his obsession, even though they ascribed lower motives to his tactics. Pan-Africanism was the overarching purpose of his life. Nkrumah applied those tactics that he had already seen unite diverse peoples in the 1930s and 1940s toward achieving the goal of uniting the thousands of disparate African linguistic and ethic groups. From New York to Philadelphia, Father Divine had united his multiracial following in their belief in his Christhood. Blacks, whites, Christians, and Jews were frequently not on sociable terms outside of Divine's Peace Mission. But inside his arenas of love, his "Heavens" and "Promised Lands," the "Divinites" became "Angels." And Angels recognized only the human race. Each communal Promised Land was like an independent nation that he and his followers had liberated from America's historical hatreds. At the center of his combat ideology, like a hub holding together multidirectional spokes, was his personal divinity. Like the twelve disciples of Christ, his thousands of followers owned everything in a common. This interracial communism led to repeated threats upon Divine's life by the Ku Klux Klan.[27] Even so, Divine never flinched from pursuing his ultimate vision of creating an egalitarian society that recognized no differences in race or class. Sweet Daddy Grace, Sufi Abdul Hamid, the Reverend Adam Clayton Powell, Jr., and several others were prominent in black America during Nkrumah's sojourn in the West. Learning from all of them and practicing his preaching techniques in black American churches honed his skills for the task he faced. Nkrumah believed that he understood the nature of African peoples and he constructed his appeal to that spiritual nature:

> The traditional face of Africa includes an attitude toward men which can only be described, in its social manifestation, as being socialist. This arises from the fact that man is regarded in Africa as primarily a spiritual being, a being endowed originally with certain dignity, integrity and value. It stands refreshingly opposed to the Christian idea of the original sin and degradation of man.[28]

Nkrumah, the ordained Christian minister, once again defied the orthodoxy of his faith, just as he had been doing since his childhood. He would not allow outer doctrines to overrule his inner understandings. A leader of such a movement could not be raised up by his people. Like other epic African heroes, he had to be divinely born for the mission. Long before Gandhi's birth, heroes like Nkrumah arrived in West African societies as agents of change. They used their occult powers to challenge and overturn the status quo. While realizing their divine destinies, they altered the destiny of entire societies. Throughout their life missions they earned and received verses of adulation from their contemporaries.[29] Those verses became part of the folklore and popular poetry of oral societies.

African Power and the Politics of Foreign Subversion

In 1949 Nkrumah repeatedly demanded that the British amend the new constitution to include the CPP demands. Otherwise he would launch a campaign of boycotts and nonviolent civil disobedience.[30] The full weight of the significance of Nkrumah's threat to the British is evident if one considers two other British colonies. Violent anticolonial movements had begun to rise in Malaya and Kenya. Malaya's rebels armed themselves and launched a long guerilla war for independence.

Kenya's violent nationalist Kikuyu organization, the Mau Mau, began first stirring in 1950. These thorns in the side of the British Colonial Office were another coincidence accompanying Nkrumah's rise. During the first years of the 1950s, A. Creech Jones, the British secretary of state for the colonies, saw stark and bloody eventualities should Her Majesty's government refuse to accede to the popular wishes of the Africans in the Gold Coast colony. Violence in two other parts of the empire influenced Britain in negotiating the independence of Ghana.

Nkrumah wrote a letter on December 15, 1949, to the Gold Coast colonial governor insisting that the colonials amend the Coussey Constitution. His main demand was for immediate self-government. Then he turned up the pressure. He published an article on the front page of the *Accra Evening News* with the bold headline "The Era of Positive Action Draws Nigh." In this article he gave the British two weeks to accept the demand for a "CONSTITUENT ASSEMBLY through a General Election to determine a Full Self-Government Constitution for the country."[31] The British decided to address Nkrumah directly at this point. They invited him to a meeting with the Gold Coast colonial secretary R. H. Saloway.

By then the British had concluded that Nkrumah was permanently outside their control. Back in London, in 1949, Colonial Secretary A. Creech Jones had written a secret letter inquiring about the possibility of co-opting or buying off Nkrumah. He wrote to the chief commissioner of the Gold Coast colony, T. R. O. Mangin:

> I wonder whether there is any positive and constructive work which can be offered to Nkrumah to divert his energies into better and more helpful ways? I don't mean government employment but something in which he can take an interest and turn his thoughts into useful channels?[32]

Commissioner Mangin's reply to Jones discloses the Machiavellian nature of the British strategy to hold on to the Gold Coast colony. Dividing as many Africans from Nkrumah as possible must become an immediate British priority. Mangin concluded that Nkrumah's call for self-government was rooted in his race hatred and desire for mob rule. This was incompatible with the goals of "Africans of substance." These Africans were led by the UGCC. "Thus we have the open and, one hopes final split between the Convention and Nkrumah's new party."[33] Mangin's letter further reveals the glee with which the British now greeted any weakening of Nkrumah's less-compromising brand of nationalism. Nevertheless, the commissioner accompanied his growing hostility toward Nkrumah with a sober and begrudging assessment. Regrettably, Nkrumah was incorruptible:

> I fear that it would be impracticable to adopt your suggestion of finding employment for Nkrumah. He is obdurately and fanatically withdrawn from communication with Europeans, especially officials . . . Much thought has been given to the possibility of fitting him into some niche where he would do less harm and tentative enquiries of one kind or another have in fact been made. They all indicate that he is unlikely to be attracted by anything that could be offered.[34]

The British commanded considerable wealth and could have offered Nkrumah large amounts of cash in their efforts to induce him to leave politics and fit into a less troublesome slot. But they concluded that nothing would tempt Nkrumah off his path. Nkrumah was incorruptible because nothing the British had to offer was more valuable to him than achieving an independent Ghana and a unified Africa.

The public depictions of Nkrumah by the Western powers and their media in the coming years would not match their secret assessment of his incorruptibility. When Nkrumah began to demand true African independence, as opposed to neocolonialism, the Western media would demonize him as the worst example of Africa's endemic corruption. Periodically a voice of truth has stepped outside the propaganda boundaries of the campaign to destroy Nkrumah's government in the past and his reputation permanently. Years after Nkrumah's death, Willard De Pree, the principal officer of the U.S. Embassy in Accra (1964–1968) ventured off script. He revealed a truth that contradicted the images of corruption that his own embassy had contributed to spreading. De Pree candidly reflected that during his years of living in Ghana he had witnessed no "blatant or pervasive corruption." He further stated that although Nkrumah perhaps diverted some funds his own way, it was "not so much for his own personal gain, as to promote his political wishes throughout Africa."[35] This truthful assessment runs intermittently through decades of declassified documents from the British Foreign Office, the U.S. State Department, and the CIA. Nkrumah was an ascetic whose reason for living was his political goals. He selflessly poured most of the resources that he personally accrued into his vision.

The sole purpose of Gold Coast Colonial Secretary Saloway's meeting with Nkrumah was to convince him to stop his Positive Action campaign. He insisted that it would bring the Gold Coast nothing but chaos and disorder. Saloway next warned Nkrumah of dire personal consequences should bloodshed result. Then he concluded with an insult that must have raised Nkrumah's ire: "Now take India . . . The Indian was used to suffering pains and deprivations but the African has not that spirit of endurance. Mark my words, my good man: within three days the people here will let you down—they'll never stick it."[36]

Nkrumah interjected that Positive Action would commence if the British did not accede to the resolutions of the Ghana People's Representative Assembly and amend the new constitution. The British refused to make concessions during this and a subsequent meeting, so Nkrumah proclaimed the start of Positive Action. The British media then announced that Positive Action had been called off and that Africans in other areas were not boycotting or striking. They succeeded for a while in stirring enough confusion to diminish the effectiveness of the campaign. But the African epic hero rises above unforeseen challenges. Nkrumah walked to Accra's Arena and hundreds of Africans joined him. By the time he reached the Arena, it looked like the whole population of Accra had arrived. After his two-hour speech, nothing the British put in their media could turn back the nationalist tide.[37]

Civil disobedience spread: no work, no trains, no government services, and no stores. The colony ceased to function economically. The colonial authorities responded by censoring and shutting down the indigenous press. They imprisoned the leaders of the CPP, the most prominent person being Nkrumah himself. During this time, Joseph Danquah spoke for the elite Joint Provincial Council of Chiefs and the black petite bourgeoisie. He justified the repression of Positive Action by saying, "It is my opinion that those who go against constitutional authority must expect to pay for it with their neck."[38] Danquah would later remind Nkrumah of his position during these times. He viewed the sacrifices that brought independence as avoidable, even though Danquah's own gradualist policies before Nkrumah's Positive Action, had brought few results.

I reminded the President that an outcome of the Positive Action declared by him in January, 1950, was the killing of two policemen by mobs in Accra. In addition, many a bread-winner lost their occupations, and quite a number of prominent people were tried in Court for organizing an illegal strike, found guilty, convicted and sentenced to terms of imprisonment.[39]

Danquah, evidently, believed that the British would relinquish the Gold Coast, their rich gold- and cocoa-producing colony, without African political pressure or sacrifices. Rising nationalists in Accra fought against brutal British repression and killed two policemen. To Danquah, these African resistance fighters were a "mob." He found the British violence against Nkrumah's nonviolent Positive Action campaign unworthy of condemnation. Frantz Fanon's observations of Danquah's social stratum in Africa during these years are relevant here:

> During the period of unrest that precedes independence, certain native elements, intellectuals, and traders, who live in the midst of that imported bourgeoisie, try to identify themselves with it. A permanent wish for identification with the bourgeois representatives of the mother country is to be found among the native intellectuals and merchants.[40]

Fanon needed only to add to his description of Danquah's social class that they not only identified with the British, but that the British also identified with them. Moreover, the British far preferred turning over their colony to them than to uncontrollable idealists like Nkrumah. The colonizer knew that the indigenous elite shared his belief in the profit motive as life's highest purpose. Time and again the former colonial powers' assessment of the black petite bourgeoisie would prove true throughout Africa in the coming decades. The indigenous merchant class, like the colonialists, refused to allow pesky "socialist" demands for schools, electricity, potable water, roads, or hospitals to reduce their profits. As conscienceless as the departed Europeans, these darlings of the West lived then and live now in mansions of obscene splendor, not far from families in dirt-floor hovels. Danquah and the other members of the African elite harbored a secret wish that was fundamentally incompatible with Nkrumah's vision. After independence they intended to replace the British as the privileged power. They did not seek to alter the system that impoverished the Africans at the expense of the colonial elite. They only wanted to change the color of the privileged while the color of the unprivileged remained as unchanged as their socioeconomic conditions.

The British put Nkrumah on trial for charges associated with his endeavoring to "coerce the government of the Gold Coast."[41] Two courts convicted Nkrumah of a total of three felonies connected to the Positive Action campaign and sentenced him to three years in prison. His prison conditions were so onerous that they were tantamount to mental if not physical torture. They had given up on buying or co-opting him. Now their prison would break his mind and body.

During Nkrumah's confinement, the British Foreign Office commissioned a study on the influence of Communism in West Africa. The report stated that Dr. Danquah was strongly against Communism and that his "programme, and that of his supporters, is essentially one of Gold Coast 'nationalism.'" Nkrumah, on the other hand, "a former member of the British Communist Party, is a much more dangerous character." The report stated that Nkrumah had joined the British Communist Party in 1945. He and two other CPP leaders were "all at various times . . . in touch with either British or 'iron curtain' Communists."[42] This opinion informed British involvement in Ghanaian politics for the next five years.[43] Danquah was the "moderate" anti-Communist and Nkrumah was the "extremist" pro-Communist villain.

The British apparently thought that with Nkrumah behind bars, the Opposition forces of Danquah would sweep to power in the 1951 elections. Nkrumah's subordinate leader in the CPP, K. A. Gbedemah, ably represented the nationalist cause during the months of Nkrumah's prison ordeal. He followed Nkrumah's directive to have CPP candidates contest every office in the election. The result was a landslide. The people elected Nkrumah as a representative of Accra Central. He received the largest percentage of votes in the colony's history, 22,780 votes out of 23,122 cast.[44] Ironically, the UGCC opponent he defeated was the same Ako Adjei who had first recommended him for the leadership of the UGCC.

By nighttime on February 9, 1951, the vote count showed that the CPP had soundly defeated almost all opponents. They had won thirty-four out of thirty-eight seats in Accra and the rural areas. The CPP election victory forced the British to release Nkrumah from prison on February 12. He had spent fourteen months in prison, less than half his sentence. Vast and jubilant crowds welcomed him back to Accra. As leader of the majority party, Nkrumah assumed the title "Leader of Government." A year later the British changed the Coussey Constitution and Nkrumah assumed the title Prime Minister. From then on the British colonial governor had to consult with Nkrumah before making appointments for government offices. For the first time the British gave real powers to an African leader. The Gold Coast was not yet independent Ghana, but Nkrumah's party's electoral victory in 1951 led directly to the next package of events that brought independence.

The amended Coussey Constitution still left the prime minister with partial power. This status was only a step toward the ultimate goal of full independence. The election victory did not unify all Africans behind Nkrumah. It marked a crucial stage that would reverberate to the detriment of the country's democracy for years to come. Nkrumah accurately described the Opposition response to the CPP victory:

> The U.G.C.C. leaders never forgave me and my associates for proving the rightness of our policy of "Self-Government Now" in the results of the 1951 election. Thereafter their opposition amounted to a virtual denial of independence and a reluctance for the British to leave. They were prepared to sacrifice our national liberation if that would keep me and my colleagues out of government.[45]

They launched a secessionist movement in Ashantiland. They used their media to spread anti-Nkrumah propaganda to discredit him with the people. All of their stratagems failed. So overwhelming was the CPP victory that Danquah and the other Opposition figures knew that victory at the ballot box was permanently outside their grasp. A campaign of assassination attempts, collaboration, and subversion offered the only possibility of achieving the power they believed that a mere upstart had usurped. How and when foreign intelligence agencies recruited members of the Opposition such as Joseph Danquah and Kofi Busia is not possible to determine. Recently declassified documents omit this information on entirely blacked-out paragraphs and pages. What is certain is that during the Cold War, the standard policy of the West was to secure agents of their interests within countries that they deemed at risk of turning Communist.

Recruiting African allies who shared the Western world viewpoint that was procapitalist and antisocialist was the logical thing for Western intelligence agencies to do. Antisocialism was not the same as anti-Communism. Forms and degrees of democratic socialism had come to power in various European countries. The British Labour Party was a socialist party. The West German Social Democratic Party could more properly have been named the "Democratic Socialist Party." These parties supported New Deal reforms of the kind that President Roosevelt had initiated in the United States. They advocated a mixed economy that included the best of capitalist financial incentives and the best of socialist protections for the workers and the poor. Their ideal welfare state drew more inspiration from the ideals of Eugene Debs and George Bernard Shaw than from Marx and Lenin. None of them advocated a Soviet- or Chinese-style "Dictatorship of the Proletariat." Neither did Nkrumah. But in the former colonies, expensive welfare state reforms meant that the governments would draw money from the profits of foreign corporations and from the local merchant class. These business interests conflated socialism and Communism as one system, both of which impinged on their profit margins. These economics contributed to the permanent split in worldviews between Nkrumah and his Opposition. To overcome their hostility, Nkrumah would have had to convince them to stick to non-violently countering his political party and program as a Loyal Opposition. He failed to win them to this pledge. This marked an important failure of the Akan hero's ability to overcome obstacles. The men who first hired him to run the UGCC could not view their former employee as a legitimately elected prime minister, no matter how large and unbeatable his voting majorities. Their ever sharing an increasingly popular belief that he was Africa's political Messiah was out of the question. Danquah and Busia were from royal Ashanti lineages and the small and relatively well-to-do African elite. Nkrumah's egalitarian pronouncements could only have deepened their alienation from his government and from him personally. Even though some of the UGCC members did eventually join the CPP, Nkrumah could not produce a combination of words to convince the Danquah-Busia trend to support the CPP.

As long as Danquah and the other UGCC leaders brooded and plotted on the outer edges of power, Nkrumah and his regime was in danger. The Opposition began to foment tribal separatism in Ashantiland as a means of stopping Nkrumah's consolidation of power. They also began to stir the chiefs against Nkrumah by accusing him of usurping their hereditary powers.[46] J. B. Danquah's notions of independence were considerably different from Nkrumah's. Two items that Danquah insisted that the UGCC include in its constitution stand out. First, "that when the time came, the government of the country should pass into the hands of the people 'and their Chiefs.'" Second, "that the type of self-government I stood for was not to be outside the Commonwealth, but self-government as understood and accepted in the Statute of Westminister."[47] Some of these chiefs were direct descendants of the men who sold slaves to the British in the eighteenth and nineteenth centuries. Many had been tools of indirect rule. Turning over power from a white elite to this black elite was not Nkrumah's idea of freedom.

Nkrumah could not decolonize the minds of his conservative Opposition, because they were no longer colonized. Their minds were, by 1953, *neo*colonized. The Opposition had already decided that the country should not become independent in the way that Nkrumah envisioned. They also disdained his Pan-African dream. They wanted to continue a relationship with Britain that did not challenge either foreign political or economic domination of the country. Rather, as members of the elite, they wanted a larger share of the economy for themselves and their social class after the country received a limited version of independence. Nkrumah had read Vladimir Lenin's book *Imperialism: the Highest Stage of Capitalism*. He knew that the Opposition's form of independence was only a new form of dependency. As Lenin put it:

> Not only are there two main groups of countries, those owning countries, and the colonies themselves, but also the diverse forms of dependent countries which, politically, are independent but in fact are enmeshed in the net of financial and diplomatic dependency.[48]

Neocolonized Africans behaved as if their financial and personal interests coincided with this net of financial and diplomatic dependency because they did. The elite, had no hope of achieving their political goals without aligning themselves with foreign political and business interests. Nkrumah could have successfully united both left and right factions of Ghanaian political opinion only if he could have *de*-neocolonized the minds of his conservative opponents. This petit bourgeois minority would have had to renounce its elite social status and identify with the interests of Ghana's majority—Amilcar Cabral's *class suicide*. The obduracy of the Opposition caused Nkrumah to give up on securing their loyalty. Instead he concentrated his communicative gifts on de*colonizing* African minds across the continent.

Like previous epic African heroes, Nkrumah had successfully heard the call. He had prepared himself while a youth for his quest for the Golden Fleece. Then he succeeded, during his quest, in securing the knowledge needed to win African sovereignty. But now, during the return, the epic hero began to falter. He accepted Lenin's analyses of colonialism and imperialism. His humanism blocked him from accepting Lenin's brutal precepts of revolution.

> The dictatorship of the proletariat imposes a series of restrictions on the freedom of the oppressors, the exploiters, the capitalists. We must suppress them in order to free humanity from wage slavery, their resistance must be crushed by force; it is clear that where there is suppression, where there is violence, there is no freedom and no democracy.[49]

After the fifth attempt to assassinate Nkrumah with bullets or bombs—and the deaths of 30 innocent bystanders and the wounding of over 300—he signed the Preventive Detention Act on July 18, 1958. Nkrumah stated that the law should not alarm anybody who was not "attempting to organise violence, terror, or civil war, or who are acting as fifth columnist for some foreign power."[50] In addition to the dead bodies, Nkrumah's intelligence agents had given him reason to suspect that certain men in the Opposition were engaging in each of these behaviors. Evidence available now proves that this was a correct assessment.

Reginald Reynolds Amponsah and Modesto Apaloo were members of Parliament and leading members of the Opposition who tried to organize an anti-Nkrumah coup in 1958. A coconspirator revealed their plot to an Nkrumah loyalist. When the police went to Amponsah's house to arrest him, at 1:00 a.m., they found him in the company of Kofi Busia, Joseph Danquah, Joe Appiah, and Victor Owusu. They were the foremost Opposition figures in the country. After their arrests, throughout colonial Africa and the Western world, heaps of denunciations pummeled Nkrumah for his "dictatorial and undemocratic measures." Danquah, Busia, and the rest loudly, and sometimes eloquently, proclaimed their innocence. Nevertheless, their behavior after the 1966 coup suggests otherwise. As a unit, these men (without Danquah who died in 1965) immediately identified with the new neocolonial military regime soon after Nkrumah's overthrow.[51]

The renowned African American anthropologist and educator, St. Clair Drake (1911–1990), discovered one reason for the Preventive Detention Act's denial of a trial for detainees for up to five years. He wrote about the power of the African occult overweighing judicial authority in the Ghanaian mind during the middle years of Nkrumah's regime. He was at the University of Ghana from October 1958 to February 1961 and remembered talking for an hour to Geoffrey Bing, Ghana's attorney general. Bing explained to Drake that he had lost cases against persons who were known "plotters of political murder because his witnesses had been so terrified by 'witch doctors' that they changed their stories."[52] Drake's recollection is a reminder that Nkrumah had to battle his opponents on both natural and supernatural battlefields. This was true for most of Africa's epic heroes of the last thousand years.

Despite the strong evidence of Opposition plots to kill and overthrow him, Nkrumah did not liquidate them by force, because he was not aiming to install a "dictatorship of the proletariat." He did not want to kill, exile, and imprison the business class; he wanted them to remain loyal, peacefully contend for electoral power, and help build the country's economy. Violence against the CPP cadres and numerous deaths during repeated attempts to assassinate him caused Nkrumah to reflexively confine them, but not to kill them as Lenin, Stalin, and Mao advocated.

Nkrumah gave his famous "The Motion of Destiny" speech before the country's parliament on July 10, 1953. It was possibly the finest expression of his vision for Ghana and Africa that he gave during his entire life. He recounted the glorious civilization of the kingdom of Ghana and announced that the country would now officially take its name from that ancient empire. One section of his speech sounded as if Nkrumah directed the words specifically at the "old ideas" of Danquah and the Opposition. He highlighted ideas as the basis of the political hostilities that had begun to embroil the country. Nkrumah renounced both violence in international affairs and violence in Ghana's domestic politics. The men whose ideas kept them "trammeled in greed" shared neither his new ideas nor his passion for an economic system that was not based on greed. He correctly predicted that the future would not record such men as heroes. The true hero's loyalty to the highest humanistic principles would lead Africa to this egalitarian vision. The African Messiah would auger in a new era of Christian socialism:

> Thus may we take pride in the name of Ghana, not out of romanticism, but as an inspiration for the future . . . For we repudiate war and violence. Our battles shall be against the old ideas that keep men trammeled in their own greed; against the crass stupidities that breed hatred, fear and inhumanity. The heroes of our future will be those who can lead our people . . . into the valley of light where purpose, endeavor and determination will create that brotherhood which Christ proclaimed two thousand years ago, and about which so much is said, but so little done.[53]

Martin Luther King, Jr., would describe a similar vision and call it *The Beloved Community*. King in 1953 was two years away from beginning his life as a human rights activist. Nevertheless, Nkrumah's metaphors and Christian allusions sounded distinctly Kingian, or, rather, King's speeches sounded as if he had studied Nkrumah. One reason for this might have been that King had graduated from the Crozer Theological Seminary in Chester, Pennsylvania. When Nkrumah studied for the ministry, he worked as a counter for the Sun Shipbuilding Yard in the same city.[54] He attended and spoke in churches in this area of Pennsylvania.

He possibly picked up some of the same methodologies for moving people with metaphor that King would observe and emulate a decade later. Like Nkrumah, King did not cling to his campus. He also ventured into the black communities of Chester and Philadelphia, where he met and intermingled with the locals and attended churches where his parents' friends were ministers.

The Vision of the Bandung Conference

The next package of events in Nkrumah's life was another giant step toward his eventual destiny. The famous conference of African and Asian nations in Bandung, Indonesia (April 18–24, 1955), intensified Western fears and made an Afro-Asian power bloc a fearsome possibility. The Bandung Conference brought together the leaders of twenty-nine nations newly independent from colonialism. The conveners were Burma (now Myanmar), Ceylon (now Sri Lanka), India, and Pakistan. Nkrumah represented Ghana, and the term "spirit of Bandung" permanently entered his vocabulary. That spirit was first of all that of nonalignment. The Nonalignment Movement (NAM) was a Third Way during the Cold War. The Soviet Communists and the Western capitalists had split the world into a bipolar war between their respective ideologies. By remaining nonaligned, Africa and Asia could resist the Communists' and capitalists' coercion to follow them toward mutually assured nuclear destruction. "Decisions of the Asian-African Conference" was the official document that the participating countries agreed upon. It was harmless, in that it did "not preclude either the desirability or the need for cooperation with countries outside the region, including the investment of foreign capital." Nevertheless, recommendations five and six uplifted a vision that could only have horrified the West.

5. The Asian-African conference recommended that *collective action be taken by participating countries for stabilizing international prices* of and demand for primary commodities through bilateral and multilateral arrangements, and that as far as practicable and desirable they should adopt a unified approach on the subject in the United Nations Permanent Advisory Commission on International Commodity Trade and other international forums. [emphasis added]
6. Asian-African countries should diversify their export trade by *processing their raw materials* whenever economically feasible before export. . . . [emphasis added]

7. The Asian-African conference attached considerable importance to shipping and expressed concern that shipping lines reviewed from time to time their freight rates often to the detriment of participating countries.

It recommended a study of this problem and *collective action thereafter to put pressure* on the shipping lines to adopt a more reasonable attitude. [emphasis added][55]

The West would have found the realization of points five, six and seven alarming. Points eight and nine would have been shocking. Point eight sought to eliminate the Western banking monopolies in Asia and Africa by the formation of regional banks. Point nine stated that the "conference felt that the exchange of information on matters pertaining to oil, such as remittance of profits and taxation, might lead to the formation of a common policy." This was a call for an Asian-African oil cartel two decades before the formation of the Organization of Petroleum Exporting Countries (OPEC).

An Asian–Pan-African alliance that implemented these recommendations would have altered centuries of inequitable economic relations between Asia, Africa, and the West. Nkrumah left Bandung with his vision of a united Africa enhanced. He added to the potential Asia-Africa alliance the inclusion of Latin America in the future: "A strengthening of the Afro-Asian Solidarity Organization and the spirit of Bandung is already under way. To it, we must seek the adherence on an increasingly formal basis of our Latin American brothers."[56] His advocacy of African–Asian–Latin American solidarity would only have enhanced his image in the West as dangerous. But he went even further and stated that neocolonialism was the enemy of this unity. He gave the appearance that the Nonaligned Movement was establishing a third power in the world that would not join the Communist world, but would, like them, oppose the interests of the West.

The Western powers could logically have seen this unity as a second power bloc opposing them. To the United States and the European colonial powers, whether or not the Bandung nations sided with the Soviets in the Cold War was of secondary importance. Even without a formal friendship treaty between a coalition of Asia, Africa and Latin America, and the Soviets, their forming a third bloc outside Western hegemony removed the West from its position of world dominance. The main benefit of international white supremacy was controlling the politics, markets, and resources of Asia, Africa, and Latin America. The Spirit of Bandung was to permanently end this imbalance and alter forever the world so that the first would be last and the

last would be first. Bandung was reminiscent of the epochal call by
Dr. Belsidus in George Schuyler's "Black Empire" serials in the 1930s
to permanently end worldwide white supremacy.

Nkrumah's drive to unify Africa caused the most friction between
him and the British and later between him and the United States. All
sorts of reasons for animus for Nkrumah run through the next twenty
years of declassified documents from the British Colonial Office, and
later from the U.S. State Department and the CIA. But at the core of
what the Western powers regarded as the "Nkrumah Problem" was
Nkrumah's relentless pursuit of a unified, egalitarian Africa. The
Western media would disseminate a plethora of negative portrayals of
Nkrumah. However, behind each accusation of corruption, wasteful
spending, communist sympathies, vanity, instability, and so forth, was
a singular Western understanding and goal. They, above all else, had
to discredit Nkrumah and kill the potential of a unified Africa. After
Bandung, Pan-Africanism looked like a causal step toward the "Third
World" turning the tables and becoming the world's foremost economic and political force. Bandung meant a permanent shift in the
world balance of power from north to south and east. But Bandung
would never be possible if the West assured that the causal link to
Pan-Africanism stayed impossible.

Nkrumah's vision for Ghana and Africa never needed his trickster's
skills more than after Ghana's Independence Day, March 6, 1957. The
Western powers now understood what they could lose and what postcolonial Africa could win. Nkrumah was the chief spokesperson for
an unstoppable movement for African independence. But he
demanded more than parliamentary democracy. The West promoted
the ballot box as a new fetish that required quadrennial obeisance
from Africans to cure all their social ailments. Nkrumah declared that
political power without economic control was just neocolonialism.
True liberation would arrive only when Africa united and owned and
controlled its resources.

The West's centuries of stupendous profits sucked from the veins of
the mighty continent were now threatened by Nkrumah's dream of a
socialist Union of African States. The former colonial masters could
not placate him with bribes. Nor would he borrow from their banks
and lose independence by national debt peonage. More than parched
deserts, squalid hovels and fetid jungles were at stake, although these
were the images of Africa still peddled by the Western media. The
coordination with their governments and corporations to secure
Africa's continuing servility was uninterrupted. The Western powers

never tired of the rhetoric of democracy and freedom. These they faithfully supported, so long as democrats did not meddle with the gold and diamond mines, the rich deposits of bauxite and uranium, the fields of cacao and palm oil-bearing trees. For the West, democracy in Africa was always a tactic, not a strategy. The next decade after Ghana's independence would prove this point repeatedly. When democratically elected or politically popular leaders of liberation movements failed to serve Western interests, they were overthrown and replaced by antidemocratic dictators, whom the West embraced with loans and "aid." When antidemocratic dictators opposed Western interests (and this rarely happened), the West supported "democratic change" to rid themselves of the problem.

Nkrumah understood even before independence that where voting took place but not ownership, and, therefore, not real political control, there was no true independence. This scenario was in fact the foundation of neocolonialism. But independence brought more issues than foreign interference in Africa's internal affairs. Now all the internal contradictions within Ghana itself were exposed. The epic hero faced new challenges from all strata of his own people.

Ghana was still a dependency of the United Kingdom after 1951 and was under the suzerain power of the British Crown. Traditions and treaties limited other countries' entrée into the politics of British colonies. Independence in 1957 ended Ghana's British-dependent status. Independence placed the new country in the dangerous realm of competitive Cold War power politics. One entity that began to pay special attention to Ghana was the CIA. The CIA commissioned a comprehensive economic and political intelligence "outlook" on Ghana in 1957. It assessed that economically Ghana produced large amounts of cocoa, timber, diamonds, gold, and manganese. The country contained one-third of the world reserves for bauxite, the highly important "strategic mineral" from which aluminum is smelted.[57]

It is at this point that Max Weber's dictum comes into play: "Every charismatic leader marches on a road from a turbulently emotional life that knows no economic rationality to a slow death by suffocation under the weight of material interests."[58] The charismatic African hero must magnify his spiritual power to counter the growing challenge of adverse material forces. The CIA Intelligence Estimate described the hurdles Nkrumah had to leap over. The report stated that Nkrumah encouraged free enterprise and foreign investment. He was "attempting to fulfill demands created by the rapid transition from a subsistence to an exchange economy." Even so, Nkrumah was "extending government control over an ever-widening sector of the economy. While foreign interests (mostly British) still dominate such fields as commerce and mining, all public utilities are owned by the government which also engages in commercial banking services and owns various enterprises."[59]

These economic policies brought problems for which charismatic authority offered no answer. To maintain the colony's dependency on them, the British colonialists had educated just enough Africans to perpetuate indirect rule. They had taught relatively few Africans the types of technical and bureaucratic knowledge necessary to manage an independent government and economy. The CIA accurately assessed the result: "The growing scale of government economic operations is resulting in the operation of many public projects at a loss, due to their uneconomic nature and the lack of managerial talent."[60]

The shortage of trained and talented managers was an essential part of the uneconomic nature of the projects. Even if a project carried potential profitability, an untrained managerial force would have a difficult time developing a profit-making strategy. Here is where the hero's ambitions for his country began to surpass his people's abilities. The CIA noted that despite Nkrumah's training in Catholic and Protestant theology, "he still consults fetish oracles."[61] Nevertheless, fetishes and charisma alone could not overcome the objective realities now challenging him. Despite these problems, the CIA predicted that Nkrumah's "quasi-mystical identification with the struggle for independence is likely to preserve his popular support for at least the next year or two."[62] Nkrumah's nonalignment policy did not escape the CIA's perceptive eye. They noted it as a form of trickerism. Nkrumah was a "fanatical nationalist" who was determined "to manipulate all issues—including the conflict between the Soviet bloc and the West—to the betterment of Ghana's position."[63]

The CIA analysis took further note of Nkrumah's Pan-Africanism. It would cause him to play an increasingly larger role in continental affairs. They did not yet see Pan-Africanism—what they called "Nkrumaism"—as a mortal danger to Western interests that they would proclaim it four years later in their 1960 "National Intelligence Estimate" of Ghana. In 1957 it was not Pan-Africanism that would change Africa, but the new epoch brought by Ghana's independence itself. This they accepted fatalistically. "The very fact of Ghana's existence heightens the pressures for independence in other African

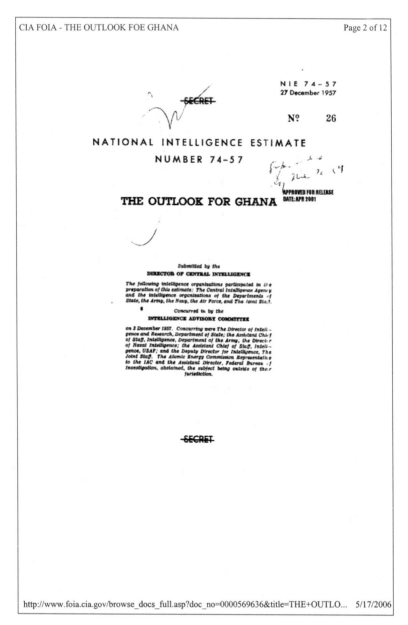

Figure 10   CIA FOIA Document – National Intelligence Estimate Number 74–57.

territories."[64] This truth would make Ghana the immediate target of vengeful colonial forces that viewed its existence as a threat to their futures in Africa. But the CIA correctly predicted that the very nationalism that Nkrumah had unleashed on the continent would militate against his Pan-African dream. The rank-and-file workers and farmers in the nationalist movements "acclaim Nkrumah's achievements." But the elite "leaders—especially in nearby West African areas—are suspicious of the possible effects of his influence on their countries."[65]

Nkrumah had outorganized the Danquah-Busia nexus of neocolonized elitists in Ghana. They had no chance of constitutionally assuming the country's leadership, because the people had repeatedly rejected them overwhelmingly at the ballot box. Members of their neocolonized social class in nearby states such as Togo and Ivory Coast had observed their defeat. When members of the African merchant class assumed power in these countries, they resolved that despite the popularity of full Nkrumah-style independence, they would not spend their wealth on welfare state reforms. Nor would they allow the uncontested growth of Pan-African consciousness within their countries. In the coming decades, Africa's corrupt ruling merchant and military petite bourgeoisie would rarely display Nkrumah's merciful humanism against their enemies. The West supported their murderous suppression of socialists and Pan-Africanists as necessary to win the Cold War. The 1957 CIA report included Nkrumah's nonalignment as a further threat. He increasingly pursued a mixed capitalist/socialist economy, with the socialist side beckoning the rest of Africa toward a radical break from Western ideological domination.

The Reverend and the Osagyefo: Highways across the Diaspora

That March midnight in 1957, Martin Luther King, Jr., stood on Accra's Polo Grounds, along with half a million other weeping and cheering people, when Nkrumah declared Ghanaian independence. The pastor of Abyssinian Baptist Church, Adam Clayton Powell, Jr., stood on King's right, beside United Nations Deputy Secretary Ralph Bunche. Nkrumah had met Bunche while visiting Howard University when he was a student in the United States and Bunche was an esteemed professor there. The strongly pro-Africa black Congressman from Detroit, Charles Diggs, stood on King's left. Nearby was Horace Mann Bond, the first black president of Lincoln University; Dr. Mordecai

Johnson, the president of Howard University; and long-time black activist, union leader, and socialist A. Phillip Randolph. Vice President Richard Nixon also shared the privileged space near the front.[66] Grand Master John W. Dobbs of Georgia represented Prince Hall Freemasonry. He later described with pride his meeting with Nkrumah, his brother Master Mason.[67]

For Martin Luther King, Jr., the ceremony brought an epiphany. He stood on free African soil less than four months after the terrifying yet exhilarating saga of leading and winning the victory of the Montgomery, Alabama, bus boycott. Mrs. Rosa Parks had launched the battle that would grow to a protracted campaign for black civil and human rights. But the huge phenomenon of the civil rights movement was all ahead of King this night. All he knew was that he had led the defeat of the fearsome forces of Jim Crow in one southern city. The U.S. Supreme Court had struck down segregated seating in public accommodations. That one victory still did not signal that anything earth-shattering had occurred in the black world. But to King, the raising of Ghana's red, gold, and green flag was "the symbol of a new age coming into being."[68] Nkrumah also had reached across the Atlantic into the diaspora when he placed the black star in the center of the flag. This was Marcus Garvey's symbol of the worldwide unity of African peoples.

Tears streamed down King's face while he watched Africans for the first time in modern history take control of their country. More impressive than anything else for him was Nkrumah and his fellow ministers and members of Parliament walking onto the stage wearing their prison caps. Nkrumah also wore his prison coat. "Often the path to freedom will carry you through prison," King concluded.[69] He summed up the international significance of Ghana's independence. It "would give impetus to oppressed people all over the world." And it "would become a symbol of hope for hundreds and thousands of oppressed peoples all over the world."[70] For King, personally, Ghana's birth renewed his belief in the inexorable victory of the people who resist injustice. It made him more certain that "somehow the universe itself is on the side of freedom and justice. This gave new hope to me in the struggle for freedom."[71] King here placed himself in the mode of premodern Africa and spoke of the universe—not of God—as a living, pantheistic entity. King's universe was alive and thinking. It consciously chose to support some causes and to oppose others. King, later that year, asserted that Ghana's birth would influence the situation in the American South. And he called these words of Nkrumah a great statement: "I prefer self-government with danger, to servitude with tranquility."[72]

Both King and Nkrumah had discovered the power of nonviolent Gandhian activism. Nkrumah had won a country with it; King would return home to try to win his people civil and human rights. After Ghana's independence, King would prefer to quest for black freedom in danger and would, like Nkrumah before independence, eschew the tranquilities of the diversionary offerings of personal wealth and official status. But the deepest impressions that Nkrumah made on King are perhaps most visible in King's frequent use of language that sounded similar if not identical to Nkrumah's vocabulary. On May 17, 1956, soon after he returned to the United States from Ghana, he spoke at the Cathedral of St. John the Divine in New York. He titled his sermon "The Death of Evil Upon the Seashores." Africa was on his mind. "The great struggle of the Twentieth Century has been between the exploited masses questing for freedom and the colonial powers seeking to maintain their domination."[73]

Later that year in Montgomery, Alabama, he delivered an address titled "Facing the Challenge of a New Age." He drew unmistakable parallels between Africa and black America. For centuries African peoples had been "dominated politically, exploited economically, segregated and humiliated . . . But there comes a time when people get tired." The people have freed themselves from "the Egypt of imperialism and colonialism."[74] He would for the rest of his life link these two words, "imperialism and colonialism," in his speeches and sermons just as Nkrumah did.

Both King and Nkrumah were ordained Christian ministers. The viewpoints of the two men converged most profoundly over the question of Marxism and socialism. Nkrumah had declared himself a nondenominational Christian and a Marxist socialist. "I have not found any contradiction between the two," he wrote.[75] He sought to blend two seemingly contradictory philosophies in a vision that would take the best from each. His vision would perhaps be best represented by the democratic socialist systems today in Norway and Sweden.

King had already come to similar conclusions long before meeting Nkrumah. He was a student at Crozer Seminary in 1951 when he wrote a criticism of the "fallacy" in Marxism, but accepted what he deemed true in Marxism. He criticized capitalism for failing to meet the needs of the masses.[76] The Socialist Party journal *Socialist Call* published at least two of King's speeches during the 1950s. He also made statements supporting democratic socialism and remained critical of capitalism throughout his life. According to his friends, he made it clear in private that "he considered himself what he termed a Marxist."[77] Evidently, like Nkrumah, he saw no contradiction between Marxism and his Christianity. King, consistently, during the thirteen years of his life on the public stage, referred to the *intrinsic worth* of the human being. He abhorred atheistic communism, but viewed socialism as a counter to the capitalist concept that the profit motive and market forces should rule societies, even to the detriment of persons whom Jesus referred to as "the least of these." For him the Malthusian and social Darwinist side of capitalism placed profit as a higher good than the intrinsic worth of the human being:

> An intelligent approach to the problems of poverty and racism will cause us to see that the words of the Psalmist—"The earth is the Lord's and the fullness thereof"—are a judgement upon our use and abuse of the wealth and resources with which we have been endowed . . . True compassion is more than flinging a coin to a beggar; it understands that an edifice which produces beggars needs restructuring.[78]

The planet's resources are not the province of a handful of profiteers. They are the divine provision for all of humanity. The distribution of wealth and resources as the Lord intended required restructuring the social edifice. Unavoidably, King would have kept abreast of events in Nkrumah's Ghana as Nkrumah became Africa's preeminent voice for the social restructuring that King advocated. Similarly, no matter how busy his schedule, Nkrumah could not have missed observing King's triumphs and travails as black America's foremost champion of civil and human rights. For these two men the Atlantic served as a highway and not a barrier between Africa and black America.

Like Nkrumah, King had entered the world arena in the mode of the African epic hero whose calling is to overturn society and bring a new epoch. His vehicle would be the social gospel. Humanity would realize his highest vision for a new society through the Beloved Community. This was a society where greed did not supersede need and people focused more on making a life than on making a living. The convergence of the fundamental philosophies of the African and the African American hero presaged the twenty-first century Black Atlantic crosscurrents of ideas when the cyber age advanced Pan-Africanism toward Black Globalism.

Independence: The End of the Beginning and the Beginning of the End

The Kenyan writer Okot p'Bitek captured both the euphoria and the dangers in the African attitude toward *uhuru,* postcolonial freedom.

> Did someone tell you
> That on the morning of uhuru
> The dew on the grass
> Along the village pathways
> Would turn into gold
> That the leaves
> Would become banknotes
> And be scattered by the wind
> Among the villagers?[1]

Ghanaians now expected Nkrumah to perform this alchemy because he had amazingly vanquished the British Empire. Ghanaians looked forward to Nkrumah, that is, independence, transforming their lives of dirt and sweat into lives of gold and gin, or silver and beer at the least. The prime minister was an Nzima, after all. Had not the Akan God, *Onyame,* endowed Nzimas with the mystic gift of acquiring wealth easily? Once man has turned into Messiah, he cannot turn back into man. And so in the heady days following independence, Ghana's people expected the Messiah to bring manna from heaven. Ghana needed a miracle to work its way out of the debilitating economic webs spun by foreign domination. Nkrumah had only a limited amount of time before his charisma would "suffocate under the weight of material interests," as Max Weber predicted. Colonialism was a system that extracted raw materials like cocoa from Ghana but never built a factory for making chocolate. It left the country dependent on this single cash crop for its national income.[2] This left Ghana dependent on factors totally outside its own control. The foreign chocolate makers in the United States and Europe set the prices. They maintained stocks to dump on the market and force down prices at will. Western consumers' cravings also influenced prices. They purchased items like chocolate depending on the fluctuations of their own economic lives. When their countries' economies turned downward, the price of chocolate had to follow. Add to this quandary the fact that Ghana was a marketplace for Britain's high-priced manufactured goods and one can readily see why Nkrumah placed so much emphasis on pulling Ghana out of this iniquitous economic predicament.

Other problems immediately became evident and forced Nkrumah to make perilous compromises:

> The first problem in Ghana at the time of independence was to make use of our pitifully small stock of professional and technical experts. Whatever their political views they had to be utilized to the full in the interest of the newly emerged Ghana State. From the start I had to bring not only into my cabinet but had to appoint to important posts in the judiciary, the civil service and the universities, individuals who had been active opponents of the Party in colonial days.[3]

The scholar St. Clair Drake assessed Nkrumah's cabinet the year before independence. He concluded that every one of them had a Western orientation.[4] A year later Nkrumah had not changed the political makeup of his cabinet, because he could not. His left-wing critics routinely overlooked the actual circumstances in which he functioned when they attacked his slow pace toward the socialist revolution that they deemed Ghana needed.[5] What they did not understand was that Nkrumah could not make a revolution without revolutionaries. The literacy level of the people and the traditional political conservatism of the chiefs and the educated black elite and merchants left him few supporters to rely on. Other left-wing critics denounced Nkrumah for resorting to "undemocratic methods" when he imprisoned Danquah and other Opposition members following assassination attempts against him and attacks on CPP cadres in Ashanti territory.[6] They did not know what we know now: declassified British and American government files reveal the unseen hands of foreign subversives colluding against and lurking over Ghana, plotting, manipulating, and buying Ghanaians as traitorous slaves of their interests.

Appointing his enemies to high public office did not make them allies. These appointments moved closer to him persons who wanted his government to fail and, eventually, wanted him to die or go into exile. The pool of educated persons in Ghana was so small that

Nkrumah had no choice but to rely on them. In 1954 only 14 percent of the members of Ghana's national legislature held a college degree. Only 42 percent had some secondary schooling, while 44 percent had attended only elementary school.[7]

The main danger was the army and the police. Nkrumah recognized the hazards but from the beginning the circumstances wedged him into a perilous corner. He would later assess the problem. "I could have dismissed many of the higher police officers about whose loyalty I had doubts. But whom could I have put in their place?"[8] Here is where Nkrumah's new environment acted upon his judgment. As a student in the United States, an activist in England, and a nationalist in the Gold Coast colony, Nkrumah's incoming stimuli were not too overwhelming for his intuitive and intellectual filters to make balanced judgments about which direction to take. As the prime minister of his country, however, his new milieu presented a never-ending welter of sages and genies. His inability to determine which voices were, in the African epic tradition, "divinely-sent" with the correct advice indicated his lack of ability to carry out his heroic mission. His confidante, Genoveva Marais, offered a personally observed perspective on the hero's limitation:

> Because of his impatience to get things done quickly he was liable to put his schemes into effect perhaps too soon. Most people flattered him and he enjoyed their flattery, as perhaps is natural; but it blinded him to the more constructive advice others might offer.[9]

Some advisers wanted him to behave more radically and ruthlessly than his temperament allowed. Leftists offered a solution to the problem of an elite army officered by British holdovers: sack the Brits and abolish the army. They wanted him to organize an "African Legion," a people's militia of armed workers and farmers, in its place.[10] They presumed that Nkrumah was a Communist like Castro and Mao, even though he had consistently described himself as a Christian Socialist. They also did not take into account that Cuba and China had revolutionary vanguard parties full of committed Reds who educated and politically guided the people's militias at all levels. Ghana had too few literate citizens with revolutionary knowledge to make such a policy possible. In hindsight, the army's role in the coming disasters, first, for Congo's Prime Minister Patrice Lumumba, and, later, for Nkrumah, might lead some persons to believe that the leftist solution for the army was correct. But we need look no further than Marxist-Leninist Ethiopia in the 1970s to see what happened when Africans used the repressive Leninist and Maoist modus operandi of state terror. Nkrumah let his opponents live. Although he acceded to political pressures that demanded the Preventive Detention Act, his humanist principles opposed the death penalty for even the men who repeatedly attempted to assassinate him.

On the other hand, in the 1970s, Ethiopia's Marxist-Leninist leader, Mengistu Haile Mariam, created an organ of institutionalized terror called the *Dergue* (Committee). Had Nkrumah turned to violent repression, his Red Terror would have swallowed up thousands of Ghanaians in a raping, murdering, torturing gulag, as in 1970s Ethiopia.[11] A Ghanaian *Dergue* would have kept a man in power, but that man would not have been Nkrumah. He would no longer have been the Christian Socialist and humanist Nkrumah who believed what he wrote in *Consciencism*. So instead of repression, he attempted to reason with the military and to appeal to their patriotism and idealism. On May 18, 1961, he addressed the cadets of the Ghana Military Academy. His talk was titled "Politics Are Not for Soldiers." Nkrumah told the cadets that it was not their duty as soldiers to interfere in any way with Ghana's political affairs. Their role was not to criticize the government, but to serve it and the Ghanaian people loyally. He concluded by telling them that as military officers, their loyalty should be first to the government and to fellow soldiers. But if "ever there is any conflict, it is your self interest which must be sacrificed."[12] The somewhat naive character of these remarks exhibit either an incomplete understanding of Marxist-Leninism or a complete disregard of Leninist teachings of the state. These words show that Nkrumah was far, far away from being the doctrinaire Communist that some suspected. A fundamental tenet of the Marxist-Leninist faith was that the military and the police were political institutions by their very nature. The Marxist-Leninist considered influencing the military's politics to the left to be of primary importance, not idealistically denying that military life is political.

Nkrumah was fundamentally an idealist who adhered unflinchingly, during his years in power, to certain lofty principles. He acted as if he believed that his using Leninist means would destroy the Afrotopian beauty of his idealistic ends:

> The socialism of a liberated territory is subject to a number of principles if independence is not to be alienated from the people. When socialism is true to its purpose, it seeks a connection with the egalitarian and humanist past of the people before their social evolution was

ravaged by colonialism; it reclaims the psychology of the people, eras-
ing the "colonial mentality" from it; and it resolutely defends the independence and security of the people.[13]

Liberation, nonalienation, egalitarianism, humanism, independence, and security—these were ends that Nkrumah knew could be
destroyed by using the wrong means. (How "egalitarian" precolonial
Africa actually was is a whole other issue that is not the province of
this study.) He could no more have turned to terror and remained
Nkrumah, than Martin Luther King, Jr., could have turned to violence
and remained Dr. King. A *Dergue* would have transformed Nkrumah
into a Stalin impersonator.[14] He would have been a Stalinist voodoo
zombie, with a spiritually dead heart, acting under the reincarnated
will of the totalitarian monster.

Not taking the leftists' advice to abolish the army secured his fate,
however. The CIA documents show their knowledge in February
1965, exactly one year before the coup, that "plotting is actively
underway to oust Nkrumah." The CIA noted that only the army
could successfully oust him, because it was "one of the few power
groups not yet under party control."[15]

Because he neither politically indoctrinated the army nor abolished
it, Nkrumah lost his presidency. On the other hand, Ethiopia's
Colonel Mengistu Haile Mariam took the leftists' advice and his name
has died while his heart is still beating. Addis Ababa contains no
memorials honoring Mengistu's years in power. He presently resides
in Zimbabwe. Ethiopia has tried and convicted him in absentia for
genocide, homicide, and war crimes.[16] Nkrumah, in contrast,
remained true to his own path. His splendid memorial in Accra sym-
bolizes the love that Africans, at home and abroad, have for him. Like
Martin Luther King, Jr., his stalwartness for his humanist principles
has made him immortal.

Rather than purge the army and police, Nkrumah blamed the colonial education system for why so few Ghanaians could read or write.
He responded by proclaiming free public education for all Ghanaian
youths through their third year of secondary school. He included in
this literacy training political education in Nkrumaism. Moreover, he
mobilized Ghana's women. They had always been the backbone of his
movement. Women had hidden him from the police during the early
days of the independence movement and women had spread his mes-
sages through the markets. On July 18, 1960, he gave the opening
address to an "All-Ghana Conference of Women." He praised them

for their fervent support of the cause of Ghanaian nationalism. Then he linked their full liberation with the freedom and unification of Africa. Women had fought side by side with men in Ghana to hoist high the red, green, and gold banner of freedom. They were not second to men but rather their equals. They would continue in this role until all of Africa was free.[17] He appointed women to important posts, elevating them to become directors of corporations, pilots, members of parliament, government ministers, and graduates of Nkrumah's political party school.[18]

Despite all of his socialist pronouncements, reality dictated that he pursue a cautious economic path. By 1961 he still had to warn against left-wing socialist speechifying that was unsuited for Ghana's postcolonial economy. He could not make socialism without industry in a primarily agrarian economy. Nor was it practicable for him to press the issue with a cabinet and political party full of capitalists:

> At this juncture, Ghana is not a socialist state. Not only do the people as yet not own all the means of production and distribution, but we have still to lay the actual foundations upon which socialism can be built, namely, the complete industrialization of our country. All talk of socialism, of economic and social reconstruction, is just empty words if we do not seriously address ourselves to the question of basic industrialization and agricultural revolution of our country, just as much as we must concentrate on our socialist education.[19]

Max Weber's clock was ticking. Nkrumah had to educate a generation to produce the Pan-African revolutionaries who would carry forward the dreams of Du Bois, Padmore, Garvey, and himself. By 1963 Ghana was spending a larger percentage of its gross national product on education than any other nation in the world. Nkrumah was making a revolution in education.[20] Pending mass education, he still urgently had to hold his people's loyalty and attention. His newspaper echoed in print the method CPP cadres used for this purpose:

> [Nkrumaism is] the highest form of Christianity . . . in an age of greed and hypocrisy which teaches that you must remove all these root causes of hate and jealousy among haves and have-nots in order to make it humanly possible to "love one's neighbor as one's self" in a more enduring way.[21]

Sam Nyako remembered his trip with other Young Pioneers to see Nkrumah in his office. "Nkrumah had a halo around him like Jesus," he said. "Everything that Nkrumah did was the best. He dressed better, talked better, looked better, fought the white man better. . . . Man, when I was a boy wasn't anybody better than Osagyefo Kwame Nkrumah."[22] Belief in Nkrumah's messianic mission and seeing signs of that divinity were, evidently, interrelated.

The ideals of the revolution were the ideals of the Bible that the new, radiant Messiah had come to earth to implement. The Opposition and the Western media might periodically denounce the Osagyefo for his Marxist-Leninist leanings. Nevertheless, he worked daily to realize in Ghana what Martin Luther King, Jr., described in the United States as the Beloved Community.

Nkrumah, Lumumba, and the Assassination of Pan-Africanism

Nkrumah prepared for a future Africa free of Western economic and political domination. The West was watching, plotting, assuring that they and not he would construct Africa's future. The next package of events in the life of the hero involved challenges that he would have had to meet and outmaneuver if he were to achieve his revolutionary goals. Sages at different stages of the hero's life bring advice to assist him to avoid disaster. When he fails to heed this advice, he loses divine favor and can lose his head.

Nkrumah enjoyed relatively good relations with the United States until the two countries conflicted over the fate of Patrice Lumumba and the Congo in 1960. A full review of the Lumumba tragedy, from which stemmed the ongoing tragedy of the Congo, is beyond the parameters of this study. A brief review is necessary, however, to contextualize Lumumba and the Congo as they relate to the life of Nkrumah.

Nkrumah hosted representatives from sixty-two nationalist organizations for an "All-African People's Conference" in Accra in December 1958. It was like a Bandung Conference with mainly Africans attending. Congo was not yet independent. Patrice Lumumba was its leading nationalist figure. His experience in Accra of the fellowship of African nationalists and his exposure to Nkrumah's Pan-Africanist ideas inspired him from then on to talk about Pan-African unity, as did Nkrumah. He spoke at the Accra Conference with words familiar to every Pan-Africanist. "We are particularly happy to see that this conference has set as its objective the struggle against all the internal and external factors standing in the way of the emancipation of our respective countries and the unification of Africa." He concluded by condemning the two enemies of Africa in the order that Rev. Martin Luther King, Jr., continually denounced them after he left Ghana. "Down with colonialism and imperialism!" Lumumba exclaimed.[23] The CIA was present and recording the event.

Lumumba also spoke at the University of Nigeria in Ibadan in March 1959. At the closing session of an international seminar organized by the Congress for the Freedom of Culture, he reiterated his allegiance to Africa's Pan-African future. He urged African leaders to "get to know each other and draw closer together in order to create that union that is indispensable for the consolidation of African unity."[24] Furthermore, he added, "African solidarity must take concrete form in facts and acts. We must form a bloc in order to demonstrate our brotherhood to the world."[25] Lumumba's use of the term "bloc" would reinforce fears in the West of a unified Africa creating another oppositional power center like the Eastern bloc. Lumumba's public statements are important for understanding how the United States came to view such a mild-mannered nationalist as dangerous.[26]

In the fateful month of August in 1960, Lumumba creatively conflated two of Nkrumah's main ideas. "The African personality must express itself. That is what our positive neutralism means."[27] The African personality would return to the decolonized African mind. These New Africans would have to maintain their personal and political autonomy by nonalignment and independence from both the Eastern and Western blocs.

The Democratic Republic of the Congo was (and still is) blessed with some of the world's most mineral-rich land. According to the *CIA World Factbook*, the country is one-fourth the size of the United States and is rich in gold, coltan (the mineral for making capacitors), cobalt, copper, niobium, tantalum, petroleum, industrial and gem diamonds, silver, zinc, manganese, tin, coal, hydropower, and timber. Plus, it holds the world's greatest deposits of uranium. This, especially, was a prize that East and West vied for during the height of the Cold War nuclear arms race.

Congo became independent on June 30, 1960. Nine days later Nkrumah and Lumumba signed a secret agreement that committed both countries to a "Union of African States." The agreement stipulated a republican form of government within a federal framework. This single government would be responsible for the foreign affairs, defense, common currency, and economic planning and development

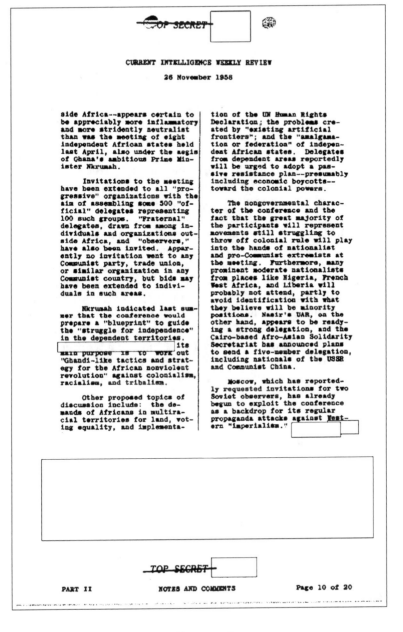

CURRENT INTELLIGENCE WEEKLY REVIEW

26 November 1958

side Africa--appears certain to be appreciably more inflammatory and more stridently neutralist than was the meeting of eight independent African states held last April, also under the aegis of Ghana's ambitious Prime Minister Nkrumah.

Invitations to the meeting have been extended to all "progressive" organizations with the aim of assembling some 500 "official" delegates representing 100 such groups. "Fraternal" delegates, drawn from among individuals and organizations outside Africa, and "observers," have also been invited. Apparently no invitation went to any Communist party, trade union, or similar organization in any Communist country, but bids may have been extended to individuals in such areas.

Nkrumah indicated last summer that the conference would prepare a "blueprint" to guide the "struggle for independence" in the dependent territories. its main purpose is to work out "Ghandi-like tactics and strategy for the African nonviolent revolution" against colonialism, racialism, and tribalism.

Other proposed topics of discussion include: the demands of Africans in multiracial territories for land, voting equality, and implementation of the UN Human Rights Declaration; the problems created by "existing artificial frontiers"; and the "amalgamation or federation" of independent African states. Delegates from dependent areas reportedly will be urged to adopt a passive resistance plan--presumably including economic boycotts--toward the colonial powers.

The nongovernmental character of the conference and the fact that the great majority of the participants will represent movements still struggling to throw off colonial rule will play into the hands of nationalist and pro-Communist extremists at the meeting. Furthermore, many prominent moderate nationalists from places like Nigeria, French West Africa, and Liberia will probably not attend, partly to avoid identification with what they believe will be minority positions. Nasir's UAR, on the other hand, appears to be readying a strong delegation, and the Cairo-based Afro-Asian Solidarity Secretariat has announced plans to send a five-member delegation, including nationals of the USSR and Communist China.

Moscow, which has reportedly requested invitations for two Soviet observers, has already begun to exploit the conference as a backdrop for its regular propaganda attacks against Western "imperialism."

Figure 11   "Current Intelligence Weekly Review."

of both countries.[28] A giant step toward unifying the entire continent would have been achieved had Congo and Ghana been able to implement this treaty. Guinea, certainly, and Mali, likely, would have joined Ghana and Congo. Joining the Union of African States would have been on the agendas of all of the African liberation movements still battling colonialism. They would have had the choice of joining the union upon independence or staying outside it. National liberation and Pan-Africanism together were a powerfully inspirational force in the 1960s. With Congo on board, and the union seeking joint or sole ownership of Congo's stupendous wealth from Western corporations, the union would also come closer to true independence than any postcolonial African country could hope for alone. For the West, the best way to stop this continental unification was to ensure that the Congo would not even accomplish national unity. Nkrumah had to quell a separatist movement of the Ashanti in the heart of Ghana. Eleven days after Congo's independence, Katanga, the most mineral-laden province in the Congo, seceded from the country.[29] The Belgians sent in their soldiers and duplicitously assured the world that they had arrived only to ensure the safety of the lives and property of the Belgian citizens. The Katangan elite, under Moise Tsombe, sought and received arms and other material support from the Belgian soldiers.[30] Lumumba asked the United States government for assistance to maintain his democratically elected government and received none.[31] The United Nations passed resolutions requesting the withdrawal of Belgian troops, but UN Secretary-General Dag Hammarskjold vacillated instead of doing anything to enforce the resolutions.

Lumumba's desperation to keep his young nation together caused him to make a desperate request for military equipment and advisers from the Soviet Union. The Soviets sent him trucks, weapons, planes, and military advisers. This was the first time that the Soviets had sought to use force to alter Africa's future. This alarmed the White House. Congo's strategic minerals were so important to the West that President Eisenhower and his advisers believed that losing the country would shift the balance of power in the whole world.[32] Lumumba had never declared himself a Communist. He did not advocate Communism, nor did he seek to form a Congolese Communist Party, which was a doctrinal prerequisite for establishing a Soviet-style dictatorship of the proletariat. Nevertheless, on July 21, 1960, CIA director Allen Dulles declared to the National Security Council (NSC) that Lumumba was in the employ of the Soviet Union. He was "a Castro or worse."[33] On August 18, a CIA officer in Leopoldville, Congo, cabled CIA headquarters in Washington:

EMBASSY AND STATION BELIEVE CONGO EXPERIENCING CLASSIC COMMUNIST EFFORT TAKEOVER GOVERNMENT . . . WHETHER OR NOT LUMUMBA ACTUALLY IS COMMIE OR IS PLAYING COMMIE GAME TO ASSIST HIS SOLIDIFYING POWER . . . THERE MAY BE LITTLE TIME LEFT IN WHICH TO TAKE ACTION TO PREVENT ANOTHER CUBA.[34]

The fear that a black Fidel Castro would run one of the most mineral-rich countries in the world and form a Pan-African power bloc with Ghana and Guinea generated strong currents of Cold War paranoia throughout the national security establishment. The 1975 Senate Intelligence Committee testimony of NSC member Robert Johnson suggests that Dulles conveyed the cabled Congo information to President Eisenhower on the same day he received it. Johnson took notes during the August 18, 1960, NSC meeting. He recalled seeing President Eisenhower turn to Dulles "in the full hearing of all those in attendance and saying something to the effect that Lumumba should be eliminated. . . . There was a stunned silence for about 15 seconds and the meeting continued."[35]

On August 26, Allen Dulles signed a cable to the Leopoldville, Congo, CIA station chief, stating that Lumumba's "REMOVAL MUST BE AN URGENT AND PRIME OBJECTIVE."[36] But Lumumba refused to surrender or die easily. Bronson Tweedy was the head of the CIA Africa Division. He complained in a cable to Leopoldville on September 13 that "LUMUMBA'S TALENTS AND DYNAMISM APPEAR OVERRIDING FACTORS IN REESTABLISHING HIS POSITION, EACH TIME IT SEEMS HALF LOST. IN OTHER WORDS, EACH TIME LUMUMBA HAS CHANCE HAVE LAST WORD HE CAN SWAY THINGS HIS WAY."[37]

Men whose media portrayed their government as the world's number one purveyor of democracy refrained from using the word "popular" when discussing Lumumba's resilience. For if the Congo's legitimately elected leader was popular, then they were the ones thwarting democracy to establish a dictatorship and not the Communists. Nkrumah never read the following telegram from the American embassy in Leopoldville to the State Department in Washington, but surely he sensed his Pan-African dream slipping out of reach with each mounting danger to Lumumba's government.

EVIDENCE HAS STEADILY ACCUMULATED THAT GHANA, GUINEA, AND THE UAR [the short-lived Egypt–Syria Union] HAVE BEEN PUTTING CONTINUOUS AND MOUNTING PRESSURES [for the] REESTABLISHMENT OF STATUS QUO ANTE LUMUMBA . . . I BELIEVE THIS MOVE SPARKPLUGGED BY NKRUMAH WHO CLINGS TO DREAM OF GHANA-GUINEA-CONGO UNION AS STEPPING STONE TO NKRUMIZATION OF AFRICA. IF LUMUMBA IS OUT OF CONGO, SO IS THAT PART OF DREAM.[38]

The "Nkrumization" of Africa, of course, was the Union of African States. Interestingly, U.S. government representatives viewed thwarting this dream as their specific duty. Only Lumumba's removal would satisfy their fears of the revival of the dream. Nkrumah eventually sent troops to Congo to help Lumumba. They were under the command of British holdovers and some of the Ghanaian officers who would eventually overthrow his own government.[39] The officers were unsympathetic to Lumumba's plight and became tools used by the United Nations to actually sabotage Lumumba's return to power. Their betrayal of Nkrumah's wishes in Congo was the first repercussion of his refusal to take the leftists' advice to abolish the old army.

Larry Devlin was the CIA station chief in Leopoldville. In an interview with the BBC in the year 2000, he recalled what happened next. The CIA headquarters had instructed him to await the arrival of "Joe from Paris." Devlin said, "I recognized him as he walked towards my car, but when he told me what they wanted done I was totally, totally taken aback." Joe from Paris was actually the CIA's chief technical officer, Dr. Sidney Gottlieb. He gave Devlin a tube of poisoned toothpaste, with instructions to get the toothpaste into Lumumba's bathroom.[40]

Before Devlin could carry out the "covert action," the troops of Joseph Mobutu had captured Lumumba. They brutally beat him and fed him a banana a day before flying him to Katanga, the stronghold of his secessionist enemies. After days of more brutality, a Belgian firing squad shot him to death on January 17, 1961. The accumulated evidence suggests that the Belgians carried out the final act, but the United States knew it was going to happen and not only did nothing to prevent it, but actively encouraged it.[41] What followed in the West was the notorious but successful Big Lie: Western governments seeded their private media with defamatory images of Lumumba as a Communist stooge and a dangerous racist dictator. They successfully tested the formula they would repeat to defame Nkrumah five years later.

Heroes are heroic because they can overcome challenges that other, "normal" people cannot. Nkrumah titled his book about the Lumumba tragedy *Challenge of the Congo*. He failed to overcome this challenge. Lumumba lost his life, and, accordingly, Nkrumah lost a degree of his heroic stature. The end of Lumumba marked the beginning of the end for Nkrumah's presidency. As the State Department wanted, Lumumba's death also ruined the chances of Africa beginning to unite in the 1960s. The conspiring Western powers fought and defeated the challenge of Pan-Africanism. In the history of the African epic hero, victory against powerful opponents is never assured. What is certain is that the hero must fight. He is compelled by forces mightier than himself to fight for the right and to attempt to vanquish the wrong. This does not mean that all of the evil that wrong represents might not triumph, at least in the short run.

In the 1950s and 1960s Nkrumah had deeply touched the lives of three great black heroes—Martin Luther King, Jr., Patrice Lumumba, and Malcolm X. When Malcolm X visited Ghana in May 1964, he spoke before parliament and to students at several colleges. He met Nkrumah in his office and remembered, "We agreed that Pan Africanism was the key also to the problems of those of African heritage."[42] During his ten remaining months of life, Malcolm X would recall this meeting with Nkrumah and advocate Pan-Africanism. His founding the Organization of Afro-American Unity was a homage to Nkrumah's central role in founding the Organization of African Unity. He would be the second hero to join Nkrumah's cause to die by gunfire. King would be the third.

By the early 1960s, Nkrumah had avoided several assassination attempts in which foreign enemies were certainly complicit. He had also evaded coup attempts that were discovered or that fizzled outside his knowledge. But the murder of his friend Lumumba affected him traumatically. Just when he came under the intensified focus of the CIA lens, he fearlessly turned his voice and his pen most compellingly against the West.

Without Congo, and with other African independence leaders too beleaguered by local problems, too corrupt, too intimidated, or too conservative to support Pan-Africanism, realization of his great dream must have felt farther away than ever. Four years after Lumumba's death, desperate to revive the Pan-African movement, needing to loudly shout obvious truths to the whole world, vengeful at the West for murdering the beloved Lumumba, all of these factors must have motivated him now. He threw caution to the wind in October 1965, and published

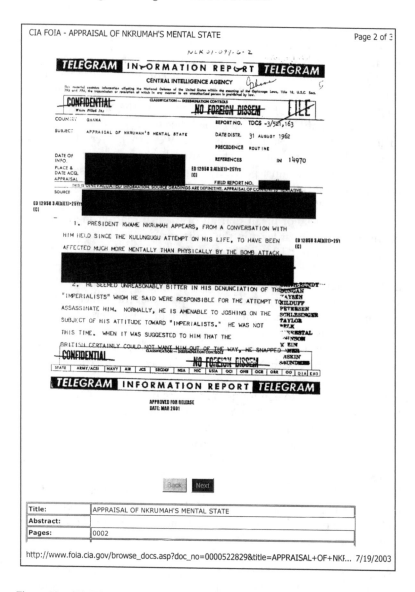

Figure 12   CIA FOIA "Appraisal of Nkrumah's Mental State."

Neocolonialism: The Last Stage of Imperialism. This book immediately brought an aggressively hostile reaction from the United States. On November 18, U.S. assistant secretary of state G. Mennen Williams delivered a "stern oral protest" to Ghana's Ambassador Ribeiro in

Washington.[43] The State Department sent a telegram about the book to all U.S. embassies in Africa. The telegram stated that Nkrumah had given copies to African chiefs of state attending the Organization of African Unity conference in Accra. "BOOK CONTAINS UNMISTAK-ABLE HOSTILE CHARGES AGAINST USG [United States Government] MOTIVES, ACTIONS, AND INTENTIONS AND IS CLEAR AND COMPREHENSIVE STATEMENT OF NKRUMAH'S FUNDAMENTAL ANTI-WESTERN, ANTI-US BIAS." The telegram stated further that Ghana had been informed that the book's "PROVOCATIVE AND ANTI-AMERICAN TONE ARE 'DEEPLY DISTURBING AND OFFENSIVE' TO USG."[44]

The next State Department documents reported that Assistant Secretary Williams issued a threat to Ghana's Ambassador Ribeiro. Punitive consequences would be forthcoming for Ghana that would "undoubtedly become evident in due course."[45] Due course was only two days, because on November 20, 1965, the United States officially informed Nkrumah that it had turned down his request for $100 million in surplus food. The documents again threatened Ghana with additional punitive measures.[46] Two months later the CIA files reveal their knowledge, if not their complicity, in the organizing of both a plan to assassinate Nkrumah and to overthrow his regime.

Nkrumah had written the book despite receiving previous advice from one of his sages, George Padmore, against being "too outspoken" when criticizing the Big Powers.[47] C. L. R. James was another sage from Nkrumah's days in the United States. He warned Nkrumah after Lumumba's death in 1961 that a crisis was imminent for his own regime.[48] What had Nkrumah written that brought these unprecedented reactions? Neocolonialism: The Last Stage of Imperialism is a devastatingly penetrating, irrefutable dissection of the modes and means by which the West maintained its inequitable economic relationship with Africa. It showed the fundamental economics of imperialism[49]. The West had swapped the African slave trade for a system that replaced human beings, as Africa's main export, for more profitable raw materials and cash crops mined and grown by cheap (and for decades forced) labor. Moreover, it had closed their respective colonies' markets to refined products from other possibly competing countries. The colonial powers simultaneously blocked Africans' industrial development. Without industry to develop their raw materials, Africans had no choice but to remain perpetual markets for European refined products.

Moreover, the book highlighted the disastrous impact of the perpetual balkanization of Africa into competing ministates. Africans' senseless competition with one another drove their countries' incomes down further. At the same time, the Western powers were not competing against each other. They colluded in drawing the maximum income from Africa's abundant human, agricultural, and mineral resources: "So long as Africa remains divided it will therefore be the wealthy consumer countries who will dictate the price of African cash crops."[50] Before Nkrumah wrote this book, the words "neocolonialism" and "imperialism" were abstract concepts for many black people on the continent and in the diaspora. His book linked these concepts to the concrete realities of Africa so that their truths were inescapable.

The book provided statistics to solidify his points. In 1957, Africa provided much of the Western world's tin, iron, manganese, copper, bauxite, chrome ore, asbestos, cobalt, antinomy, cotton, iron ore, zinc ore, lead, and phosphates. "Yet," Nkrumah wrote, "in none of the new African countries is there a single integrated industry based upon any one of these resources."[51] The colonial powers had prevented the Africans' development of industry so that they would remain perpetually in a subordinate and dependent status. Colonialism had geared all of Africa to serve the interests of dominating foreign capital. The United States had entered the game relatively late, but its large corporations, like the Europeans, now dominated whole sections of Africa's economy. This was basically the same system from which the American colonists declared independence in 1776. The metropole had locked the subordinate countries in parasitically inequitable economic relations. *Neocolonialism: The Last Stage of Imperialism*, combined with Nkrumah's 1963 book, *Africa Must Unite*, details Africa's solutions to postcolonial dependency: political and economic unification, industrialization, and ridding Africa of neocolonized black puppets whom the Western powers conspired to keep as Africa's leaders to guard their interests.

CIA documents reveal the next level of punitive measures. Ghana's economy was suffering a downturn because of low cocoa prices. If the United States had not cancelled the $100 million worth of surplus food going to Ghana, then the crisis would not have struck the country so hard. The American embassy noted that in the past, coup rumors intensified during economic tension. On February 10, 1965, the embassy reported to the deputy director of the CIA that the plot to overthrow Nkrumah was underway but incomplete.[52] Evidently the CIA source held a seat in the meetings of the coup-plotters at each stage of the planning progress. "During the spring and early summer of 1965 a group of senior military and police officers continued to develop coup plots, to discuss tentative dates and occasions for overthrowing Nkrumah."[53]

But, like Lumumba, Nkrumah would not cooperate in his own demise. On July 28, 1965, the CIA lamented that he had abruptly retired Ghana's defense chief, Otu, and his deputy, Ankrah. "Both men had been involved in coup plotting for several months but vacillated too long and gave Nkrumah the chance to act first."[54]

In January 1966 the State Department moved to ensure that Nkrumah would drop his guard. They appointed Franklin Williams as Ghana's first African American ambassador. Williams was a 1942 graduate of Lincoln University. They probably believed that his graduating from Nkrumah's alma mater would make Nkrumah less suspicious of U.S. designs. However, Williams having been the chief of the Peace Corps Division of Private Organizations would have aroused Nkrumah's suspicions.[55] In his book *Neocolonialism*, Nkrumah accused the Peace Corps of functioning as a cover for American intelligence operations in Africa. Next came the significant words on February 17, 1966. The CIA's clandestine source reported, "There is another plot afoot to kill Nkrumah and take over the government."[56] The official record does not show anybody in the U.S. national security establishment ever broaching the topic of warning him at any time during the planning of his murder and overthrow.

Nkrumah reported the allegation that the CIA had used Ambassador Williams to maintain contact with the coup-plotters. Williams had offered Nkrumah's generals $13 million to overthrow his government. "Afrifa, Harlley, and Kotoka were to get a large share of this if they would assassinate me at the Accra airport as I prepared to leave for Hanoi."[57] Only these three men's cowardly fear of the consequences of failure prevented Nkrumah's murder.

Ambassador Williams was as subservient as Danquah, Afrifa, and Busia to anti-African interests. Unlike them, however, he had graduated like Nkrumah from a historically black university. Nevertheless, he had eagerly betrayed Africa's future. While attendance at an African American learning center in the diaspora influenced such men as Nkrumah, Williams's treachery proves that environmental factors alone did not account for the difference in mentalities between Nkrumah and his Sandhurst- and Oxford-bred adversaries. The key determinant of the black student's future course in life is whether he or she maintains an attitude of resistance toward the combat ideologies of Western indoctrination regardless of the location of schooling. The white administrators of Lincoln University sought to create black bearers of the white man's burden in Africa. They trained Lincoln's African students to return home not with the

Golden Fleece, but with a moth-eaten, rigid, and conservative whole cloth of Christian ideology that declared all African forms of worship heathen and all Western culture superior. When Nkrumah defiantly defended his pouring libations to African deities in honor of James Aggrey, he demonstrated the strength of his will to resist the debilitating combat ideology of his benefactors, even at the risk of losing their patronage. He was saying to them, I will not be the kind of Christian you think. I will assert my independent mind and spirit into all of my future endeavors. I will not just be an uncritical believer; I will be a critical thinker, infused with the love of my own people and their ancient understanding of God before I love your Eurocentric version of the divine. I will furthermore not submit to your self-serving paternalistic "guidance" of my peoples' economic and political future. Independent of your interest, I will weigh and assess strategies and policies based on how they improve the lives of Africans and not the profit margins of rapacious foreign corporations.

Nkrumah was not alone among Lincoln University graduates to display this will to resist. Oscar Brown Jr. Langston Hughes, Nnamdi Azikiwe, and Thurgood Marshall also left Lincoln determined never to serve any power inimical to their peoples' uplift. Unlike them, Franklin Williams lacked a will to resist an education that manufactured black stooges. For this reason he accepted a career serving American imperialism. The difference between Lincoln University and Oxford or Sandhurst was the easy access Lincoln provided to an attractive critical mass of African American racial pride, progressive politics, and an ethos of African American social uplift such as existed in no English center of higher learning. Even so, a student at this historically black college had to have a will to resist to become an Nkrumah as opposed to a Franklin Williams.

W. E. B. Du Bois delivered his "Talented Tenth Memorial Address" at Fisk University in 1948. He stated that he had hoped that when he coined the term "Talented Tenth" that one-tenth of black Americans would devote their talents to uplifting the rest of black America. However, when he graduated from Fisk his idealism was shaken by another realization:

> I realized that it was quite possible that my plan of training a talented tenth might put in control and power, a group of selfish, self-indulgent, well-to-do men, whose basic interest in solving the Negro problem was personal; personal freedom and unhampered enjoyment and use of the world, without any real care, or certainly no arousing care, as to what became of the mass of American Negroes, or of the mass of any people.[58]

Only such a negative identity could have motivated Williams to write a letter on February 25, 1966, to Bill Moyers, who was then a special assistant to President Johnson, stating, "The way it looks now, we have been extremely fortunate in what has occurred here. All the personalities associated with the coup are strong friends of ours. . . . Bill this is the kind of change people like you and I hope for."[59] Williams's celebration of the anti-Nkrumah coup explained

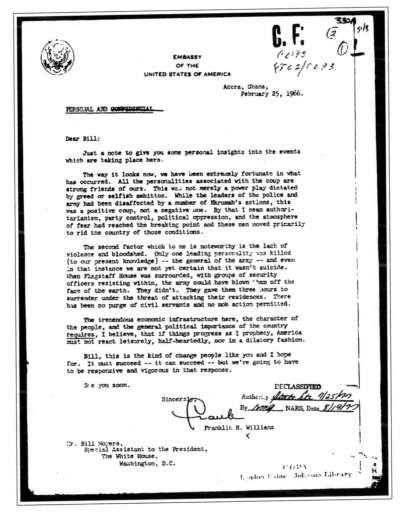

Figure 13   Letter to Bill Moyers.

his mindset. He was a person "like you." He sought, like the CIA hit squads dispatched to kill Lumumba, to demolish forever the dream of a unified and self-sufficient Africa. His Africa, locked in dependency, would perpetually beg the West for aid. Africa would not unite, nor would individual countries seize control of a share of their overabundant riches. While improving African lives, indigenous ownership would lower the stupendous profit margins of multinational corporations. Hence it was against the interests of "persons like you and I."

Consequently, the world's poorest people would continue to live on the world's richest continent. Two tragic events guaranteed the continuation of this state of affairs into the twenty-first century. The first was the murder of Patrice Lumumba and the second was the coup that overthrew Nkrumah.

Williams was a black pioneer in the U.S. State Department. His betrayal of Africa's future portended the type of black mentality that future administrations would seek for placement in high State Department positions. These would be individuals from the talented tenth akin to those about whom Du Bois warned: conscienceless careerists willing to lie to the world and overthrow democracies that opposed U.S. business interests and install dictatorships in their place. All the while, they would glow before the world with the rhetoric of freedom and democracy. Speaking to the generation of Nkrumah and Williams, Du Bois elaborated that their "generation must learn that the object of the world is not profit but service and happiness. They must therefore be directed away from careers that are anti-social and dishonest."[60]

The letter Williams wrote to Bill Moyers celebrating the coup shows that his identity was not shaped by Du Bois's advice. His antisocial and dishonest depiction of the aftermath of the coup demonstrated his indoctrination in the State Department propaganda techniques used successfully after Lumumba's murder.

The numerous assassination attempts on Nkrumah's life had failed. Now the character assassination campaign had begun. Nkrumah lamented that it was "particularly disgraceful that it should be an Afro-American ambassador who sold himself out to the imperialists and allowed himself to be used in this way. It was this same man who deliberately lied when he publicly described the coup as "bloodless."[61] The international media ignored the widespread strikes and civil disobedience by miners, farmers, factory workers, and students, in protest against the new regime. Instead they relished reporting the "spontaneous" anti-Nkrumah demonstrations of what Nkrumah partisans like Kwame Ture described as "CIA rent-a-crowds."[62] Against a steady stream of calumnies, Nkrumah defended himself with facts:

It has been said that the fabrication of the "big lie" is essential in the planning of any usurpation of political power. In the case of Ghana, the big lie told to the world was that Ghana needed to be rescued from "economic chaos." Various other lies were hinged on this central lie. The country was said to be hopelessly in debt and the people on the verge of starvation. Among the lies aimed against me personally was the one that I had accumulated a large private fortune; this was to form the basis for an all-out character assassination attempt. But these lies were subsidiary to the one big lie of "economic mismanagement," which was to provide an umbrella excuse for the seizure of power by neo-colonialist inspired traitors.

If Ghana was in such a serious economic condition, why was there no lack of investment in her growing industries? Investors do not put their money into mismanaged enterprises and unstable economies. Why did the imperialist powers try to exert an economic squeeze on Ghana? No one in his right mind bothers to attack an already-dying concern.[63]

Nkrumah then explained the true motivation for foreign backing of the coup. Franklin Williams, the U.S. State Department, and the Western media had monopolized explaining this. Each of their explanations provided another layer of lies. Nevertheless, few people knew any other reasons than the ones they gave. Even many of Nkrumah's supporters were left by the anti-Nkrumah media campaign with unanswered questions about him and his years as Ghana's leader. From exile in Guinea, Nkrumah refuted his critics' defamatory distortions and answered the questions of an awaiting world:

Who made up the figures of Ghana's supposed "debt"? Why was only one side of the ledger shown—why no mention of assets? How can the obvious evidence of the modernization and industrialization of Ghana, such as the new roads, factories, schools and hospitals, the harbour and town of Tema, the Volta and Teffle bridges and the Volta dam be reconciled with the charge of wasted expenditure? If the Ghanaian people were starving, why no evidence of this, and why no popular participation in the "coup"? How was it that Ghana had the highest living standard in Africa per capita, the highest literacy rate, and was the nearest to achieving genuine economic independence? All these questions, and many related to them, are now being asked. An examination of our development plans and of their implementation reveals the truth—that it was their success and not their failure which spurred our enemies into action. Ghana, on the threshold of economic independence, and in the vanguard of the African revolutionary struggle to achieve continental liberation and unity, was too dangerous an example to the rest of Africa to be allowed to continue under a socialist-directed government.[64]

Nkrumah understood that the fabrications against his regime and his character were but updates of the combat ideologies of colonialism. Indigenous Africans had opposed foreign domination for five hundred years. And for that entire span of time, the foreigners periodically adjusted and rewrote their combat ideologies. If a defiantly independent Ghana prospered, without submitting itself to neocolonial domination, then the other African countries would have an example of independence to follow that conflicted with the model that the West preferred for them.

Europe and the United Stated had to continually imbue their own citizens with a sense that world domination was their proper, if not divinely ordained, destiny. The Western combat ideology also had to convince Africans that foreign domination was best for them. Ghana's true record under Nkrumah refuted their lies. That is why not even a year had passed with the generals in power when General Akwasi A. Afrifa wrote, "The irony of the present situation in Ghana is that it is quite probable that President Nkrumah and the CPP would command the support of a majority of the electorate, even in genuinely free elections."[65] The peak of this irony, for this architect of the coup, resided in his helping to paint a false image of the results of Nkrumah's rule, when he knew that the Ghanaian people wanted Nkrumah's return precisely because they knew that Afrifa and his Western masters were lying. An even more striking irony was the public rhetoric of democracy and freedom loudly proclaimed by the Western backers of the successive unpopular juntas. Simultaneously, they privately colluded with the generals to keep Nkrumah out of power, even though they also knew that he was the Ghanaian people's democratic choice.

After Williams's letter to Moyers, the historical record contains CIA Deputy Director Richard Helms's handwritten note to McGeorge Bundy, dated February 28. Bundy was special assistant for National Security Affairs to Presidents Kennedy and Johnson from 1961 to 1966. The note alludes to a talk between Bundy and Helms on February 25. It suggests that Bundy had expressed an interest in the progress of the coup against Nkrumah. "I am particularly pleased to send you a favorable report on your last day," Helms wrote.[66] Helms informed Bundy that a military junta called the National Liberation Council had seized power while Nkrumah was flying to Peking.

On March 12, Robert Komer, acting special assistant for National Security Affairs, summed up the United States' attitude in a letter to President Johnson. "The coup in Ghana is another example of a fortuitous windfall. Nkrumah was doing more to undermine our interests than any other black African. In reaction to his strongly pro-Communist leanings, the new military regime is almost pathetically pro-Western."[67] Calling Ghana's new rulers "pathetically pro-Western" portended a coming phenomenon. Although the West despised Nkrumah, they did respect him for standing up fearlessly for his principles. Men like Afrifa and others in the so-called National Liberation Council, who groveled before Western money and power, often got money and power, but never respect. Just as their Western benefactors did not respect them in the first days of the coup, so a majority of Ghana's people recognized them as champions only of themselves and their own financial interests.

Nkrumah had championed the welfare of Ghanaians and all Africans. As one Ghanaian stated on the streets of Accra to this author, "Nkrumah sometimes was too much African and too little Ghanaian." Meaning, Nkrumah had focused too much on the liberation of the whole continent and too little on his own nation. This was but one perspective among Ghanaians for why the military successfully seized power. Nkrumah loyalists resisted throughout the country and many of them met death under the guns of a new and ruthless power, which, unlike Nkrumah, harbored few qualms against shedding Ghanaian blood.

After the coup, Nkrumah flew from China to Guinea, whose president, Ahmed Sekou Toure, quickly appointed him "co-President" of the country. The position was largely symbolic, but the symbolism was courageous. The complicity of the West in Nkrumah's overthrow was widely suspected in Africa. Most leaders kept their distance from Nkrumah, fearing that associating with him could bring down Western wrath upon them too. But President Toure attached Nkrumah to himself as co-president, thus telling the African world that the ideals that Nkrumah lived for made supporting him worth the danger.

In Guinea Nkrumah appointed the African American revolutionary Kwame Ture (Stokely Carmichael) as his political secretary. Ture recalled in his autobiography their "almost daily" discussions in which Nkrumah talked about the coup in Ghana, his belief that he would eventually return to power, the African American struggle,

Pan-Africanism, and the mistakes Nkrumah had made in Ghana. Those mistakes weighed heavily upon him during his final years. But he expressed no regrets for having devoted his life to the liberation of Ghana and the unification of Africa. He had made his mistakes always while fighting to improve the lives of Africans. Among his mistakes was not building vast villas in Switzerland or the Riviera, like the African dictators whom the West embraced and supported. "The only people who never make mistakes are people who never try to do anything. The thing to do is to learn from your mistakes," he said.[68]

Nkrumah died of cancer in Romania on April 27, 1972. He did not live long enough to return to Ghana. The misrule of the regimes that followed him made even the Ghanaians who had opposed him eventually come to see him in a different light. When sufficient time had passed to compare the performance of the different governments and leaders, in contrast to the dwarfs who succeeded him, Nkrumah began to look like a giant. Nothing ever said against Nkrumah's government even remotely compared to the brutality, corruption, ignorance, and greed of the series of military and civilian anti-Nkrumah regimes. Nkrumah's achievements also defended his reputation in the eyes of his people. They were constant reminders that even if some members of his government were corrupt, Ghana once had a leader who poured money into developing the country rather than sifoning all of it into officials' pockets. Chief among the concrete benefits of Nkrumah's rule is the Volta Dam that supplies energy to four countries. Next are the roads and ports he built. Throughout his rule his detractors ridiculed these as "prestige projects" and "Nkrumah's folly." These roads, schools, bridges, and other projects are now the mainstays of the country's economy. Without them the Ghanaian standard of living would have fallen precipitously low. They are one reason why the country can now compete successfully in the various trades that bring in money.

Fed up with the ineptitude and corruption of Nkrumah's successors, Flight Lieutenant Jerry Rawlings first seized power in Ghana in 1979.[69] He then turned over the country to civilians. But because they continued the corrupt ways of old, Rawlings again seized power in 1981. He respected and honored the positive aspects of the Nkrumah legacy. Rawlings told Paa Kwame (Leroy Mitchell) that he would have brought Nkrumah back to Ghana had he lived but nine more years.[70] According to scores of Ghanaians to whom this author spoke, Ghana's welcome for Nkrumah would have rivaled the one Nelson Mandela received when South Africa's apartheid regime released him from prison. During this celebration Ghanaians would have honored Nkrumah again as the "Osagyefo," the epic hero who devoted his life to redeeming Ghana and all of Africa. And not only Ghanaians would have welcomed Nkrumah's return to power. The BBC polled its African listeners in December 1999 for their choice of "Africa's Man of the Millennium." Throughout Africa and the diaspora people voted for and eventually selected Kwame Nkrumah.[71]

The word "epic" stems from the etymological Greek root word *epos*. Orality was inherent in this original meaning. The scientific nature of the BBC polling may be disputed. What is indisputable is that despite decades of pejoratives piled atop Nkrumah's reputation in the West, a popular counter discourse has continued. In Africa and the diaspora, oral renditions of the Nkrumah epic have countered anti-Nkrumah television documentaries, newspaper and journal articles, and books. The Western media and some scholars have intermittently denounced Nkrumah's ideals as the source of the beginning of Africa's postcolonial failures. Nevertheless, the African and diasporic "grapevine" has placed before the minds of successive generations the positive achievements of Nkrumah's quests.

This ongoing oral tradition, like the epics of Africa's medieval heroes, continues to embellish and expand the Nkrumah Epic. Each story that this author heard about Nkrumah on the streets and in homes in Ghana, Guinea, Mali, and Senegal—as well as in the United States—added paragraphs if not chapters to his epic. These continuing oral transmissions are acts of discursive power that challenge and refute the defamations of those powerful forces that murdered Lumumba and overthrew Nkrumah.

Remembrance of ancestors in the West African traditions has often appeared to the Western eye like ancestor worship. The African belief actually is that as long as an ancestor is remembered, spoken about, even "receives" a plate of food at family functions, then the ancestor is not truly dead. Ultimately the enduring oral epic of the life of Osagyefo Kwame Nkrumah follows this African mystical tradition. The *epos* keeps his ideas and his spirit alive.

Notes

Foreword

1. Kwame Nkrumah, *Revolutionary Path* (New York: International Publishers, 1973), p. 121.
2. Ibid.
3. See T. Peter Omari, *Kwame Nkrumah: The Anatomy of an African Dictatorship*, with a foreword by Nii Amaa Ollennu (New York: Africana, 1970); and Trevor Jones, *Ghana's First Republic 1960–1966: The Pursuit of the Political Kingdom* (London: Methuen, 1976).
4. For a critique of Nkrumah in the genre of conservative black put-down literature, see George B. N. Ayittey, *Africa Betrayed* (New York: St. Martin's Press, 1992), p. 159–171; also see Robert H. Jackson and Carl G. Rosberg, *Personal Rule in Black Africa: Prince, Autocrat, Prophet; Tyrant* (Berkeley: University of California Press, 1982). Adu Boahen offers an equally negative interpretation in *Ghana: Evolution and Change in the Nineteenth and Twentieth Centuries* (London: Longman, 1975).
5. Henry Bretton, *The Rise and Fall of Kwame Nkrumah: A Study of Personal Rule in Africa* (New York: Praeger, 1966), p. 30.
6. Ibid., p. 31. The marginalia on a page in the Nkrumah Papers at Howard University's Moorland-Spingarn Research Center displays Nkrumah's awareness of Bretton's animus. In 1970, after Nkrumah had been in exile for four years in Guinea, Bretton sent him a copy of his essay "The Overthrow of Kwame Nkrumah." Handwritten at the top of the title page are the words "This from that Bretton man who wrote—The Rise & Fall of K.N. You will [*missing word*] it amusing."
7. Interview, Paa Kwame, Detroit, Michigan, May 2003.
8. See Maxwell Owusu, *Uses and Abuses of Political Power: A Case Study of Continuity and Change in the Politics of Ghana* (Chicago: University of Chicago Press, 1970).
9. Akwasi A. Afrifa, *The Ghana Coup: 24th February 1966* (London: Frank Cass, 1966), pp. 32–37.

Introduction

1. Hugh Seton-Watson, "Fascism, Right and Left," *Contemporary History,* January 1, 1996, p. 196.
2. Ali Mazrui, "Nkrumah: The Leninist Czar," *Transition,* nos. 75/76, 1966, pp. 106–126.

3. *Black Spokesman, Selected Published Writings of Edward Wilmot Blyden,* ed. Hollis R. Lynch (London: Frank Cass, 1971), p. 286.
4. Albert Memmi, *The Colonizer and the Colonized* (Boston: Beacon Press, 1965), p. 88.
5. Carl Von Clausewitz, *Principles of War,* ed. and trans. Hans W. Gatzke (Harrisburg, PA: Military Service Publishing Company, 1942), p. 15.
6. Kwame Nkrumah, *Ghana: The Autobiography of Kwame Nkrumah* (New York: International Publishers, 1971), p. viii.
7. Ibid.
8. Linda Tuhiwai Smith, *Decolonizing Methodologies: Research and Indigenous Peoples* (New York: Zed Books, 2002), p. 1.
9. Nkrumah, *Ghana,* p. vii.
10. Africans are only "illiterate" in comparison with the conquering European culture of "literacy." The *il*-ness in the pejorative "illiterate" invalidates the indigenous educational culture of preliterate Africans. Although many sub-Saharan Africans could read and write either Arabic or indigenous scripts when the Europeans arrived, preliterate Africans grew up learning in memory-based systems of orality. They could hold the equivalent of many books in their memories. Yet the European culture of written as opposed to oral literacy still counted them as ignorant.
11. *Daily Gazette,* March 3, 1966.
12. Genoveva Marais, *Kwame Nkrumah: As I Knew Him* (Chichester: Janay Publishing Company, 1972), p. 34.
13. Kwame Nkrumah, *Consciencism: Philosophy and Ideology for Decolonization and Development with Particular Reference to the African Revolution* (London: Heinemann, 1964), p. 62.
14. Kwame Nkrumah, *Class Struggle in Africa* (London: Panaf Books, 1970), pp. 50, 51.
15. Heinz Eulau, *The Behavioral Persuasion in Politics* (New York: Random House, 1963), p. 67.
16. Jurgen Habermas, *Communication and the Evolution of Society* (Boston: Beacon Press, 1970), p. 20.
17. Kwame Nkrumah, *Dark Days in Ghana* (New York: International Publishers, 1968), p. 66.
18. See Earl Lewis, "To Turn as on a Pivot: Writing African Americans into a History of Overlapping Diasporas," *American Historical Review* 100 (June 1995): 765–787.
19. See Stephen M. Oberhelman, Van Kelly, and Richard J. Golsan, eds., *Epic and Epoch: Essays on the Interpretation and History of a Genre* (Lubbock: Texas Tech University Press, 1994).
20. See Isidore Okpewho, *The Epic in Africa* (New York: Columbia University Press, 1979), p. 84.

Chapter I

1. Isidore Okpewho, *The Epic in Africa* (New York: Columbia University Press, 1979), p. 86.
2. Ibid., p. 86, 87.

3. Clyde W. Ford, *The Hero with an African Face: Mythic Wisdom of Traditional Africa* (New York: Bantam Books, 2000), p. 72.

4. Otto Rank, *The Myth of the Birth of the Hero: A Psychological Interpretation of Mythology*, trans. Dr. F. Robbins and Dr. Smith Ely Jelliffe (New York: Robert Brunner, 1957), p. 4.

5. Kwame Nkrumah, *Ghana: The Autobiography of Kwame Nkrumah* (New York: Nelson, 1957), p 4.

6. Kwame Nkrumah, *Axioms of Kwame Nkrumah*, from an undated speech (London: Thomas Nelson and Sons, 1967), p. 47.

7. See Steven J. Salm and Toyin Falola, *Culture and Customs of Ghana* (London: Greenword Press, 2002)

8. *Evening News,* September 22, 1959, p. 8.

9. *Evening News,* September 24, 1959, p. 2. Paa Kwame stated that the uncertainty of Nkrumah's paternity was widely known in Ghana during the years of Nkrumah's leadership.

10. See Kwame Nkrumah, "Primitive Education in West Africa," Nkrumah Papers, 1–4 (Lincoln University, January 1941), pp. 88–89.

11. Okpewho, *Epic in Africa*, p. 86.

12. Interview, Accra, Ghana, July 1999.

13. Nkrumah, *Ghana*, p. 8.

14. Ibid., p. 9.

15. Okpewho, *Epic in Africa*, pp. 105, 106.

16. *The Epic of Askia Muhammad*, recounted by Nouhou Malio, ed. and trans. Thomas A. Hale (Bloomington and Indianapolis: Indiana University Press, 1996), p. 23.

17. Nkrumah, *Ghana*, p. 9.

18. Some market women in Kumasi harbored resentment toward Nkrumah because of his policies of forcing down prices to make their goods affordable to the poor. Witches only become "damned" in Akan society when their supernatural powers fail to bring profitable results or deliberately cause harm. Witches who usher in prosperity and good luck are never the recipients of spite.

19. Interview, Bowie, Maryland, April 2003.

20. The Gaa are non-Akan people who migrated from the Lake Chad region in the sixteenth century.

21. Library of the Congress of the United States, *Country Studies.*

22. Interview, Cleveland, Ohio, October 2003.

23. H. Debrunner, *Witchcraft in Ghana* (Accra: Presbyterian Book Depot, 1961), p. 182. The anthropologist Karen E. Fields explained the routine character of an ever-present knowledge and expectation of witchcraft in the African mind. Despite the Westerner's view of witchcraft as something extraordinary, for African villagers not to routinely believe in witchcraft would have required them to "escape a texture of life which sustained the idiom of witchcraft." See Karen E. Fields, "Political Contingencies of Witchcraft in Colonial Central Africa: Culture and the State in Marxist Theory," *Canadian Journal of African Studies* 16, no. 3 (1982): 567–593.

24. The name of the Akan subclan, spelled here as both Nzima and Nzema, has several different spellings. These include Nzeemah, Nzimah, and Nzimeh.

25. George P. Hagan, "Nkrumah's Leadership Style—An Assessment from a Cultural Perspective," in *The Life and Work of Kwame Nkrumah*, Papers of a symposium organized by the Institute of African Studies, University of Ghana, Legon, edited by Kwame Arhin (Accra: Sedco Publishing Limited, 1991).

26. Interview, Kumasi, Ghana, July 1999.

27. T. O. Beidelman, *The Kagaru* (New York: Holt, Rinehart and Winston, 1971), pp. 131–132.

28. Max Weber, *Theory of Social and Economic Organization* (New York: Oxford University Press, 1947), p. 359.

29. See Karl Loewenstein, *Max Weber's Political Ideas in the Perspective of Our Time* (Amherst: University of Massachusetts Press, 1966), p. 74.

30. Emmanuel Kotoka was one of the leading generals who overthrew Nkrumah. He expressed this African attitude that contradicts Weber one month after the February 1966 coup. Addressing the Ghanaian army on March 20, he said, "But for God, who had already finished the job, it would have been impossible for the army and the police to overthrow Nkrumah." Quoted in Peter Barker, *Operation Cold Chop: The Coup that Toppled Nkrumah* (Accra: Ghana Publishing Corporation, 1969) p. 106.

31. Nkrumah, *Ghana,* pp. 11–12.

32. This process of internalization and replication is visible in the revolutionary symbolism of the personage of Ernesto Che Guevara. The individual heroic epic of Che became the inspiration for thousands of Cubans to fight for Angola's independence as *internationalistas*. They emulated the internationalism of Che, who, although a native of Argentina, had fought for socialist revolutions in Cuba, the Congo, and finally, fatally, in Bolivia.

33. *Black Spokesman, Selected Published Writings of Edward Wilmot Blyden*, ed. Hollis R. Lynch (London: Frank Cass, 1971), p. 288.

34. John A. Hardon, S. J. Pocket Catholic Dictionary, http://www.therealpresence.org/cgi-bin/getdefination.pl/

35. See Frantz Fanon's books, *Black Skin, White Masks* (New York: Grove Press, 1968); *The Wretched of the Earth* (New York: Grove Press, 1967); *A Dying Colonialism* (New York: Monthly Review Press, 1965); and *Toward the African Revolution* (New York: Grove Press 1969) for in-depth expositions of the psychology of the colonizer and colonized.

36. Even presently in Ghana, all pictures that vendors sold of Christ, God, angels, Mary, and Joseph that this author observed were European in appearance. When I asked the vendors whether they had any pictures portraying Jesus, Mary, Joseph, and the angels as black people, as is done in black America (or even as tanned, dark-haired Jews), they were invariably puzzled by my question. "I had never thought of that," one vendor stated.

37. Most black American Christians long ago answered the echoing call of Marcus Garvey and began depicting and interpreting God in their own black image. According to Dhoruba Bin Wahad, a resident of Accra, had Nkrumah remained in power, Ghanaians would have changed the colors of their imported gods like the black Americans. But their cultural and spiritual awakenings were arrested by Nkrumah's overthrow. Hence white Christian iconography in Ghana today provides a snapshot of the colonial mentality that Nkrumah resisted.

"Ghanaians believe that a white Jesus and Mary are more powerful than if they were black, because the white man and white woman are more powerful than the black," Sam Nyako explained.

38. *Black Spokesman*, p. 290.
39. Aimé Césaire, *Discourse on Colonialism*, trans. Joan Pinkham (New York: Monthly Review Press, 1972), p. 11. Originally published as *Discours sur le colonialisme* (Paris : Presence Africaine, 1955).
40. Gustav Jagoda, *White Man* (London: Oxford University Press, 1961), p. 77.
41. M. J. Field, *Social Organization of the Ga People* (London: The Crown Agents for the Colonies, 1940), p. 100.
42. Jagoda, *White Man*, p. 77.
43. For a superb recent critique of Western research methods in the developing world, see Linda Tuhiwai Smith, *Decolonizing Methodologies: Research and Indigenous Peoples* (London: Zed Books, 2002).
44. The word "genie" comes from the Arabic term *jinn*. Jinns were the primordial spirit beings of pre-Islamic Arabia. Arabs continued to believe in them after the coming of Islam. The *Qur'an* states that jinns are beings "created by Allah from fire" (Sura 15; Ayat 27). Jinns have no independent will, but can only act as ordered by Allah, who is their sole master. These spirits can appear in human form and can also perform the evil deeds of devils. The Islamic vocabulary entered West Africa with the coming of Islam in the eleventh century. When Islam arrived, belief in spiritual forces analogous to jinns was already extant. Africans incorporated Islamic terminology and beliefs into their pre-existing belief systems.
45. Kaarta was located in an area north of present-day Bamako, Mali. Kaarta had formerly been part of the Songhay empire.
46. John William Johnson, Thomas A. Hale, and Stephen Belcher, eds., *Oral Epics from Africa: Vibrant Voices From a Vast Continent* (Bloomington: Indiana University Press, 1997), p. 58.
47. Ibid., p. 61.
48. In the future, opponents of Nkrumah would accuse him of blending Muslim fetishism with indigenous Akan occult practices. They attacked him not for his usage of the occult but for betraying his nationalist and Akan roots by additionally incorporating "foreign" Islamic spiritualism to achieve his goals.
49. William M. Macartney, *Dr. Aggrey: Ambassador For Africa* (London: SCM Press, 1948), p. 106.
50. Nkrumah, *Ghana*, p. 14.
51. Edwin W. Smith, *Aggrey of Africa: A Study in Black and White* (London: Student Christian Movement Press, 1929), p. 13.
52. Nkrumah, *Ghana*, p. 14.
53. Magnus Sampson, *Makers of Modern Ghana*, vol. 1 (Accra: Anowuo Educational Publications, 1969), p. 144.
54. African Students Association (U.S.A.), *Know This of Aggrey: Unpublished Monograph of Things Said by and of Aggrey* (New York, 1942), p. 1, Moorland-Spingarn Research Center, Howard University.
55. Aggrey has been credited with originating this allegory. However, this author heard a virtually identical version of it during his youth at the Antioch Baptist

Church in Chicago. Seventy-three-year-old Junie Irwin, a deacon in this church on Chicago's south side, stated to this author that he heard this parable used in a sermon back in the 1930s. One of the most famous sermons of Reverend C. L. Franklin, the late father of the soul singer Aretha Franklin, is titled "The Eagle Stirreth in her Nest."

56. Smith, *Aggrey of Africa*, pp. 57, 58.
57. See Swami Prabhavananda and Christopher Isherwood, *How To Know God: The Yoga Aphorisms of Patanjali* (New York: New American Library, 1953), pp. 89, 90.
58. Nkrumah, *Ghana*, p. 14.
59. Albert Luthuli, *Let My People Go* (New York: McGraw-Hill, 1962), p. 41.
60. Quoted in Smith, *Aggrey of Africa*, p. 181.
61. See Kenneth King, *Pan Africanism and Education: A Study of Race Philanthropy in the Southern States and East Africa* (Oxford: Clarendon Press, 1971).
62. During my interview with Paa Kwame, he related that he had started teaching at Achimota in 1965, in the last year of Nkrumah's rule. He affirmed that even when Nkrumah was in power, Achimota was a bastion of British conservatism. In the mode of Aggrey, pro-Nkrumah Africans "kept their heads down" in the presence of the white administrators who had the power and the money. But out of their presence, they were fiery for Nkrumah's revolution. After the February 1966 coup that overthrew Nkrumah, the British headmaster of Achimota refused to renew Paa Kwame's contract. He did not like Paa Kwame's pro-Nkrumah attitude. The headmaster had been waiting for Nkrumah's demise to "clean house." Paa Kwame next taught at the Kwame Nkrumah University at Kumasi. Two of his students were Jerry Rawlings and Rawlings's future wife, Nana. Paa Kwame shared with Rawlings his understanding of Nkrumah's socialist and Pan-Africanist ideals. This was at a time when all media sources coordinated their attacks on Nkrumah's legacy with Ghana's new rulers.

In 1979, as a flight lieutenant in Ghana's air force, Jerry Rawlings would be the selected leader of soldiers who overthrew Ghana's government. With more than a hint of satisfaction, Paa Kwame noted that his former student eventually ordered the arrest of the leaders of the coup that overthrew Nkrumah and had them shot.

These executions and the rehabilitation of Nkrumah as a national hero changed Ghana's political chemistry. Some of those politicians who supported Nkrumah's demise refused this author's request for interviews, even though they live in the United States. Now that it is they who have been portrayed as traitors for opposing Nkrumah, their reluctance to draw attention to their now-unpopular past political positions is understandable. According to one anti-Nkrumah Ghanaian politician who is currently living in the Metropolitan Washington, D.C., area, the executions of Nkrumah's enemies makes feasible his own execution some day. This man was in the cabinet of Prime Minister Kofi Busia in Ghana's Second Republic. He fears that although the executions have ended and Rawlings is gone, some future regime could arrest him. He too could be executed for the crime of overthrowing a man who has become a legend.
63. Nnamdi Azikiwe, *My Odyssey* (London: C. Hurst & Company, 1970), p. 280.

64. Nkrumah, *Ghana*, p. 14.
65. See Robert H. Brisbane, *The Black Vanguard, Origins of the Negro Social Revolution 1900–1960* (Valley Forge: Judson Press, 1970), pp. 50–52.
66. Herbert Aptheker, ed., *The Correspondence of W. E. B. Du Bois*, vol. 1, *Selections, 1877–1934*(Amherst: University of Massachusetts Press, 1977), p. 182.
67. Ibid. According to Aptheker, although no response to Aggrey's letter survives, both men knew and respected each other. David Levering Lewis wrote that Aggrey never did come to New York to work on *Crisis*. Nevertheless, Aggrey entered New York's Columbia University in 1918 and stayed until 1920. No records of his interaction with Du Bois have survived, but this would have given him ample time to interact with Du Bois.
68. Ibid., pp. 183, 184.
69. William Wells Brown, *Three Years in Europe or, Places I have Seen and People I have Met* (*Documenting the American South*, Electronic Edition, University of North Carolina at Chapel Hill Library), p. 99.
70. . E. Casely Hayford, *Gold Coast Native Institutions, With Thoughts upon a Healthy Imperial Policy for the Gold Coast and Ashanti* (London: Sweet and Maxwell, 1903), pp. 235, 236, 237, 238.
71. See George M. Frederickson, *Black Liberation: A Comparative History of Black Ideologies in the United States and South Africa* (Oxford: Oxford University Press, 1995), p. 147.
72. Aptheker, *Correspondence*, p.182.
73. Daniel Walden, ed., *W. E. B. Du Bois: The Crisis Writings* (Greenwich, CT: Fawcett, 1972), p. 60.
74. See Deuteronomy 32:11.
75. Aggrey Papers, Moorland-Spingarn Collection, Howard University. Box 1, 143–3.
76. Smith, *Aggrey of Africa*, p. 118.
77. All this being so, Aggrey's presence at Achimota must still be attributed to the uncommon administration of the Gold Coast governor, Sir Frederick Gordon Guggisberg (1919–1927). Guggisberg allocated hundreds of thousands of pounds to build and staff the college at Achimota. This he did when colonizers in other parts of Africa neglected and discouraged with suspicion higher education for black people. Guggisberg also insisted that indigenous Africans receive medical education. Then he had these black doctors appointed to posts where white British colonials had to utilize their medical skills or go untreated. Despite the white men's strong objections to their wives being treated by black male doctors, Guggisberg refused to change his policy. See Adell Patton, Jr., *Physicians, Colonial Racism, and Diaspora in West Africa* (Gainesville: University of Florida Press, 1996). Nonetheless, for all of his progressivism, Guggisberg was, in the end, an administrator of a system of institutionalized black inferiority maintained by armed force. No "progressivism" on the part of Ghana's British colonial masters could cover the reality that colonialism was ultimately maintained by Europeans' possession of more technologically lethal systems of violence than indigenous Africans could muster. Without this advantage, neither Guggisberg nor his predecessors or successors could have overstayed their welcome in the Gold Coast or any African colony.

78. See George Padmore, *The Gold Coast Revolution* (London: Dennis Dobson, 1953).
79. Nkrumah, *Ghana*, pp. 21, 22.
80. Ibid., pp. 22, 23. Azikiwe and Nkrumah would become estranged years later when each man assumed leadership of his country and pursued different policies. In 1966 Azikiwe's moderating advice to Nkrumah would not prevent the overthrow of his own government by a military coup d'état.
81. Nnamdi Azikiwe, *Renascent Africa* (New York: Negro Universities Press, 1969), p. 157. Azikiwe cites as his source Carter G. Woodson's *The Negro in Our History*, 6th ed. (Washington, D.C.: Associated Publishers, 1966), pp. 230–231 and 461–467.
82. For definitions of Pan-Africanism, taking into account a wide swathe of literature, see D. Sizwe Poe, *Kwame Nkrumah's Contribution to Pan-Africanism: An Afrocentric Analysis* (New York: Routledge, 2003).
83. Azikiwe, *My Odyssey*, p. 275.
84. Kwame Nkrumah Papers, Lincoln University Archives.
85. Lincoln University Archives.
86. Andrew E. Murray, "The Founding of Lincoln University," *Journal of Presbyterian History* (Winter1973).
87. Basil Davidson, *Black Star* (London: Allen Lane, 1971), p. 29.

Chapter 2

1. Gloria House, *Tower and Dungeon: A Study of Place and Power in American Culture* (Detroit: Casa De Unidad Press, 1991), p. 2.
2. Edwin W. Smith, *Aggrey of Africa: A Study in Black and White* (London: Student Christian Movement Press, 1929), p. 122.
3. Memorandum, Federal Bureau of Investigation, *Re: Adam Clayton Powell Jr., History and Background,* July 10, 1942.
4. Adam Clayton Powell, *Adam by Adam: The Autobiography of Adam Clayton Powell, Jr.* (New York: Kinsington, 1971), pp. 54, 244.
5. Kwame Nkrumah, *Ghana: The Autobiography of Kwame Nkrumah* (New York: Nelson, 1957), p. 28.
6. Ibid., p. 19.
7. African American Christians refer to these possessions by various names, such as getting happy, getting the Holy Ghost, and getting the spirit. These spirit-possessions bear a close resemblance to the spirit-possessions in diasporic religions more closely associated with their African roots. These are known as *Condomble* in Brazil, Voo Doo (or *Vou Doun*) in Haiti and New Orleans, and *Santaria* in Cuba.
8. W. E. B. Du Bois, *The Autobiography of W. E. B. Du Bois* (New York: International, 1958), p. 343.
9. However, Frazier's observations, showing the alienation from African and even black American culture of a portion of the black middle class in New York in the 1920s, coincide with the class division between Du Bois and Garvey partisans, respectively. See E. Franklin Frazier, *On Race Relations,*

Selected Papers, ed. G. Franklin Edwards (Boston: Beacon Press, 1969), pp. 262, 265.

After some years of living in the United States, Nkrumah added his voice to this debate about African retentions in black America. For him the two poles of sociological thought were between Professor E. Franklin Frazier at Howard University and Melville Herskovits, Professor of Anthropology at Northwestern University. Nkrumah wrote, "The Howard school of thought maintained that the Negro in America had completely lost his cultural contact with Africa and the other school, represented by Herzkovits [*sic*], maintained that there were still African survivals in the United States and the Negro of America had in no way lost his cultural contact with the African continent. I supported, and still support, the latter view and I went on one occasion to Howard University to defend it" (Nkrumah, *Ghana*, p. 44).

10. Marcus Garvey, *Philosophy and Opinions of Marcus Garvey* (London: Frank Cass, 1923), p. 50.

11. See David Levering Lewis, *W.E.B. Du Bois, A Reader*, "The Conservation of the Race" (New York: Henry Hold and Company, 1995), pp. 20–27.

12. Nkrumah, *Ghana*, p. 44.

13. See Leon Litwack and August Meier, eds., *Black Leaders in the Nineteenth Century* (Urbana: University of Illinois Press, 1988).

14. Representative of these speakers was Martin Delaney. Even as far back as 1852 Delaney stated a premise of pride that the rising vanguard of New Negroes and African nationalists would propagate as truisms in the twentieth century. "No people . . . can ever attain to greatness who lose their identity. We shall ever cherish our identity of origin and race, as preferable in our estimation, to any other people." He spoke these words three years after U.S. Supreme Court Justice Roger B. Taney had stated in the *Dred Scott* decision that black people had no rights that white people were bound to respect. Rather than join a headlong rush away from a caste-plagued blackness, Delaney affirmed the cursed color. In so doing, he articulated racial identity politics in 1852 with sophistication equal to any theoretician of U.S. black power or African postcoloniality a century later.

15. Alain Locke, ed., *The New Negro* (New York: Atheneum, 1980), p. 6.

16. Ibid., p. 7.

17. Ibid.

18. As quoted in Willard Scott Thompson, *Ghana's Foreign Policy, 1957–1966* (Princeton: Princeton University Press, 1969), p. 417. To contextualize this quote, Thompson wrote that on March 23, 1968, Jones-Quartey wrote this citation to elaborate on and clarify the notes he had taken in an interview with Jones-Quartey on February 3, 1966.

19. See Clyde W. Ford, *The Hero with an African Face: Mythic Wisdom of Traditional Africa* (New York: Bantam Books, 2000), p. 19.

20. Schuyler wrote both "The Black Internationale" and "Black Empire" under the pen name Samuel I. Brooks. He possibly chose to do this to give verisimilitude to his revolutionary nationalist fictional characters. The ideas of these characters differed sharply from the often caustically negative and unprogressive opinions he expressed under his real name in the *Courier*. Writing these

two sagas of black supremacy and mental decolonization under the name George Schuyler would have been, at minimum, confusing to his readers.

21. The archives at Lincoln University contained no records of which newspapers were in the Lincoln library during the years of Nkrumah's matriculation. The archivist advised that the conservatism of the all-white Lincoln administrators in the 1930s and 1940s made the inclusion of such a publication as the *Pittsburgh Courier* improbable. Nevertheless, students were free to individually acquire subscriptions. The newspaper was truly a national newspaper and was ubiquitous in African American communities throughout the country in those years.

22. Francis Nkrumah, "Negro History," *Lincolnian* 5, no. 2 (January 18, 1938).

23. Nkrumah, *Ghana*, p. 45.

24. Amy Jacques Garvey, comp., *The Philosophy and Opinions of Marcus Garvey, Or, Africa for the Africans* (London: Frank Cass, 1967), p. 53.

25. The nationalist dream was also the opposite of the assimilationism promoted by Schuyler under his own name. Schuyler's autobiography, *Black and Conservative*, includes chronological excerpts from his writings. Yet *Black and Conservative* did not mention the *Courier* series. His autobiography was highly detailed because he, evidently, viewed most moments of his life as significant. One probable reason for his not mentioning his literary Pan-Africanism was that he argued against the very positions he took in "Black Empire" and "The Black Internationale" throughout his autobiography. Hence it is the conclusion of this writer that Schuyler wrote these two serials purely for profit. Schuyler wrote for a living and had to cater to what was popular in black America to continue to make a living. He directed *Black and Conservative* to a readership that would be attracted to the word "conservative" in the title—the white conservative reading public. The writings in his autobiography against black unity, the back-to-Africa movement, socialism and communism, and opposing black nationalism were counter to the collective ethos of the 1930s black reading public. They were the ones buying and reading the *Courier*. Schuyler wrote his Pan-Africanist serials for his black readers because he was an intellectual entrepreneur. Like a vegetarian selling meat, he peddled what the market demanded, even though he would never personally consume the product that he sold.

26. *Pittsburgh Courier*, November 26, 1936.

27. Ibid.

28. Ibid., December 5, 1936.

29. Ibid., July 3, 1937.

30. Ibid.

31. This scenario bears a striking resemblance to the contemporaneous elevation of Elijah Muhammad in the Nation of Islam. Muhammad too grew up in Georgia and heard the teachings of itinerant Christian preachers. His god in Detroit was W. D. Fard, who proclaimed Elijah Muhammad his messenger. See Claude Clegg, *An Original Man: The Life and Times of Elijah Muhammad* (New York: St Martin's Griffin, 1998).

32. John William Johnson, Thomas A. Hale, and Stephen Belcher, eds., *Oral Epics from Africa: Vibrant Voices From a Vast Continent* (Bloomington: Indiana University Press, 1997), p. 58.

33. Robert Weisbrot, *Father Divine and the Struggle for Racial Equality* (Urbana: University of Illinois Press, 1983), p. 53.

34. Nkrumah, *Ghana*, p. 40.

35. Ossie Davis and Ruby Dee, *With Ossie and Ruby: In This Life Together* (New York: HarperCollins, 1998), p. 104.

36. Akwasi A. Afrifa, *The Ghana Coup: February 24th 1966* (London: Frank Cass 1967), p. 123.

37. One striking example of Anglophilia relates to the Rhodesia crisis. Nkrumah threatened to use Ghana's army to assist black Rhodesians to achieve their freedom from the racist white minority regime. Afrifa opposed Nkrumah's interventionism. He wrote, "I personally knew that Her Majesty's Government of the United Kingdom was quite capable of dealing with the Rhodesia situation." (See Afrifa, *The Ghana Coup*, p. 22.) Afrifa failed to explain how he personally was privy to the inner counsels of the British government. Considering that the British overtly and covertly supported Rhodesia's white minority government for another decade, Nkrumah's anticolonialist analysis proved correct. Britain did deal with the situation, but in ways that were not in the interests of Rhodesia's black people. Afrifa's peculiarly monarchist and pro-imperialist groveling permeates his entire memoir.

38. See Richard Wright, *Black Power* (New York: Harper, 1954), p. 228.

39. Ghana's military controlled the elections in 1969 and banned Nkrumah partisans from running for office. The economy collapsed under Busia and the social system deteriorated. On January 13, 1972, the military under Colonel Ignatius Kutu Acheampong executed another coup and overthrew Busia. See Godfrey Mwakikagile, *Military Coups in West Africa Since the Sixties* (Huntington, NY: Nova Science Publishers, 2001).

40. Afrifa, *The Ghana Coup*, p. 20.

41. A female defector from Divine's commune charged in explicit detail that Divine was not personally practicing the celibacy that he imposed on his followers.

42. Interview, Conakry, Guinea, 1997.

43. *Evening News*, October 2, 1965, as quoted in Afrifa, *The Ghana Coup*, p. 20.

44. Interview, Popenquine, Senegal, July 1997.

45. Interview, Bowie, Maryland, April 16, 2003.

46. Manning Marable asserts that Nkrumah derived his ambivalent attitude toward orthodox Communists from George Padmore. No doubt, Padmore reinforced these tendencies. However, Nkrumah first observed this manipulation of Communists, using them as a tool instead of being used by them, in the practices of Father Divine.

47. See Ali Mazrui, "Nkrumah: The Leninist Czar," *Transition*, no. 26 (1966), pp. 8–17.

48. Letter to Dean Johnson, September 20, 1941, Kwame Nkrumah Papers, Lincoln University.

49. See David Rooney, *Kwame Nkrumah: The Political Kingdom in the Third World* (New York: St. Martin's Press, 1988), p. 266.
50. See *New Day*, August 2, 1958, p. 29, and August 9, 1958, p. 23.
51. File #1000-21745, FBI Archives, J. Edgar Hoover Building , Washington, D.C.
52. Garvey, *The Philosophy and Opinions of Marcus Garvey*, pp. 69, 70.
53. Ibid., p. 68. In 1920 the Chicago office of the Bureau of Investigation falsely reported to the Washington D.C. headquarters that Marcus Garvey had been arrested during a raid of a meeting of the International Workers of the World (IWW). Known as the Wobblies, the IWW was one of the most radical anticapitalist organizations in the United States. See Emory J. Tolbert, "Federal Surveillance of Marcus Garvey and the U.N.I.A.," *Journal of Ethnic Studies* 14, no. 4 (1987): 17.
54. Garvey, *The Philosophy and Opinions of Marcus Garvey*, p. 72.
55. Francis Nwia-Kofi Nkrumah, "Education and Nationalism in Africa," *Educational Outlook* (November 1943), School of Education, University of Pennsylvania, Philadelphia, p. 5.
56. Ibid., p. 8.
57. For details on Nkrumah's financial hardships at Lincoln and during his years in the United States, see Marika Sherwood, *Kwame Nkrumah: The Years Abroad 1935–1947* (Legon, Ghana: Freedom, 1996).
58. Nkrumah, *Ghana*, p. 44.
59. Leon Trotsky (1879–1940) had been first a Menshevik opponent, and then a Bolshevik protégé of Lenin and Stalin. He helped to organize the Communist Revolution that seized power in Russia in 1917. After the revolution, as Commissar of the Red Army, he led it to victory over the "White" counterrevolutionary forces, including invading troops from the United States and Britain. From 1923 to 1933, he challenged Stalin's policies as the "left opposition" in the Soviet Communist Party. Stalin eventually engineered the expulsion of Trotsky from the party. Trotsky then went into exile. An agent of Stalin axed Trotsky to death in Mexico in 1940. See *Encyclopedia of Marxism: Glossary of People*, http://www.marxists.org/glossary/people/t/r.htm#trotsky-leon.
60. See C. L. R. James, *Nkrumah and the Ghana Revolution* (Westport, CT: Lawrence Hill, 1977).
61. C. L. R. James, "The Rise and Fall of Kwame Nkrumah," in *The C.L.R. James Reader*, ed. Anna Grimshaw (Oxford, UK: Blackwell, 1992), p. 355.
62. Ibid.
63. Interview, Detroit, Michigan, January 2004.
64. Interview, Ann Arbor, Michigan, August 2000.
65. Harold Cruse elaborated on his negative impressions of West Indians in his famous book *The Crisis of the Negro Intellectual* (New York: Morrow, 1967).
66. Nkrumah, *Consciencism: Philosophy and Ideology for Decolonization and Development with Particular Reference to the African Revolution* (London: Heinemann, 1964), p. 68.
67. Interview, Kwame Ture (Stokely Carmichael), Detroit, March 1998.
68. Nkrumah, *Ghana*, p. 166.

Chapter 3

1. John W. Roberts, *From Trickster to Badman* (Philadelphia: University of Pennsylvania Press, 1989), pp. 5, 6.
2. "The Heart of Africa, Interview with Julius Nyerere on Anti-Colonialism," *New Internationalist Magazine*, January–February 1999.
3. Nkrumah made his presence felt when he visited Howard University. He often spoke at forums concerning problems of colonialism and Africa's future.
4. J. B. Danquah, *The Akan Doctrine of God, a Fragment of Gold Coast Ethics and Religion* (London: Frank Cass, 1944).
5. Manthia Diawara, *In Search of Africa* (Cambridge: Harvard University Press, 1998), p. 32.
6. Peter Abrahams, "The Last Word on Nkrumah," *West African Review* 25 (1954): 913.
7. Kwame Nkrumah, *Revolutionary Path*, 1st U.S. ed. (New York: International Publishers, 1973), p. 46.
8. Ibid., p. 50.
9. See V. I. Lenin, Lenin Collected Works, vol. 5, *What Is to Be Done* (Moscow: Foreign Languages Publishing House, 1961), pp. 347–530.
10. Acts 10:38, 39.
11. Peter Abrahams, "Nkrumah, Kenyatta, and the Old Order," in *African Heritage*, ed. Jacob Drachler (London: Collier Books, 1964), p. 138.
12. Ibid.
13. Richard Wright, *Black Power* (New York: Harper, 1954), p. 228.
14. Ibid.
15. L. P. Mair, *Native Policies in Africa* (New York: Negro Universities Press, 1936), p. 56.
16. Hans Kohn and Wallace Sokolsky, *African Nationalism in the Twentieth Century* (New York: Von Nostrand Reinhold Co., 1965), p. 30.
17. Geoffrey Gorer, *Africa Dances: A Book about West African Negroes* (London, 1935), in *Africa Reader: Colonial Africa*, ed. Wilfred Carty and Martin Kilson (New York: Vantage Books, 1970), pp. 103, 104; and Lord Malcolm Hailey, *Native Administration and Political Development in British Tropical Africa* (London, 1943). See also Chinua Achebe, *Things Fall Apart* (New York: Anchor Books, 1994). In this novel Achebe vividly describes an incident in which the British employ a "foreign" African ethnic group that does not sympathize with the Ibos to suppress and subdue Ibo resistance to British colonial domination.
18. Asiata Vaai, "The Idea of Law: A Pacific Perspective," *Journal of Pacific Studies* 21(1997): 226.
19. Ibid.
20. Kwame Nkrumah, *Ghana: The Autobiography of Kwame Nkrumah* (New York: Nelson, 1957), p. 303.
21. Kwame Nkrumah, "Dialectics of Materialism and Sociology," Seminar Paper, University of Pennsylvania, 1942, p. 5.
22. Ibid.

23. Nkrumah, *Ghana*, p. 31. For information on the origins of Prince Hall Freemasonry, see Martin R. Delaney, *The Origin and Objects of Ancient Freemasonry; Its Introduction into the United States and Legitimacy among Colored Men* (Pittsburgh: W. S. Haven, 1853), and Harold Van Buren Boorhis, *Negro Masonry in the United States* (Bensenville, IL: Lushena Books, 2003), pp. 7–13.

24. See Malcolm C. Duncan, *Duncan's Ritual of Freemasonry* (New York: Crown Publishers, n.d.)

25. See William A. Muraskin, *Middle-Class Blacks in a White Society: Prince Hall Freemasonry in America* (Berkeley: University of California Press, 1975), p. 56.

26. See *Who's Who in Colored America: A Biographical Dictionary of Notable Living Persons of African Descent in America, 1933–1937* (Brooklyn: Thomas Yenser, 1937).

27. Nkrumah, *Revolutionary Path*, p. 49.

28. See George E. Simons, *Standard Masonic Monitor of the Degrees of Entered Apprentice, Fellow Craft, and Master Mason* (Richmond, VA: McCoy Publishing and Masonic Supply Co., 1984).

29. Duncan, *Duncan's Ritual*, p. 97.

30. See Gordon S. Wood, *The Radicalism of the American Revolution* (New York: Vintage, 1993), p. 223. See also Edith J. Steblecki, *Paul Revere and Masonry* (Boston: Paul Revere Memorial Association, 1985), and Steven C. Bullock, *Revolutionary Brotherhood, Freemasonry and the Transformation of the American Social Order* (Chapel Hill: University of North Carolina Press, 1996).

31. Joseph Appiah, *Joe Appiah: The Autobiography of an African Patriot* (New York: Praeger, 1990), p. 164.

32. Letter to Phillip Brown, July 17, 1942, Ghana National Archives, SC/1/44.

33. Appiah, *Joe Appiah*, p. 210.

34. Paa Kwame stated further that Kwabina grew up to be an unscrupulous trickster. The Ghanaian police arrested him for importing counterfeit currency into the country. He died in jail from an illness he contracted there.

35. *Frantz Fanon: Black Skin, White Masks*, cowritten and directed by Isaac Julien (Normal Films, 1995).

36. Frantz Fanon, *Black Skin, White Masks* (New York: Grove Press, 1968), p. 63.

37. Appiah, *Joe Appiah*, pp. 192, 193.

38. Ibid., p. 194.

39. Roi Ottley, *No Green Pastures* (New York: Charles Scribner's Sons, 1951), pp. 51, 52.

40. The future Mrs. Peggy Cripps Appiah would mature to have a more incisive understanding of racial issues when she moved to Kumasi to live with her husband Joseph (d. 1990). She bore four children and integrated herself into the daily life of Africa. She became a philanthropist and was one of the principal financial backers of a school for the blind. She also became an avid student of Ashanti culture and a collector of thousands of Ashanti proverbs. She authored several children's books that beautifully illustrated the Aesop-like wisdom contained in Ashanti folklore. She died on February 11, 2006, at the age of 84, beloved of and respected by many people in Ashantiland and throughout the African World. See http://www.telegraph.co.uk/news/main.jhtml?xml=/news/2006/02/24/db2401.xml.

41. Ottley, *No Green Pastures*, p. 52.
42. Peter Abrahams, *A Wreath for Udomo* (New York: Collier Books, 1971), pp. 46–47.
43. Nkrumah, *Ghana*, p. 56.
44. Erica Powell, *Private Secretary (Female Gold Coast)* (New York: Palgrave Macmillan, 1984), p. 50.
45. Abrahams, "Nkrumah, Kenyatta, and the Old Order," pp. 143–144.
46. "The Heart of Africa," *New Internationalist Magazine*, no.309, January–February 1999 .
47. Campbell, Joseph, *The Hero with a Thousand Faces* (New York: Princeton University Press, 1968), p. 30.
48. Rudyard Kipling, *American Notes*, http://whitewolf.newcastle.edu.au/words/authors/K/KiplingRudyard/.
49. See K. L. Little, *Negroes in Britain, A Study of Racial Relations in English Society* (London: Kegan Paul, 1947), p. 217.
50. Cited in Edward Scobie, *Black Britannia, A History of Blacks in Britain* (Chicago: Johnson, 1972), p. 149. See also Hakim Adi, *West Africans in Britain, 1900–1960* (London: Lawrence and Wishart, 1998).
51. Wright, *Black Power*, pp. 233–234.
52. Ahmed Sekou *Toure, The Political Leader Considered as the Representative of Culture* (Newark: Jihad Productions), p. 6.
53. See Amilcar Cabral, "National Liberation and Culture," in *Return to the Source: Selected Speeches of Amilcar Cabral* (New York: Monthly Review Press, 1973), pp. 239–256.
54. For a contrary point of view, see the book by Joe Appiah's son, Kwame Anthony Appiah, *In My Father's House: Africa in the Philosophy of Culture* (Oxford: Oxford University Press, 1992).
55. Apparently, the CIA did not inform the American ambassador to Ghana, William P. Mahoney, about Joseph Danquah's being on the CIA payroll. A book written by Mahoney's son states that his father discovered this when Danquah came to the embassy asking why the CIA had missed his payments. Mahoney summoned the CIA station chief for an explanation of why he was not informed about Danquah's employment. After receiving an answer that he regarded as inadequate, Ambassador Mahoney flew to Washington, D.C., and personally informed President Kennedy about the matter. See Richard D. Mahoney, *J.F.K.: Ordeal in Africa* (New York: Oxford University Press, 1983), pp. 184, 185. For information about the dysfunctional relationship between the State Department and the CIA during the 1960s, see D. Wise and T. B. Ross, *The Invisible Government* (New York: Random House, 1964).
56. Wright, *Black Power*, p. 219.
57. Ibid., p. 220.
58. Ibid., p. 222.
59. K. A. Busia explained his world outlook in his books *The Challenge of Africa* (New York: Praeger, 1964) and *Africa in Search of Democracy* (New York: Praeger, 1967).
60. Joe Appiah was once an ally of Busia. He confirmed Busia's treason by quoting in his autobiography the letter thanking Busia for his assistance that

apartheid South Africa's Prime Minister Balthazar Johannes Vorster wrote and signed. Busia left the "Secret and Confidential" letter in his office after his overthrow. His successor, General Acheampong, gave Appiah a copy. See Appiah, *Joe Appiah*, pp. 335, 336.

61. Kenyatta's disdain for the "primitive" was contradicted by the photo of himself on the cover of his 1942 book, *Facing Mt. Kenya.* The photo shows him wearing only an animal skin. One of his shoulders is naked. His left hand grips the shaft of a spear. His eyes rest upon the fingers of his right hand, which caresses the spear point. The 1940s were the heyday of the Tarzan movies. This photo could only have reinforced the pernicious stereotype of the primitive and half-naked African spear-bearer.

62. Quoted in Oginga Odinga, *Not Yet Uhuru: The Autobiography of Oginga Odinga* (New York: Hill & Wang, 1967), p. 101.

63. George Padmore, *History of the Pan-African Congress* (London: Hammersmith, 1947) p. 32.

64. Ibid., p. 27.

65. Ibid., p. 13.

66. Ibid., pp. 21, 22.

Chapter 4

1. Joseph Campbell, *The Hero with a Thousand Faces* (New York: Princeton University Press, 1968), p. 71.

2. See, C. A. Ackah, *Akan Ethics* (Accra: Ghana University Press, 1998).

3. Kwame Nkrumah, *Revolutionary Path,* 1st US ed. (New York: International Publishers, 1973), p. 51.

4. Ibid., p. 13.

5. See C. G. Baëta, Prophetism In Ghana: A Study of Some "Spiritual" Churches (London: SCM Press, 1962).

6. Kwame Nkrumah, *Ghana: The Autobiography of Kwame Nkrumah* (New York: Nelson, 1957), p. 66.

7. *African Morning Post*, January 21, 1948.

8. Kwame Nkrumah, *I Speak of Freedom* (London: Panaf Books, 1961), p. 5.

9. Ibid.

10. Ibid., p. 3.

11. H. B. Martinson, *Ghana, The Dream of the Twenty First Century, Politics of J. B. Danquah, Busia and Kufuor Tradition* (Accra: Norcento Press, 2001), p. 35.

12. Joel H. Wiener, ed., *Great Britain: Foreign Policy and the Span of Empire 1689–1971: A Documentary History*, vol. 2 (New York: Chelsea House/McGraw-Hill, 1972), pp.1192–1193.

13. Atlantic Charter: Declarations by Members of the War Cabinet, National Union of Conservative and Unionist Associations (UK), 1942.

14. Nkrumah, *Ghana*, p. 71.

15. Danquah and other UGCC leaders would eventually denounce Nkrumah and accuse him of deceitfully gathering power in his hands as UGCC general secretary. However, these experienced lawyers and businessmen could not credibly

claim such naïveté as they were the ones who had appointed Nkrumah to the position. Nkrumah then became the de facto leader of all affiliated Ghanaian organizations. Members of these organizations naturally viewed him as the national leader of the Gold Coast independence movement. The UGCC founders' complaints against Nkrumah mask the fact that in a culture that adored the trickster figure Ananse, men who thought that they had chosen a man whom they could manipulate and control found that they were outsmarted. Like the master manipulator in an Ananse tale, Nkrumah had turned the tables on them.

16. Nkrumah, *Ghana*, p. 72.
17. Ibid.
18. Ibid.
19. Ibid., p. 73. Some UGCC leaders would falsely claim to the Watson Commission that they had voted against Nkrumah's program.
20. Telegram from Sir G. Creasy, February 28, 1945. Richard Rathbone, ed., *British Documents on the End of Empire*, vol. 1, *Ghana*, Part 1, 1941–1952 (London: HMSO Publications Centre, 1992), page 61.
21. Ibid., p. 66.
22. Ibid., p. 67.
23. Ibid., p. 68.
24. Ibid.
25. Ibid., p. 69.
26. Ibid., pp. 68, 72.
27. Letter from Sir C. Arden-Clarke to Sir T. Lloyd, January 13, 1954. *British Documents on the End of Empire*, vol. 2, *Ghana*, p. 81.
28. Richard Wright, *Black Power* (New York: Harper, 1954), pp. 90–92.
29. Interview, Bowie, Maryland, April 16, 2003.
30. New York Herald Tribune, May 24, 1956.
31. *Jet* Magazine, June 7, 1956, p. 59.
32. William Shakespeare, *Othello*, 3.5.
33. Sidney Hook, *The Hero in History: A Study in Limitation and Possibility* (Boston: Beacon Press, 1955), p. 22.
34. Max Weber, *Economy and Society*, ed. G. Roth and C. Wittich (New York: Bedminster, 1968), p. 1120.
35. Genoveva Marais, *Kwame Nkrumah: As I Knew Him* (Chichester: Janay Publishing Company, 1972), pp. 19, 20.
36. Ibid., pp. 22, 23.
37. John William Johnson, Thomas A. Hale, and Stephen Belcher, eds., *Oral Epics from Africa: Vibrant Voices From a Vast Continent* (Bloomington: Indiana University Press, 1997), pp. 71, 72.
38. Interview, Lansana Kaba, Chicago, 1998.

Chapter 5

1. John William Johnson, Thomas A. Hale, and Stephen Belcher, eds., *Oral Epics from Africa: Vibrant Voices From a Vast Continent* (Bloomington: Indiana University Press, 1997), pp. 211–223.

2. Ibid., p. 223. For a detailed historical account of the saga of Lat Dior see Boubacar Barry, *Senegambia and the Atlantic Slave Trade*, translated from the French by Ayi Kwei Armah (Cambridge: Cambridge University Press, 1998). See also James F. Searing, *"God Alone is King":Islam and Emancipation in Senegal* (Oxford: Heinemann, 2002).
3. The Jesus epic introduced the world to Christian ideals of faith, hope, and charity. The world still awaits Christ's physical return. Rev. Dr. Martin Luther King, Jr., preached that believers returned to Christ themselves whenever they worked to build a society that would win Christ's approval. King called this society the Beloved Community. People move closer to Jesus when they work to institutionalize his ideals by building this new egalitarian social system. Each brick placed on top of another toward building the Beloved Community is a realization of the Christian ideal.
4. "The Heart of Africa, Interview with Julius Nyerere on Anti-Colonialism," *New Internationalist Magazine*, 309 (January–February 1999).
5. Interview, Muhammad Gueye, Dakar, Senegal, July 1998.
6. Kwame Nkrumah, *Neocolonialism: The Last Stage of Imperialism* (London: Nelson, 1965), p. 259.
7. See Nii Bonne, *Milestones in the History of the Gold Coast; Autobiography of Nii Kwabena Bonne III, Osu Alata Mantse, also Nana Owusu Akenten III, Oyokohene of Techiman, Ashanti* (London: Diplomatist Publications, 1953), pp. 63, 64.
8. Ibid., p. 66.
9. Ibid., p. 64.
10. Ibid., p. 65.
11. Ibid., p. 66.
12. Ibid., p.74.
13. Kwame Nkrumah, *Ghana: The Autobiography of Kwame Nkrumah* (New York: Nelson, 1957), p 75.
14. Bonne, *Milestones*, p. 86.
15. Ibid., p. 87
16. Ibid., p. 84.
17. Kwame Nkrumah, *Revolutionary Path*, 1st US ed. (New York: International Publishers, 1973), p. 55, See also *Ghana*, p. 77.
18. *Revolutionary Path*, p. 55.
19. Memorandum by R. Scott on the Gold Coast Government's View of the Causes of the Riots and the Steps to be Taken to Restore Law and Order, CO 96/795/6, no. 84, March 5, 1948.
20. [Gold Coast Riots]: Outward Circular Intelligence Telegram no. 121 from FO to HM Diplomatic Posts on the Detention of Political Activists, CO 96/795/7, no. 132, March 19, 1948.
21. Henry Morton Stanley, *My Early Travels and Adventures in America and Asia* (London: Sampson, Low, Marston and Co., 1895), 1:x–xi. See also Henry Morton Stanley, *Through the Dark Continent*, 2 vols. (London: Sampson, Low, Marston, Searle and Rivington, 1878).
22. West African tour—1948: Report by Mr. Rees-William to Mr. Creech Jones, Conclusions and Recommendations, CO 537/3226, no. 1, September 27, 1948.

Chapter 6

1. Kwame Nkrumah, *Ghana: The Autobiography of Kwame Nkrumah* (New York: Nelson, 1957), p. 84.
2. Ibid., p. 86.
3. Ibid., p. 87.
4. Ibid., p. 86.
5. Ibid., p. 92.
6. Despatch [*sic*] from R. Scott to Mr. Creech Jones on the Agitation for Self-Government. Minutes by E. G. G. Hanrott, L. H. Gorsuch, and A. B. Cohen, CO 537/4638, no. 1, March 10, 1949, p. 42.
7. Ibid.
8. Ibid., p. 3.
9. So many coup leaders, torturers, and murderers have received training at the United States Army's School of the Americas in Fort Benning, Georgia, that in the developing world the base has earned the popular moniker "School of the Assassins."
10. R. Scott to Mr. Creech Jones, pp. 4–5.
11. *Ghana*, p. 108.
12. Kwame Nkrumah, *I Speak of Freedom: A Statement of African Ideology* (London: Heinemann, 1961), p. 19.
13. *Accra Evening News*, January 14, 1949.
14. Kwame Nkrumah, *Revolutionary Path*, 1st U.S. ed. (New York: International Publishers, 1973), p. 93.
15. As quoted in *Revolutionary Path*, p. 92.
16. See Telegram from American Embassy, Leopoldville, to the State Department, Leopoldville, September 22, 1960, in *Foreign Relations of the United States, 1958–1960*, vol. 14 (Washington, D.C.: GPO, 1992), p. 501.
17. Nkrumah, *Ghana*, p. 87.
18. J. B. Danquah, *The Ghanaian Establishment: Its Constitution, Its Detentions, Its Traditions, Its Justice and Statecraft, and Its Heritage of Ghanaism*, ed. Albert Adu Boahen (Accra: Ghana Universities Press, 1997), p. 95.
19. Ibid.
20. Nkrumah, *Ghana*, p. 113.
21. *Accra Evening News*, January 17, 1950.
22. Nkrumah, *Ghana*, pp. 224–225.
23. *New York Amsterdam News*, December 23, 1931, p. 1.
24. Prime Minister's *Personal Minute*, Public Record Office Reference: PREM 11/2587, pp. 2–3.
25. Timothy Bankole, *Kwame Nkrumah: His Rise to Power* (London: George Allen & Unwin, 1955), p. 81.
26. See Vittorio Lanternari, *The Religions of the Oppressed: A Study of Modern Messianic Cults*, translated from the Italian by Lisa Sergio (New York: Mentor Books, 1963).
27. *Pittsburgh Courier*, March 13, 1937.
28. Kwame Nkrumah, *Consciencism: Philosophy and Ideology for Decolonization and Development with Particular Reference to the African Revolution* (London: Heinemann, 1964), p. 68.

29. See Charles S. Bird and Martha B. Kendall, "The Mande Hero, Text and Context," in *Explorations of African Systems of Thought*," ed. Ivan Karp and Charles S. Bird (Bloomington: Indiana University Press, 1980), p. 13.
30. Nkrumah, *Revolutionary Path*, p. 94.
31. *Accra Evening News*, December 16, 1949.
32. Letter from Mr. Creech Jones to T. R. O. Mangin on the Agitation for Self-Government, CO 537/4638, no. 8, May 24, 1949.
33. Letter (Reply) from T. R. O. Mangin to Mr. Creech Jones on the Agitation for Self-government, the Proposed Statement and the Prospect of Finding Employment for Mr. Nkrumah, CO 537/4638, no. 19, June 9, 1949.
34. Ibid.
35. Willard De Pree, Accra, Ghana Embassy, Principal Officer (1964–1968), Georgetown University Foreign Affairs Oral History Project, box 1, fold. 36.
36. Nkrumah, *Ghana*, p. 116.
37. Ibid., p. 118.
38. Ibid., p. 120.
39. Danquah, *The Ghanaian Establishment*, pp. 95, 96.
40. Frantz Fanon, *The Wretched of the Earth* (New York: Grove Press, 1968), p. 178.
41. Nkrumah, *Ghana*, p. 124.
42. "A Survey of Communism in Africa": Foreign Office Research Department Memorandum, part 2, Regional Survey—"British West Africa," CO 537/5263, no. 49, June 1950.
43. A year before independence, in 1956, a second British assessment would conclude that Nkrumah's anti-Communist policy had resulted in no Communists working in Ghana's civil service. See "Assessment of 'Anti-Communist Propaganda'": Memorandum by the United Kingdom Information Office in the Gold Coast, CO 554/1177, no. 16, April 23, 1956.
44. Nkrumah, *Ghana*, p. 134.
45. Kwame Nkrumah, *Africa Must Unite* (New York: International Publishers, 1963), p. 69.
46. For an in-depth exposition on the conflicts between Nkrumah and the secessionist Ashanti movement, see Richard Rathbone, *Nkrumah and the Chiefs: The Politics of Chieftaincy in Ghana, 1951–60* (Oxford, England: James Currey, 2000).
47. J. B. Danquah, *A Page from the Life of J. B.*, p. 33, quoted in Kolawole Balagun, *Mission To Ghana: Memoir of a Diplomat* (New York: Vantage Press, 1963), pp. 16–17.
48. V. I. Lenin, *Imperialism: The Highest Stage of Capitalism* (New York: International Publishers, 1939), p. 85.
49. V. I. Lenin, *The State and Revolution: Marxist Teaching on the State and the Tasks of the Proletariat in the Revolution* (Peking: Foreign Languages Press, 1965), p. 105.
50. Quoted in Dennis Austin, *Politics in Ghana* (Oxford: Oxford University Press, 1970), p. 381.
51. For the best account of this incident, and the Preventive Detention Act in general, see Geoffrey Bing, *Reap the Whirlwind: An Account of Kwame Nkrumah's Ghana from 1950 to 1966* (London: MacGibbon & Kee, 1968).
52. St. Clair Drake, "Nkrumah: The Real Tragedy," *Nation*, June 5, 1972, p. 723.

53. Nkrumah, *Revolutionary Path*, p. 108.
54. Nkrumah, *Ghana*, p. 33.
55. Modibo M. Kadalie, "Decisions of the Asian-African Conference, 1955," from Appendix A in *Internationalism, Pan-Africanism, and the Struggle for Social Change* (Savannah, GA: One Quest Press, 2000), pp.495–496.
56. Nkrumah, *Revolutionary Path*, p. 35.
57. Freedom of Information Act, Central Intelligence Agency, *National Intelligence Estimate 74–57*, "The Outlook For Ghana," December 27, 1957, p. 6.
58. Max Weber, Economy and Society, ed. G. Roth and G. Wittich (New York: Bedminster, 1968), p. 1120.
59. CIA, "The Outlook for Ghana," p. 6.
60. Ibid., p. 6.
61. Ibid., p. 3.
62. Ibid.
63. Ibid.
64. Ibid., p. 8.
65. Ibid.
66. Martin Luther King, Jr., "Birth of a New Nation," in *The Autobiography of Martin Luther King, Jr.*, ed. Clayborne Carson (New York: Warner Books, 1998), p. 112.
67. See Joseph A. Walkes, Jr., *Black Square and Compass, 200 Years of Prince Hall Freemasonry* (Richmond, VA: Macoy Publishing, 1979), p. 189.
68. King, *Autobiography*, p. 112.
69. Ibid., p. 113.
70. Ibid., 114.
71. Ibid., pp. 114–115.
72. Clayborne Carson, senior ed., *The Papers of Martin Luther King, Jr.*, vol. 4, *Symbol of the Movement, January 1957–December 1958*, ed. Susan Carson, Kieran Taylor, and Adrienne Clay (Berkeley: University of California Press, 1992), pp. 146–147.
73. Ibid., pp. 260–261.
74. James M. Washington, ed., *A Testament of Hope: The Essential Writings of Martin Luther King, Jr.* (New York: Harper & Row, 1986), p. 136.
75. Nkrumah, *Ghana*, p. 12.
76. Carson, *Papers of Martin Luther King, Jr.*, vol. 1, pp. 435–436.
77. See David J. Garrow, "The Radical Challenge of Martin King," in *The FBI and Martin Luther King, Jr.* (New York: W. W. Norton., 1981), pp. 213–215.
78. Quoted from the essay "Where Do We Go from Here," in *A Testament of Hope*, p. 630.

Chapter 7

1. Okot p'Bitek, *Song of Ocol* (Nairobi: East African Publishing House, 1970), pp. 62–63.
2. For an incisive treatment of the role of cocoa in Ghana's history, before and after independence, see Gwendolyn Mikell, *Cocoa and Chaos in Ghana* (New York: Paragon Books, 1989).

3. Kwame Nkrumah, *Dark Days in Ghana*, new ed. (New York: International Publishers, 1969), p. 65.
4. St. Clair Drake, "Prospects for Democracy in the Gold Coast," *The Annals of the American Academy of Political and Social Science* 306 (July 1956): 86.
5. For this critique, see Manning Marable, *African and Caribbean Politics: From Kwame Nkrumah to Maurice Bishop* (London: Verso Books, 1987).
6. See "The Rise and Fall of Kwame Nkrumah," in *The C. L. R. James Reader*, ed. Anna Grimshaw (Cambridge: Blackwell, 1992), pp. 354–371.
7. See H. H. Price, "The Gold Coast's Legislators," *West Africa*, May 26, 1956, p. 34.
8. Nkrumah, *Dark Days in Ghana*, p. 66.
9. Genoveva Marais, *Kwame Nkrumah: As I Knew Him* (Chichester: Janay Publishing, 1972), p. 102.
10. See T. Ras Makkonen, *Pan Africanism from Within* (New York: Oxford University Press, 1972), p. 256; Ruth First, *Power in Africa* (New York: Pantheon Books, 1970), p. 192.
11. See Andargachew Tiruneh, *The Ethiopian Revolution, 1974–1987: A Transformation from an Aristocratic to a Totalitarian Autocracy* (Cambridge: Cambridge University Press, 1993).
12. Kwame Nkrumah, "Politics Are Not for Soldiers," Lincoln University Archives, Box 14.
13. Kwame Nkrumah, *Consciencism: Philosophy and Ideology for Decolonization and Development with Particular Reference to the African Revolution* (London: Heinemann, 1964), p. 106.
14. See John Markakis, "Garrison Socialism: The Case of Ethiopia," MERIP Reports, no. 79, June 1979, pp. 3–17.
15. "Memorandum for the Deputy Director of Central Intelligence" (Helms), Washington, February 25, 1966, in *Foreign Relations of the United States, 1964–1968*, vol. 24 (Washington, D.C.: GPO, 1999), p. 250. This document contained a review of CIA inner communications about the pending coup during the year leading up to the coup.
16. See Human Rights Watch, "Backgrounders: Ethiopian Dictator Mengistu Haile Mariam," http://hrw.org/english/docs/1999/11/29/ethiop5495.htm.
17. Samuel Obeng, comp., *Selected Speeches of Kwame Nkrumah* (Accra: Afram Publications, 1979), pp. 110–115.
18. See Marais, *Kwame Nkrumah*, p. 82.
19. Kwame Nkrumah, "Address to CPP Study Group in Flagstaff House," Accra, 1961.
20. See Phillip Foster, *Education and Social Change in Ghana* (Chicago: University of Chicago Press, 1965).
21. *Evening News*, January 26, 1960, p. 2.
22. Interview, Bowie, Maryland, April 2003.
23. Jean van Lierde, ed., *Lumumba Speaks: The Speeches and Writings of Patrice Lumumba, 1958-1961*, translated from the French by Helen R. Lane. Introduction by Jean-Paul Sartre (Boston: Little, Brown, 1972), p. 58.
24. Ibid., p. 70.

25. Ibid., p. 75.
26. For a succinct display of Lumumba's ideas, see. W. A. E. Skurnik, *African Political Thought: Lumumba, Nkrumah, Toure* (Denver: University of Denver, 1968).
27. Ibid., p. 320. For Nkrumah's explanation of "Positive Neutrality," see *I Speak of Freedom, A Statement of African Ideology* (London: Heinemann, 1961), pp. 196, 199, 219.
28. Kwame Nkrumah, *Revolutionary Path*, 1st U.S. ed. (New York: International Publishers, 1973), p. 150.
29. See Conor Cruise O'Brien, *To Katanga and Back: A UN Case History* (New York: Grosset & Dunlap, 1962).
30. For an insider's account of the international machinations surrounding Lumumba and Congo's fate, see Kwame Nkrumah, *Challenge of the Congo* (New York: International Publishers, 1967). Also see the book by two Belgian professors who were in Congo during the Lumumba tragedy, G. Heinz and H. Donnay, *Lumumba: The Last Fifty Days* (New York: Grove Press, 1969).
31. Richard D. Mahoney, *J.F.K.: Ordeal in Africa.* (New York: Oxford University Press, 1983), p. 38.
32. See Madeleine G. Kalb, *The Congo Cables: The Cold War in Africa—From Eisenhower to Kennedy* (New York: Macmillan, 1982), p. xiii.
33. "Memorandum of Discussion at the 452nd Meeting of the National Security Council," July 21, 1960, *Foreign Relations of the United States, 1958–1960*, vol. 14 (Washington, D.C.: GPO, 1992), p. 339.
34. "Interim Report: Alleged Assassination Plots Involving Foreign Leaders," United States Senate Intelligence Committee, 1975, p. 14.
35. George Lardner, Jr., "Did Ike Authorize a Murder?", *Washington Post*, August 8, 2000, A23.
36. Interim Report, United States Senate Intelligence Committee, p. 15.
37. Ibid., p. 17.
38. Telegram from the American embassy, Leopoldville, Congo, to the State Department. September 22, 1960. *Foreign Relations of the United States, 1958–1960*, vol. 14, p. 501.
39. For the British officers' point of view, see. H. T. Alexander, *African Tightrope: My Two Years as Nkrumah's Chief of Staff* (London: Pall Mall Press, 1965).
40. "Who Killed Lumumba?" BBC News, http://news.bbc.co.uk/2/hi/programmes/correspondent/974745.stm.
41. See "History Will One Day Have its Say," *New African*, February 2000. Also for more recent revelations concerning the last days of Lumumba, see Ludo de Witte, *The Assassination of Lumumba*, translated from the Dutch by Ann Wright and Renée Fenby (New York: Verso, 2001).
42. Malcolm X, *The Autobiography of Malcolm X*, as told to Alex Haley (New York: Ballantine Books, 1973), p. 357.
43. United States State Department, *Foreign Relations of the United States, 1964–1968*, vol. 24, p. 250, Doc. no. 256.
44. Ibid., 256. Circular Telegram From the Department of State to Embassies in Africa, Washington, November 23, 7:26 p.m.

45. Ibid.
46. Ibid.
47. Marais, *Kwame Nkrumah*, p. 103.
48. Grimshaw, *The C. L. R. James Reader*, p. 358.
49. For a courageous exposé of the inner working of imperialism in the twenty-first century, see John Perkins, *Confessions of an Economic Hit Man* (San Francisco: Berrett-Koehler, 2004).
50. Kwame Nkrumah, *Neocolonialism: The Last State of Imperialism* (New York: International Publishers, 1965), p. 11.
51. Ibid., p. 2.
52. *Foreign Relations of the United States*, 1964–1968, vol. 24, Doc. no. 257, para. 1.
53. Ibid., para. 2.
54. Ibid., para. 3.
55. See Brenda Gayle Plummer, *Rising Wind: Black Americans and U.S. Foreign Affairs, 1935–1960* (Chapel Hill: The University of North Carolina Press, 1996), pp. 227, 309.
56. *Foreign Relations of the United States*, 1964–1968, vol. 24, Doc. no. 257, para. 4.
57. Nkrumah, *Dark Days in Ghana*, p. 49.
58. W. E. B. Du Bois, "The Talented Tenth: Memorial Address," in *W. E. B. Du Bois: A Reader*, ed. David Levering Lewis (New York: Henry Holt, 1995), p. 349.
59. Letter, Department of State, Johnson Library, White House Central File, Confidential File, CO 93. (University of Michigan: Declassified Documents Reference System). For more about Williams's response to the coup see, Kevin K. Gaines, *Black Expatriates and the Civil Rights Era: American Africans in Ghana* (Chapel Hill: University of North Carolina Press, 2006), pp. 237–239.
60. Lewis, *Du Bois*, p. 352.
61. Nkrumah, *Dark Days in Ghana*, p. 49.
62. Interview, Conakry, Guinea, 1998.
63. Ibid., p. 75.
64. Ibid., pp. 75,76.
65. Afrifa, *The Ghana Coup*, pp. 32–37.
66. Johnson Library, National Security File, Country File, Ghana, vol. 2, Cables, 3/64–2/66.
67. Johnson Library, National Security File, Memos to the President, Robert W. Komer, vol. 21, 3/3/66–3/20/66. Confidential. A handwritten "L" on the source text indicates that the memorandum was seen by the president.
68. Stokely Carmichael with Ekwueme Michael Thelwell, *Ready for Revolution: The Life and Struggles of Stokely Carmichael (Kwame Ture)* (New York: Scribner, 2003), p. 622.
69. See Kevin Shillingon, *Ghana and the Rawlings Factor* (New York: Palgrave Macmillan, 1992); also Emmanuel Hansen, "The Military and Revolution in Ghana," *Journal of African Marxists*, no. 2, August 1992.
70. Interview, Detroit, Michigan, May 2003.
71. http://www.bbc.co.uk/worldservice/people/highlights/000914_nkrumah.shtml.

Bibliography

Abrahams, Peter. *A Wreath for Udomo*. New York: Collier Books, 1971.

Ackah, C. A. *Akan Ethics*. Accra: Ghana University Press, 1998.

Adi, Hakim. *West Africans in Britain, 1900–1960*. London: Lawrence and Wishart, 1998.

African Students Association (U.S.A.). *Know This of Aggrey: Unpublished Monograph of Things Said by and of Aggrey*. New York, 1942.

Afrifa, Akwasi A. *The Ghana Coup: 24ᵗʰ February 1966*. London: Frank Cass, 1966.

Alexander, H. T. *African Tightrope: My Two Years as Nkrumah's Chief of Staff*. London: Pall Mall Press, 1965.

Appiah, Joseph. *Joe Appiah: The Autobiography of an African Patriot*. New York: Praeger, 1990.

Appiah, Kwame Anthony. *In My Father's House: Africa in the Philosophy of Culture*. Oxford: Oxford University Press, 1992.

Aptheker, Herbert, ed. *The Correspondence of W. E. B. Du Bois*. Vol. 1, *Selections, 1877–1934*. Amherst: University of Massachusetts Press, 1977.

Arhin, Kwame, ed. *The Life and Work of Kwame Nkrumah*. Accra: Sedco Publishing, 1991.

Austin, Dennis. *Politics in Ghana*. Oxford: Oxford University Press, 1970.

Ayittey, George B. N. *Africa Betrayed*. New York: St. Martin's Press, 1992.

Azikiwe, Nnamdi. *My Odyssey*. London: C. Hurst, 1970.

Baëta, C. G. *Prophetism in Ghana: A Study of Some " Spiritual" Churches*. London: SCM Press, 1962.

Barker, Peter. *Operation Cold Chop: The Coup that Toppled Nkrumah*. Accra: Ghana Publishing Corporation, 1969.

Barry, Boubacar. *Senegambia and the Atlantic Slave Trade*. Translated from the French by Ayi Kwei Armah. Cambridge: Cambridge University Press, 1998.

Beidelman, T. O. *The Kagaru*. New York: Holt, Rinehart and Winston, 1971.

Bing, Geoffrey. *Reap the Whirlwind: An Account of Kwame Nkrumah's Ghana from 1950 to 1966*. London: MacGibbon & Kee, 1968.

Blyden, Edward Wilmot. *Black Spokesman, Selected Writings of Edward Wilmot Blyden*. Edited by Hollis R. Lynch. London: Frank Cass, 1971.

Boahen, Adu. *Ghana: Evolution and Change in the Nineteenth and Twentieth Centuries*. London: Longman, 1975.

Bonne, Nii. *Milestones in the History of the Gold Coast; Autobiography of Nii Kwabena Bonne III, Osu Alata Mantse, also Nana Owusu Akenten III, Oyokohene of Techiman, Ashanti.* London: Diplomatist Publications, 1953.

Boorhis, Harold Van Buren. *Negro Masonry in the United States.* Bensenville, IL: Lushena Books, 2003.

Bretton, Henry. *The Rise and Fall of Kwame Nkrumah: A Study of Personal Rule in Africa.* New York: Frederick A. Praeger, 1966.

Brisbane, Robert H. *The Black Vanguard: Origins of the Negro Social Revolution, 1900–1960.* Valley Forge: Judson Press, 1970.

Bullock, Steven C. *Revolutionary Brotherhood, Freemasonry and the Transformation of the American Social Order.* Chapel Hill: University of North Carolina Press, 1996.

Busia, K. A. *The Challenge of Africa.* New York: Praeger, 1962.

Busia, K. A., and H. K. Akyeampong. *Ghana's Struggle for Democracy and Freedom Speeches, 1957–69.* Accra: Danquah Memorial Pub. Co., 1978.

Cabral, Amilcar. *Return to the Source: Selected Speeches of Amilcar Cabral.* NewYork: Monthly Review Press, 1973.

Campbell, Joseph. *The Hero with a Thousand Faces.* Princeton, NJ: Princeton University Press, 1968.

Carmichael, Stokely with Ekwueme Michael Thelwell. *Ready for Revolution: The Life and Struggles of Stokely Carmichael (Kwame Ture).* New York: Scribner, 2003.

Carty, Wilfred, and Martin Kilson, eds. *Africa Reader: Colonial Africa.* NewYork: Vantage Books, 1970.

Césaire, Aimé. *Discourse on Colonialism.* Translated by Joan Pinkham. NewYork: Monthly Review Press, 1972.

Clausewitz, Carl Von. *On War.* London: Penguin Books, 1982.

Danquah, J. B. *The Akan Doctrine of God: A Fragment of Gold Coast Ethics and Religion.* 2nd ed. London: Frank Cass, 1968.

Danquah, J. B., and H. K. Akyeampong. *Historic Speeches and Writings on Ghana.* Accra: G. Boakie, 1966.

Danquah, J. B., A. Adu Boahen, and University of Ghana. *The Ghanian Establishment: Its Constitution, Its Detentions, Its Traditions, Its Justice and Statecraft, and Its Heritage of Ghanaism.* Accra: Ghana Universities Press, 1997.

Davidson, Basil. *Black Star.* London: Allen Lane, 1971.

Debrunner, Hans W. *Witchcraft in Ghana.* Accra: Presbyterian Book Depot, 1961.

Delaney, Martin R., MD. *The Origin and Objects of Ancient Freemasonry, Its Introduction into the United States and Legitimacy among Colored Men.* Pittsburgh: W.S. Haven, 1853.

de Witte, Ludo. *The Assassination of Lumumba.* Translated by Ann Wright and Renée Fenby. NewYork: Verso, 2001.

Diawara, Manthia. *In Search of Africa.* Cambridge: Harvard University Press, 1998.

Du Bois, W. E. B. *The Autobiography of W. E. B. Du Bois.* NewYork: International Publishers, 1958.

————. *W. E. B. Du Bois: The Crisis Writings*. Edited by Daniel Walden. Greenwich, CT: Fawcett, 1972.

Duncan, Malcolm C. *Duncan's Ritual of Freemasonry*. NewYork: Crown Publishers, n.d.

Drachler, Jacob. *African Heritage*. London: Collier Books, 1964.

Eulau, Heinz. *The Behavioral Persuasion in Politics*. New York: Random House, 1963.

Fanon, Frantz. *Black Skin, White Masks*. New York: Grove Press, 1968.

————. *A Dying Colonialism*. New York: Monthly Review Press, 1965.

————. *The Wretched of the Earth*. New York: Grove Press, 1967.

Field, M. J. *Social Organization of the Ga People*. London: Crown Agents for the Colonies, 1940.

Fields, Karen E. "Political Contingencies of Witchcraft in Colonial Central Africa: Culture and the State in Marxist Theory." *Canadian Journal of African Studies* 16, no. 3 (1982).

First, Ruth. *Power in Africa*. New York: Pantheon Books, 1970.

Ford, Clyde W. *The Hero with an African Face: Mythic Wisdom of Traditional Africa*. New York: Bantam Books, 2000.

Foster, Phillip. *Education and Social Change in Ghana*. Chicago: University of Chicago Press, 1965.

Frazier, E. Franklin. *On Race Relations, Selected Papers*. Edited by G. Franklin Edwards. Boston: Beacon Press, 1969.

Frederickson, George M. *Black Liberation: A Comparative History of Black Ideologies in the United States and South Africa*. Oxford: Oxford University Press, 1995.

Gaines, Kevin K. *Black Expatriates and the Civil Rights Era: African Americans in Ghana*. Chapel Hill: University of North Carolina Press, 2006.

Garrow, David J. *The FBI and Martin Luther King, Jr.* NewYork: W.W. Norton, 1981.

Garvey, Marcus. *Philosophy and Opinions of Marcus Garvey*. London: Frank Cass, 1923.

————. *Philosophy and Opinions of Marcus Garvey, or Africa for the Africans*. Compiled by Amy Jacques Garvey. London: Frank Cass, 1967.

Gorer, Geoffrey. *Africa Dances: A Book about West African Negroes*. London: Faber & Faber, 1935.

Habermas, Jurgen. *Communication and the Evolution of Society*. Boston: Beacon Press, 1970.

Hailey, Lord Malcolm. *Native Administration and Political Development in British Tropical Africa*. London, 1943.

Hale, Thomas A., ed. and trans. *The Epic of Askia Muhammad*. Bloomington and Indianapolis: Indiana University Press, 1996.

Hayford, J. E. Casely. *Gold Coast Native Institutions, With Thoughts upon a Healthy Imperial Policy for the Gold Coast and Ashanti*. London: Sweet and Maxwell, 1903.

Hook, Sidney. *The Hero in History: A Study in Limitation and Possibility*. Boston: Beacon Press, 1955.

House, Gloria. *Tower and Dungeon: A Study of Place and Power in American Culture.* Detroit: Casa De Unidad Press, 1991.

Heinz, G., and H. Donnay. *Lumumba: The Last Fifty Days.* New York: Grove Press, 1969.

Jackson, Robert H., and Carl G. Rosberg. *Personal Rule in Black Africa: Prince, Autocrat, Prophet; Tyrant.* Berkeley: University of California Press, 1982.

Jagoda, Gustav. *White Man.* London: Oxford University Press, 1961.

James, C. L. R. *Nkrumah and the Ghana Revolution.* Westport, CT: L. Hill, 1977.

James, C. L. R., and Anna Grimshaw. *The C. L. R. James Reader.* Oxford and Cambridge, MA: Blackwell, 1992.

Johnson, William Hale, Thomas A. John, and Stephen Belcher, eds. *Oral Epics from Africa: Vibrant Voices from a Vast Continent.* Bloomington: Indiana University Press, 1997.

Jones, Trevor. *Ghana's First Republic 1960—1966: The Pursuit of the Political Kingdom.* London: Methuen, 1976.

Julien, Isaac, co-writer/director. *Frantz Fanon: Black Skin, White Masks.* Normal Films, 1995.

Kadalie, Modibo M. *Internationalism, Pan-Africanism, and the Struggle for Social Change.* Savannah, GA: One Quest Press, 2000.

Kalb, Madeleine G. *The Congo Cables: The Cold War in Africa—From Eisenhower to Kennedy.* New York: Macmillan, 1982.

Karp, Ivan, and Charles S. Bird, eds. *In Explorations of African Systems of Thought.* Bloomington: Indiana University Press, 1980.

Kohn, Hans, and Wallace Sokolsky, eds. *African Nationalism in the Twentieth Century.* New York: Von Nostrand Reinhold, 1965.

King, Kenneth. *Pan Africanism and Education: A Study of Race Philanthropy in the Southern States and East Africa.* Oxford: Clarendon Press, 1971.

King, Martin Luther, Jr. *The Papers of Martin Luther King, Jr.* Vol. 4, *Symbol of the Movement, January 1957–December 1958.* Edited by Clayborne Carson et al. Berkeley: University of California Press, 1992.

———. *A Testament of Hope, The Essential Writings of Martin Luther King, Jr.* Edited by James M. Washington. San Francisco: Harper & Row, 1986.

Lanternari, Vittorio. *The Religions of the Oppressed: A Study of Modern Messianic Cults.* Translated from Italian by Lisa Sergio. New York: Mentor Books, 1963.

Lenin, V. I. *Imperialism: The Highest Stage of Capitalism.* New York: International Publishers, 1939.

———. *The State and Revolution: Marxist Teaching on the State and the Tasks of the Proletariat in the Revolution.* Peking: Foreign Languages Press, 1965.

Lewis, David Levering, ed. *W. E. B. Du Bois: A Reader.* New York: Henry Holt, 1995.

Little, K. L. *Negroes in Britain: A Study of Racial Relations in English Society.* London: Kegan Paul, 1947.

Locke, Alain, ed. *The New Negro.* New York: Atheneum, 1980.

Loewenstein, Karl. *Max Weber's Political Ideas.* Translated from German by Richard and Clara Winston. Amherst: University of Massachusetts Press, 1966.

Lumumba, Patrice. *Lumumba Speaks: The Speeches and Writings of Patrice Lumumba, 1958–1961.* Translated by Helen R. Lane. Edited by Jean van Lierde. Boston: Little, Brown, 1972.

Luthuli, Albert. *Let My People Go.* NewYork: McGraw-Hill, 1962.

Macartney, William M. *Dr. Aggrey: Ambassador for Africa.* London: SCM Press, 1948.

Mahoney, Richard D. *J.F.K.: Ordeal in Africa.* New York: Oxford University Press, 1983.

Makonnen, Ra. *Pan Africanism from Within.* New York: Oxford University Press, 1972.

Malcolm X. *The Autobiography of Malcolm X, as told to Alex Haley.* New York: Ballantine Books, 1973.

Marable, Manning. *Africans & Caribbean Politics: From Kwame Nkrumah to Maurice Bishop.* London: Verso Books, 1987.

Marais, Genoveva. *Kwame Nkrumah: As I Knew Him.* Chichester: Janay, 1972.

Martinson, H. B. *Ghana, The Dream of the Twenty First Century: Politics of J. B. Danquah, Busia and Kufuor Tradition.* Accra: Norcento Press, 2001.

Mazrui, Ali. *On Heroes and Uhuru Worship.* London: Collier Books, 1967.

Memmi, Albert. *The Colonizer and the Colonized.* Boston: Beacon Press, 1965.

Mikell, Gwendolyn. *Cocoa and Chaos in Ghana.* New York: Paragon Books, 1989.

Muraskin, William A. *Middle-Class Blacks in a White Society, Prince Hall Freemasonry in America.* Berkeley: University of California Press, 1975.

Murray, Andrew E. "The Founding of Lincoln University." *Journal of Presbyterian History,* Winter 1973.

Mwakikagile, Godfrey. *Military Coups in West Africa Since the Sixties.* Huntington, NY: Nova Science Publishers, 2001.

Nkrumah, Kwame. *Africa Must Unite.* New York: International Publishers, 1970.

———. *Axioms of Kwame Nkrumah.* London: Nelson, 1967.

———. *The Big Lie.* London: Panaf Books, 1968.

———. *Challenge of the Congo.* New York: International Publishers, 1970.

———. *Class Struggle in Africa.* 1st ed. New York: International Publishers, 1970.

———. *Consciencism: Philosophy and Ideology for Decolonization and Development with Particular Reference to the African Revolution.* London: Heinemann, 1964.

———. *Dark Days in Ghana.* New ed. New York: International Publishers, 1969.

———. *Evening News.* Accra, Ghana: Star Pub. Co., 1968.

———. *Ghana: The Autobiography of Kwame Nkrumah.* NewYork: Nelson, 1957.

———. *I Speak of Freedom: A Statement of African Ideology.* London: Heinemann, 1961.

———. *Neo-Colonialism The Last Stage of Imperialism.* London: Nelson, 1965.

———. *Revolutionary Path.* 1st U.S. ed. New York: International Publishers, 1973.

———. *Towards Colonial Freedom: Africa in the Struggle against World Imperialism.* London: Heinemann, 1962.

————. *Voice from Conakry Broadcasts to the People of Ghana Made in Conakry between March and December 1966 on Radio Guinea's "Voice of the Revolution."* London: Panaf Publications, 1967.

Nkrumah, Kwame, and Samuel Obeng. *Selected Speeches.* Accra, Ghana: Afram Publications (Ghana), 1997.

Oberhelman, Stephen M., Van Kelly, and Richard J.Golsan, eds. *Epic and Epoch: Essays on the Interpretation and History of a Genre.* Lubbock: Texas Tech University Press, 1994.

O'Brien, Cruise. *To Katanga and Back: A UN Case History.* NewYork: Grosset & Dunlap, 1962.

Odinga, Oginga. *Not Yet Uhuru: The Autobiography of Oginga Odinga.* New York: Hill and Wang, 1967.

Okpewho, Isidore. *The Epic in Africa.* New York: Columbia University Press, 1979.

Omari, T. Peter. *Kwame Nkrumah: The Anatomy of an African Dictatorship.* With a foreword by Nii Amaa Ollennu. New York: Africana Pub. Corp, 1970.

Ottley, Roi. *No Green Pastures.* NewYork: Scribner, 1951.

Owusu, Maxwell. *Uses and Abuses of Political Power: A Case Study of Continuity and Change in the Politics of Ghana.* Chicago: University of Chicago Press, 1970.

Padmore, George. *The Gold Coast Revolution.* London: Dennis Dobson, 1953.

————. *History of the Pan-African Congress.* London: Hammersmith, 1947.

p'Bitek, Okot. *Song of Ocol.* Nairobi: East African Publishing House, 1970.

Perkins, John. *Confession of an Economic Hit Man.* San Francisco: Berrett-Koehler, 2004.

Plummer, Brenda Gayle. *Rising Wind: Black Americans and U.S. Foreign Affairs, 1935–1960.* Chapel Hill: University of North Carolina Press, 1996.

Poe, D. Sizwe. *Kwame Nkrumah's Contribution to Pan-Africanism: An Afrocentric Analysis.* New York: Routledge, 2003.

Powell, Adam Clayton. *Adam by Adam: The Autobiography of Adam Clayton Powell, Jr.* New York: Kinsington Publishing Corporation, 1971.

Powell, Erica. *Private Secretary Female Gold Coast.* New York: Palgrave Macmillan, 1984.

Prabhavananda, Swami, and Christopher Isherwood. *How To Know God, the Yoga Aphorisms of Patanjali.* New York: New American Library, 1953.

Rank, Otto. *The Myth of the Birth of the Hero: A Psychological Interpretation of Mythology.* Translated by Dr. F. Robbins and Dr. Ely Jelliffe Smith. New York: Robert Brunner, 1957.

Rathbone, Richard, ed. *British Documents on the Empire.* Part 1, 1941–1952. London: HMSO Publications Centre, 1992.

————. *British Documents on the End of Empire.* Vol. 2, *Nkrumah & the Chiefs: The Politics of Chieftaincy in Ghana, 1951–60.* Oxford: James Currey, 2000.

Roberts, John W. *From Trickster to Badman.* Philadelphia: University of Pennsylvania Press, 1989.

Rooney, David. *Kwame Nkrumah: The Political Kingdom in the Third World.* New York: St. Martin's Press, 1988.

Salm, Steven J., and Toyin Falola. *Culture and Customs of Ghana.* London: Greenword Press, 2002.

Sampson, Magnus. *Makers of Modern Ghana*. Vol. 1. Accra: Anowuo Educational Publications, 1969.

Scobie, Edward. *Black Britannia: A History of Blacks in Britain*. Chicago: Johnson Publishing Company, 1972.

Seton-Watson, Hugh. "Fascism, Right and Left." *Contemporary History*, January 1, 1996.

Sherwood, Marika. *Kwame Nkrumah, the Years Abroad 1935–1947*. Legon, Ghana: Freedom Publications, 1966.

Shillingon, Kevin. *Ghana and the Rawlings Factor*. New York: Palgrave Macmillan, 1992.

Simons, George E. *Standard Masonic Monitor of the Degrees of Entered Apprentice, Fellowcraft and Master Mason*. Richmond, VA: Macoy Publishing and Masonic Supply Co., 1984.

Skurnik, W. A. E. *African Political Thought: Lumumba, Nkrumah, and Ture*. Denver: University of Denver, 1968.

Smith, Edwin W. *Aggrey of Africa: A Study in Black and White*. London: Student Christian Movement Press, 1929.

Smith, Linda Tuhiwai. *Decolonizing Methodologies: Research and Indigenous Peoples*. New York: Zed Books, 2002.

Stanley, Henry Morton. *My Early Travels and Adventures in America and Asia*. London: Sampson, Low, Marston and Co., 1895.

———. *Through the Dark Continent*. 2 vols. London: Sampson, Low, Marston, Searle and Rivington, 1878.

Steblecki, Edith J. *Paul Revere and Masonry*. Boston, 1985.

Thompson, Willard Scott. *Ghana's Foreign Policy, 1957–1966*. Princeton, NJ: Princeton University Press, 1969.

Timothy, Bankole. *Kwame Nkrumah, from Cradle to Grave*. 1st ed. Dorchester, Dorset: Gavin Press, 1981.

Tiruneh, Andargachew. *The Ethiopian Revolution, 1974–1987: A Transformation from an Aristocratic to a Totalitarian Autocracracy*. Cambridge: Cambridge University Press, 1993.

Walkes, Joseph A., Jr. *Black Square & Compass: 200 Years of Prince Hall Freemasonry*. Richmond: Macoy Publishing, 1979.

Weber, Max. *Theory of Social and Economic Organization*. New York: Oxford University Press, 1947.

Weisbrot, Robert. *Father Divine and the Struggle for Racial Equality*. Urbana: University of Illinois Press, 1983.

Who's Who in Colored America: A Biographical Dictionary of Notable Living Persons of African Descent in America 1933–1937. Brooklyn: Thomas Yenser, 1937.

Wiener, Joel H., ed. *Great Britain: Foreign Policy and the Span of Empire 1689–1971: A Documentary History*. Vol. 2. New York: Chelsea House/McGraw-Hill, 1972.

Wise, D., and T. B. Ross. *The Invisible Government*. New York: Random House, 1964.

Wood, Gordon S. *The Radicalism of the American Revolution*. New York: Vintage, 1993.

Wright, Richard. *Black Power*. New York: Harper, 1954.

Personal Interviews

Ayi Kwei Armah, Popenquine, Senegal, July 1997.
Kojo Atta, Accra, Ghana, July 1999.
Boubacar Barry, Dakar, Senegal, July 1998.
Grace Lee Boggs, Detroit, Michigan, January 2004.
Harold Cruse, Ann Arbor, Michigan, August 2000.
Muhammad Gueye, Dakar, Senegal, July 1997.
Mawina Kouyate, Detroit, Michigan, December 1998.
Paa Kwame (Leroy Mitchell), Detroit, Michigan, 2003.
Sam Nyako, Bowie, Maryland, April 2003.
Kofi Ogra, Kumasi, Ghana, July 1999.
Nehanda Omowale, Detroit, Michigan, December 2000.
James Owusu, Cleveland, Ohio, October 2003.
Kwame Ture (Stokely Carmichael), Conakry, Guinea, July 1997, and Detroit, Michigan, March 1998.
Abeena Bin Wahad, Kumasi, Ghana, July 1999.
Dhoruba Bin Wahad, Kumasi, Ghana, July 1999.

Online Publications

Encyclopedia of Marxism: Glossary of People. www.marxists.org ///glossary/ people /t/r.htm#trotsky-leon.
Hardon, S.J., John A. *Pocket Catholic Dictionary.* http://www.therealpresence. org/dictionary/adict.htm.
Human Rights Watch. "Backgrounders, Ethiopian Dictator Mengistu Haile Mariam." http://hrw.org/ english/docs/1999/11/29/ethiop5495.htm.
Kipling, Rudyard Kipling. *American Notes.* http://whitewolf.newcastle.edu.au/ words/authors/K/KiplingRudyard/prose/AmericanNotes/index.html.
"Kwame Nkrumah's Vision of Africa." http://www.bbc.co.uk/worldservice/ people/highlights/000914_nkrumah.shtml.
Peggy [Cripps] Appiah, Obituary, www.telegraph.co.uk/ news/ main.jhtml?x ... ortal/2006/02/24/ixportal.html.

Newspapers

Accra Evening News, January 14, 1949.
    January 17, 1950.
    September 22, 1959.
    January 26, 1960.
    October 2, 1965.
New York Amsterdam News, December 23, 1931.
New York Herald Tribune, May 24, 1956.

Pittsburgh Courier, November 26, 1936.
    December 5, 1936.
    March 13, 1937.
    July 3, 1937.
The Washington Post, August 8, 2000.

Journals

American Historical Review 100 (June 1995): 765–787.
Canadian Journal of African Studies 16, no. 3 (1982): 567–593.
Drake, St. Clair. "Prospects for Democracy in the Gold Coast." *Annals of the American Academy of Political and Social Science* 306 (July 1956): 86.
Educational Outlook, November 1943, p. 5.
Journal of Presbyterian History, Winter 1973.
Markakis, John. *MERIP Reports,* no. 79 (June 1979): 3–17.
"Negro History," *The Lincolnian* 5, no. 2 (January 18, 1938).
Transition.

Archives

Aggrey Papers, Moorland-Spingarn Collection, Howard University.
Federal Bureau of Investigation Archives, Reading Room, J. Edgar Hoover Building, Washington, D.C.
Kwame Nkrumah Papers, Ghana National Archives.
Kwame Nkrumah Papers, Lincoln University Archives.
Kwame Nkrumah Papers, Moorland-Spingarn Collection, Howard University.
Library of the Congress of the United States.
The Martin Luther King, Jr., Center, Atlanta, Georgia.
Papers of W. E. B. Du Bois, University of Massachusetts, Amherst.
United States National Archives, College Park, Maryland.
United States National Archives, Washington, D.C.

Magazines

Drake, St. Clair. "Nkrumah: The Real Tragedy." *Nation,* June 5, 1972, p. 723.
"The Heart of Africa, Interview with Julius Nyerere on Anti-Colonialism." *New Internationalist Magazine,* no. 309, January–February 1999.
Jet Magazine, June 7, 1956, p. 59.

Official Government Documents

Circular Telegram from the Department of State to Embassies in Africa, Washington, D.C. November 23, 7:26 p.m.

Government of Great Britain. Prime Minister's *Personal Minute*, pp. 2–3.
President Lyndon Baines Johnson Library. National Security File. Country File, Ghana, vol. 2.
United States Central Intelligence Agency. "The Outlook For Ghana." *National Intelligence Estimate 74–57*. December 27, 1957, p. 6.
————. *Weekly Review*. November 26, 1958.
United States Senate Intelligence Committee. Interim Report: Alleged Assassination Plots Involving Foreign Leaders. 1975, p. 14.
United States State Department. *Foreign Relations of the United States*, 1958–1960, vol. 14 (Washington, D.C.: GPO, 1992), p. 339.
————. *Foreign Relations of the United States*, 1964–1968, vol. 24: 250. Document number 256.

Scholarly Papers

Kwame Nkrumah, "Dialectics of Materialism and Sociology." Seminar paper, University of Pennsylvania, 1942.

Index